—

Lifers

Learning from At-Risk
Adolescent Readers

—

Lifers
Learning from At-Risk Adolescent Readers

PAMELA N. MUELLER

Heinemann
Portsmouth, NH

Heinemann
A division of Reed Elsevier Inc.
361 Hanover Street
Portsmouth, NH 03801-3912
www.heinemann.com

Offices and agents throughout the world

Library of Congress Cataloging-in-Publication Data
Mueller, Pamela N.
    Lifers : learning from at-risk adolescent readers / by Pamela N. Mueller.
      p. cm.
    Includes bibliographical references (p. 157).
    ISBN 0-86709-514-8 (alk. paper)
    1. Learning disabled children—Education (Secondary)—Case studies.
    2. Socially handicapped children—Education (Secondary)—Case studies.
    3. Reading disability—Case studies. 4. Reading—Remedial teaching—Case studies. I. Title: Learning from at-risk adolescent readers. II. Title.
    LC4704.87 .M84 2001
    371.91'44—dc21   2001039159

Editors: Tom Newkirk and Leigh Peake
Production editor: Sonja S. Chapman
Cover design: Jenny Jensen Greenleaf
Manufacturing: Steve Bernier

Printed in the United States of America on acid-free paper

05 04 03 02 01 RRD 1 2 3 4 5

For years I had been appalled not only by the lack of success, in terms of interest and skills, of the ninth-grade students who were assigned to remedial reading, but also by their lack of progress out of remedial reading. Once labeled and placed in remedial programs, most students stayed there for their entire high school career. . . .

—JANET ALLEN,
It's Never Too Late

Contents

Contents

Acknowledgments

This book grew out of my desire to learn from a group of students I've always been drawn to, the at-risk readers who populate our high schools in increasing numbers. In working with me, they have taught me more than I can ever expect to teach them. I am grateful for all the time and energy these adolescents spent trying to make sense of their reading lives for me and for themselves.

I could never have done this work without the unwavering support of a visionary high school principal who believed as I did in the ability of all students to strive for success in a supportive community of learners. Thank you, Mark, for making me a part of your vision. And thank you as well to the First Team, without whom this vision would never have become a reality.

What I have written is the culmination of a carefully crafted doctoral program that encourages students to build on their strengths while challenging them to delve into uncharted territories. My thanks to all I learned from: John Carney, who guided me through the initial years of my studies; Grant Cioffi, Ann Diller, Jane Hansen, Paula Salvio, Tom Schram, and Bill Wansart, whose rigorous courses laid a firm foundation for my research; and Tom Newkirk, whose skillful and thoughtful mentoring brought my work to fruition.

My fellow students at the University of New Hampshire have been there every step of the way, talented and knowledgeable peers faithful in their friendship, their suggestions, and their support. Thanks especially to Pat Wilson, who obliged me as a troubleshooter by always keeping a step ahead of me in the Ph.D. process.

My family has been ever-patient and encouraging, in awe perhaps of a wife/mother who chose to return to school at fiftysomething, but confirming nonetheless. My love and thanks to Bill, Kristy, Kim, and Eric, who believed in me every step of the way.

Introduction

The horror stories are many. We've all heard them. Take this one, from a tenth grader named Joe: "The last time I read aloud was in second grade. I brought in *Green Eggs and Ham* and asked my teacher if I could read it to the class. I sat in a big chair with all my classmates around me, and I felt so proud as I turned each page. When I had finished my teacher said to me, 'You didn't read that, Joe. You memorized it.' I never read aloud again." Or Marie's (she's in the eleventh grade): "I've always known I had a problem with understanding. The words are there but they don't say anything to me. They never have, even when I was little. I can't read and I know it, but people keep asking me to do it anyway." Twelfth grader Greg remembers: "In seventh grade I couldn't keep up with the work. They thought I was slacking off. They told me to get glasses. I had to cry in front of the class before the teacher figured out I needed help." Alan, another twelfth grader, says: "I remember doing these little reading groups in third grade. I was a bad reader and I kept getting moved down. Finally they sent me to art class. I didn't have to read there."

These students are not alone. "It's stupid. Pointless. I don't see what reading workshop does. I don't know why they even have it in the school. All we do is read. We just grab a book and start reading it. You are quiet. You have to read all of these words. It's boring and it takes up my time." Banished from reading workshop because of his refusal to participate in the required half hour of silent reading, Paul sits slumped across from me in my office, trying to make sense of his uncooperative behavior. As this angry ninth grader takes a breath, the reading consultant in me launches into the all-too-familiar party line: "But, Paul, reading is an important. . . ." Before I can finish my sentence, though, this frustrated adolescent interrupts me with his continuing diatribe. "I don't like reading at all. I never have. They never teach me anything. I've been trying it for nine years now—it feels like all my life—and it still seems pointless."

As I listen to the angry words of this at-risk reader who has waged a nonstop battle with reading, I think of all the other students who have shared the same thoughts with me over the years, of adolescents who have appeared angry, sullen, cocky, or depressed as they sit in my office trying to explain their never-ending frustrations with reading. But this time something is different. Perhaps I've heard the story once too often. Perhaps it's the research project I've tackled, which requires me to listen carefully to the voice behind the words. At any rate, I hear Paul's words as if for the first time, and what he's saying is really quite simple: If I can't do it after nine years, if I still can't unlock words, if I still can't understand and remember what I've read, if I still can't keep up with my peers, if I still can't be successful in school, if nobody can ever help me do it better, then *what's the point?*

What *Is* the Point?

For the past eighteen years I have worked as a high school reading consultant, charged with developing and implementing a schoolwide literacy curriculum to meet the needs of a wide range of adolescents. During this time I have come to know all sorts of students, from National Honor Society scholars to potential dropouts. I have proofread well-developed college essays written by hopeful Ivy League applicants; I have huddled with frustrated eleventh graders hoping to make sense of *April Morning* in order to eke out a passing mark in junior English. For whatever reason, I have been drawn more and more to those students whose reading deficiencies have burdened most if not all of their educational lives.

And with good reason. The numbers of these students are growing at high schools everywhere. Year after year more and more incoming freshmen are unprepared for the literacy demands of the high school curriculum. It's not that educators know nothing about these students; there is information about them in abundance. A myriad of books and articles deal with the at-risk adolescent reader. The questions addressed are many: Who are these students anyway? What characteristics do they share? What are their social and academic backgrounds? What are the causes of their literacy struggle? What are the consequences? What can we do and what are we doing to help them? How successful are our interventions?

So What About These At-Risk Readers?

Just who are these at-risk adolescent readers I am so drawn to as a teacher and researcher? *At-risk* is a term borrowed from the insurance industry to describe students judged highly probable to become a "loss" in terms of school success and achievement. They hover on the precipice of academic failure. Lacking the literacy and learning skills to succeed in the traditional secondary classroom, they generally get poor grades, have negative relationships with teachers, and feel alienated from a place they see as unfair and a "boring waste of time." Acting out a particular role in the culture of failure in which they find themselves cast, these student "performers" do all in their power to live up to the low expectations that others have for them—and, indeed, that they have for themselves. Many are living in fractured homes that have victimized them emotionally and intellectually. Because their responsibilities toward work and family often take precedence over a high school diploma, the idea of dropping out of school is never far from their minds.

Despite "a mighty dose of reading skill-builders during their school careers" (Krogness 1995), at-risk readers have poor decoding and spelling skills, possess a weak vocabulary, and are unable to read strategically and actively. Their goal is more often than not to "get through" the text rather than make sense of it. They are often passive, much less likely than their successful peers to monitor their comprehension or tackle their comprehension difficulties head on. They have lower initial expectations of success, give up more quickly in the face of difficulty, and attribute failures to internal, static causes while attributing success to external causes. When Rosenthal (1995) interviewed poor readers, they described their reading histories with terms like frustration, lack of focus, stress, fear of failure, embarrassment and discomfort, a waste of time, low self-esteem.

How Do At-Risk Adolescent Readers Come to Be?

These students have been identified as at-risk long before high school. Poor readers are recognized as early as kindergarten or first grade, and in general, poor readers in elementary school continue to be poor readers throughout their educational careers. Rist (1970) points out that a young reader's journey through school is essentially preordained by day eight of kindergarten! According to his study, children relegated to the "slow learner" reading group during the first week of kindergarten are destined to remain there throughout their school careers, caught in a frustrating cycle of failure as they attempt to learn to read and write. The kindergarten teacher's initial expectations, which are based on family history, physical appearance, and classroom behavior rather than academic potential or performance, accurately forecast a child's future academic career.

Who's most likely to end up in this six-and-under risk pool? Allington and Cunningham (1996) list four basic factors that early on put an elementary student at risk of academic failure, factors over which a child has no control: family poverty, parental educational attainment, gender, and perceived immaturity. It's almost as if our schools are set up on a "caste system" (Rist 1970, p. 427), in which lower-class students who come to school lacking the social, linguistic, and intellectual resources deemed necessary for academic success in our democratic middle-class schoolrooms become trapped in an unescapable cistern of failure. Too often teachers do not offer explicit instruction to those students who come to school with a limited literacy history, and this omission condemns these youngsters to a life of reading and academic struggle. It's not as though these children are simply incompetent. Indeed, many of them exhibit cognitive and linguistic competence in the world outside school, yet they appear inept and slow to learn in the school setting (Au and Mason 1981, p. 117). But if school is seen as a person's first "crack" at society, then failure in school may well lead to a lifetime of more of the same.

Aren't We Already Helping At-Risk Readers?

The "at-risk" label, as objectionable as it may seem to some, at least carries the implication that all is not lost for these struggling readers, that "some sort of intervention may . . . reduce or eliminate whatever one is at risk of experiencing" (Allington and Cunningham 1996, p. 1). And so well-meaning reading and special educators give them large doses of extra reading help. Employing a medical metaphor that looks at reading disability as a learning disease (Kohl 1973), they examine the symptoms, diagnose a deficit, then prescribe a remediation. Removing the young "patient" from his healthy classmates, they offer treatment by a specialist in a clinic. Once admitted, the student is not discharged until he or she is well. For adolescent at-risk readers, though, the hoped-for cure is elusive. By high school, they have been in and out of all sorts of special intervention programs: remedial reading groups, resource rooms, retention, low-track classes—you name it, they've experienced it.

Unfortunately for these students, the cure rate of most intervention programs is limited at best. There is little evidence that participation in any of these programs helps students become better readers. Looking back at the history of reading remediation over the past thirty years, it is clear that "special programs are not special enough." At-risk high school readers are "lifers," students who despite extra help continue to qualify for reading intervention year after year (Allington and Cunningham 1996, p. 18).

Is There No Escape?

By the time I meet at-risk readers in high school, they have become lifers. Most if not all have raised the white flag in their battle against reading disability; beaten by the odds stacked against them, they are no longer willing to wage another skirmish against the written page. Seen as incurable by self, family, and school, these terminally ill readers are relegated to the "back ward" of reading clinics, a place in the special ed office reserved for those who aren't expected to read and write on their own. Or, fulfilling the destiny foretold so many years ago by their kindergarten teachers, they drop out of school, upholding the validity of the educational actuarial tables. After almost a decade of failure, these at-risk readers finally lose their struggle for school success and achievement once and for all. Their loss is ours as well.

Allington and Walmsley (1995) blame this instructional ineffectiveness on six faulty assumptions:

- Faulty assumption 1: *not all children can become literate with their peers.* By viewing individual differences as evidence of how much or how little a child is capable of learning rather than as an indicator of the amount of instruction needed, educators give the not-so-subtle message that some young children simply cannot and will not learn to read on schedule. The "slow learners" are taught less frequently, are subjected to more control-oriented behavior, and receive little or no support from the teacher.

- Faulty assumption 2: *we can measure children's literacy aptitude.* When we pass judgment on a child's innate literacy aptitude rather than offering the intensive instruction needed by those who come to school with a limited literacy history, we automatically exclude these students from membership in Smith's (1997) "literacy club." However, there is clear evidence that almost every child, even those who score low on readiness assessments, can learn to read along with their peers if given large doses of intensive and purposeful instruction.

- Faulty assumption 3: *children learn best in homogeneous groups.* As generally practiced in our schools, grouping low-ability children together more often than not leads to a literacy dead end. Expectations change, instructional approaches and pace differ, motivation drops, intellectual interaction decreases, passivity sets in, and a mentality of failure and incompetence pervades instruction. Although a seemingly logical premise, homogeneous grouping inflicts such negative effects on children's learning that the whole concept of ability grouping can be discounted as both unwise and untenable. The demeaning "sped" (special ed) label is one that students can never escape; Krogness (1995) notes that without role models and peer coaches to learn from, these students too often shut down, using their energy and intellect for counterproductive purposes—or not at all.

- Faulty assumption 4: *reading is a hierarchy of increasingly complex skills.* When arbitrary skill sequences drive instruction, more often than not the reading is left out of reading lessons. Students have few opportunities to participate in authentic literacy activities: to curl up with a book of their own choosing, to hear a skilled reader read, to share in the interactive meaning making that is at the heart of effective reading instruction. In the skill-and-drill approach, decoding is the primary emphasis. We fail to see struggling readers as comprehenders; instead we judge them as word attackers, and not very good ones at that. This focus on a hierarchy of skills is often enough to discourage and turn off even the most motivated at-risk reader.

- Faulty assumption 5: *some children need slowed-down and more concrete instruction.* Allington and Walmsley (1995) logically conclude that "slowing down the pace of instruction ensures that children will always remain behind other children whose instruction proceeds at a normal pace" (p. 8). If a student in the low reading group is only expected to get through half of the first-grade reading material in a year, how can she ever again be expected to catch up to her peers who are reading at grade level or above? On the contrary, struggling readers need *more* rather than less instruction if we expect them to learn with their classmates. In his work Stanovich (1986) points to reading volume as the key to reading success.

- Faulty assumption 6: *we should use special teachers to meet the needs of some children.* Special teachers lead to fragmented educational experiences for those who are least able to deal with this disruption. Regular class instruction is interrupted and lost. In addition, in many cases struggling readers are instructed by minimally trained paraprofessionals, a situation unlikely to accelerate learning. When Leinhart et al. (1991) studied the way class time is spent in special education classrooms staffed by special education teachers, they found that although 60 percent of the time was allocated to reading, less than a third was actually spent on it.

Where Do We Go From Here?

Can we blame the existence of at-risk readers on ineffective instructional practices alone? By addressing these six faulty assumptions, can we restructure the field of literacy instruction so that all children can become good readers? Unfortunately, the solution is not that easy. Anyone who has spent time in a classroom realizes that no two children are alike; it is logical then that all students possess unique histories as readers. While many current explanations of reading difficulty focus on the "minutiae of mental operations," we need to move beyond "the level of operations, devoid of context, goals, motive or history" (Johnston 1985, p. 175). We need to blend psychological and social determinants into our understanding of reading failure. Kos (1991) has determined four factors that prevent students from progressing: (1) their inability to use reading strategies effectively, (2) their perception of reading instruction, (3) stress related to reading, and (4) individual educational histories. Social, affective, psychological, educational, and environmental factors all play a role in adolescent readers' struggles.

Over the past three years I have begun to believe that our understanding of the at-risk adolescent reader is not complete. For as I have come to know these teenagers, whether in their classrooms or in the one-on-one privacy of my office, I have discovered a virtually untapped source of knowing: the students themselves. That they have stories to tell and knowledge to share is obvious; I hear hints of their understanding in the informal comments of Joe and Marie, of Alan and Greg. That their voices have been largely ignored up until now is equally clear; in my literature review covering thirty years of research I have thus far found only three studies whose source material is provided by the readers themselves: Johnston (1985), Kos (1991), and Rosenthal (1995). True, in the past few years teacher researchers like Janet Allen (1995) and Mary Krogness (1995) have introduced us to real at-risk pupils. However, even in these shared stories the teacher's voice and perceptions remain center stage, with the students' words and understanding cast in supporting roles. Donald Graves points out how important it is to listen to what our students have to say:

> Unless children speak about what they know, we lose out on what they know and how they know it. Through our eyes and ears we learn from them: their stories, how they solve problems, what their wishes and dreams are, what works and doesn't work, their vision of a better classroom, and what they need to learn to succeed. . . . We transform what we learn from them into an effective learning history. (1994, p. 16)

Up until now, though, the at-risk population has kept remarkably mum. As a teacher and researcher I look forward to listening to and learning from them. With this new perspective on reading failure, I hope to show firsthand what it's really like to be a lifer, academically washed up at the age of sixteen. Then, too, by making sense of each student's way of knowing, I hope to present a more intimate look into the hows and whys of reading failure. If through these adolescents' stories we gain new insight into their world of frustration, then perhaps we will begin to rethink what's gone wrong in our schools for them and others like them. Perhaps then we will begin to take steps to eradicate the category of lifers from our schools.

Where Am I Coming From?

For the past eighteen years I have been employed as a part-time high school reading consultant. A primary grade teacher who "retired" to have three children and then returned to graduate school to earn a master's degree in reading, I cut my secondary educator teeth at a rural New England high school of 375 students from mostly lower-middle-class homes. Nervous about working with an age group I knew little about, I was talked into taking the position by a persuasive principal who understood the importance that reading plays in high school and beyond and was somehow able to budget enough money to hire me. He gave me free rein to develop and implement a reading program that met the needs of the students. During my seven years there I created a reading curriculum that encompassed content area reading, recreational reading, and corrective reading. It was there that I first rubbed shoulders with at-risk adolescent readers, and I tried everything in my remedial reading bag of tricks to make a difference for these lifers. With a few I was successful; with most I was not.

Seven years after I began my secondary work, a brand new school opened its doors in a neighboring community. Its student body melded 350 adolescents from two very different places, one a sprawling blue-collar town on the outskirts of a small city and the other an affluent rural village nestled on the edge of a private college campus. Excited by the prospect of working with this economically diverse student body in concert with a handpicked staff and a visionary administrator, I took the new half-time reading consultant position. It was a decision I have never regretted.

From its inception this high school has offered an exhilarating educational environment in which to grow and learn. Indeed, the school prides itself on being a community of learners, a place where adults and adolescents work and study together, a place where every pupil is given the support he or she requires to attain academic success. Spurred on by professional development opportunities, teachers are encouraged to become innovators, trying out new ideas that may further their educational goals. Block scheduling, team teaching, performance diplomas, senior projects—you name it, we've tried it, usually with outstanding results. It is natural then that this risk-taking environment prompted me to rethink the traditional approach to corrective reading instruction. If there was another way to work with at-risk adolescent readers I wanted to find it.

In revisiting our approach to corrective reading instruction, I did a lot of thinking. I did a lot of reading. I spent a lot of time at conferences picking the brains of the few educators who had given thought to this neglected area of reading instruction. But perhaps most important, I started listening to the students who came to my office for whatever support I could give them. When the school first opened I was dealing with twenty or so lifers and had opportunities to work—and talk—with all of those who wanted my help. Eight years later though, the number of at-risk readers had doubled along with the student body; one part-time reading consultant could not serve the needs of every struggling student.

I set out on another tack, piecing together a corrective curriculum that could be taught by sympathetic English teachers willing to give up their prep period for their neediest freshmen. That class was our first attempt at developing a reading workshop. In the course of my concurrent doctoral studies, I realized that much of what I wanted to know was being voiced by the students in the crowded halls of the school where I worked. This book is based on that rather simple understanding. My hope is that you will learn from this discovery just as I did.

How Is This Book Set Up?

In order to assure anonymity, the names of the students, teachers, schools, and communities are pseudonyms. Indeed, the reading workshop students who participated in my research were delighted to have the rare opportunity to reinvent themselves, if only in name. (The administrative details of my research process are provided in the appendix A.)

The main text of this book is divided into two sections. Part 1 presents my three main themes through profiles of individual adolescents whose stories best capture the related concepts (the words of other reading workshop students reinforce the profiled student's thoughts). Chapter 1 centers on Alexis, a sullen lifer whose reading history personifies the experiences of a frustrated and disillusioned student who has had to struggle with reading from the day she started school. Chapter 2 is the story of Kayla, a fragile student whose initial love of reading is painfully extinguished as she locks horns with ineffective educational practices. Chapter 3 is about Mick, a thoughtful adolescent whose jaded and misinformed view of reading as decoding is shaken by a mindful yet mysterious journey into understanding. While this study is based on particular at-risk adolescents from specific educational backgrounds, the feelings and experiences they have shared with me no doubt exemplify the reading histories of other struggling students. Chapter 4 draws overall conclusions that readers can connect to students and classrooms they know and have known.

In part 2, I describe the elements of the reading curriculum I have devised over the past five years. As part of these chapters I offer some examples of what can happen when lifers, supported by dedicated, talented, and caring teachers, work to throw off the mantle of failure they have worn for so long.

Part I

At-Risk Adolescent Readers Speak Out: Alexis, Kayla, Mick, and Friends

*It occurred to me that we had not been listening much to children
in these recent years of "summit" conferences in education. . . .
This seems especially unfortunate because the children often are more
interesting and perceptive than the grown-ups are about the day-to-day
realities of life in school. For this reason, I decided . . . to attempt to
listen very carefully to children and, whenever possible, to let their voices
and their judgments and their longings find a place within [my] book—
and maybe too, within the nation's dialogue about their destinies.*

—Jonathan Kozol
Savage Inequalities: Children in America's Schools

The reading workshop students you will meet here are not new to the world of reading intervention. Indeed, all of them can be seen as lifers, doomed to struggle from the start in schools that despite the best of intentions have fabricated a "culture of failure" for many students (McDermott and Varenne 1995, p. 331). Year after year they have qualified for special remedial programs because of continued low achievement. And year after year they have met with continuous and mounting frustration as their peers have succeeded in school while they have been powerlessly mired in inescapable failure. They have come to school excited about reading, but their love for books has been quickly extinguished by the excruciating process of learning to read. They have been let down by the very system set up to help them. Without some effective intervention, they are at risk of dropping out of school, the first step toward failing at life as well.

1

Chapter 1

Lifers: When Readers Struggle from the Start

*No matter how well a child in the lower reading groups might have read,
he was destined to remain in the same reading group. This is, in a
sense, another manifestation of the self-fulfilling prophecy in that a
"slow learner" had no option but to continue to be a slow learner,
regardless of potential or performance.*

—RAY RIST
"Student Social Class and Teacher Expectation"

Alexis is a slender, sad-faced teenager whose sullen and silent demeanor doesn't invite conversation, either with teachers or peers. In the privacy of my office, however, her voice came alive as she gave a quietly impassioned account of an early love for books that is still intact, despite years of struggle with the reading process. Here she is, in her own words:

I've always really liked to read. I just don't. I'm not very good at it, at least not the out-loud kind of reading. When I was little I read books that were in my room. My mom would read to me. She would read them to me so many times that I would have the books memorized so when I saw the words in other books I knew what they were. I liked that. It was good when you learned to read at an earlier age. But when I went to preschool and kindergarten that didn't work. I liked the idea that someone read to me. I didn't like the idea of having to do it myself. I just stopped liking it because I was bad at it. And I wasn't doing well in school.

I went to preschool and kindergarten in one year. I was only four when I started. I went to private school because they—the teachers—said I needed help. There was a public kindergarten and there was us, and I guess in my mind I thought I wasn't smart enough to go to public school. So I went to this one. It ended up being nice. I liked my teacher. It was in her house and there were only eight people in my class. We had to draw and color and write. She taught you letters, she taught you how to add and subtract. It was like regular school. We had math and science and geography. They took us in little groups and they made us learn to read

3

and stuff. They had classes with all easy books and they made us read back to them. We had lots of hard work and it was just too much work and I got tired of it. I didn't want to do it any more. It was like third grade.

I went to private kindergarten because my mom thought my teacher would help me out more. But it didn't work because I didn't feel good about myself when I went to first grade. I could have gone to readiness but they said I was smart enough to go to first grade. When I got there I didn't feel that way. I didn't know some things. Sometimes I didn't participate in class. When I colored, yeah I colored, and when we took tests I took tests; but when she told us to read something out loud I didn't do it. I still liked my teacher, I just didn't want to do anything. I didn't understand what was going on sometimes. The teacher would be going too fast for me or something. I didn't like it. Then I would shut down and not do anything. I failed first grade.

It wasn't very hard learning to read; it was just the reading part. Because there were words I didn't know and I got frustrated. I'd like to know how do you teach somebody how to read who's frustrated? I don't know how my teacher thought she was going to do this. She would like make us read words out loud. Stuff like that. We'd have spelling tests and stuff. I thought it was all a waste of time because it wasn't helping me at all. People don't teach kids to read. They don't. Kids teach themselves. They have to.

I've never been able to read out loud. Oh, I used to be able to and then kids started showing me up. I wasn't able to read as well as everybody else so I stopped reading. We had to pick a book and read to the class. I didn't like getting up in front of my class anyway so I didn't do it. I tried but I just wasn't comfortable. I tried but I kept not doing the words right and my teacher was like "I don't know, she just. . . ." Well then my mom would ask me to read and I'd read a word and she'd say, "Alexis, when you read it all sounds the same. You never change your voice." And I was like, "Be quiet. Leave me alone." I thought my teacher felt the same way, so I never read out loud. This was going on in first grade; it's going on all my life.

The second year of first grade was better I guess. It was the best year I ever had. I liked it. I had fun. I had a different teacher. I did my work most of the time. But sometimes I got sent into the hallway and stuff like that. I yelled at my teacher. I wasn't a happy child at school. The whole thing with reading made me sick to my stomach. I didn't even like to hear that word read. I just couldn't do it if somebody told me to. If I read by myself, maybe I could do it. But once someone told me to do it I felt sick to my stomach. I stopped liking it because I was just bad at it. My feeling sick just graduated. Eventually in fourth grade I wouldn't read. I wouldn't read anything, because I didn't like to read out loud.

My cousin used to make fun of me. He told me that I was a moron because I couldn't read out loud. Once in a while I've had a teacher tell me that, not that I'm a moron but that I'm stupid, that I can't read, that I should know how to do stuff more. They just got me down. No wonder I don't want to read any more. Not being able to do it very well is hard for me. Once my mom got frustrated and she said to me, "What is wrong with you, Alexis? Why are you like this?" The teachers kept saying, "What is wrong with you? We keep trying to figure out what is wrong with you but we can't figure it out. Why are you like this? Why can't you spell? Why can't you do this? You have a learning disability. You are ADD. Why can't you be like other kids?"

From second grade up to eighth I got extra help. I was always being taken out of my normal classrooms. I hated it because my class would be doing something, our teacher would be reading us a book or something. It was an interesting book but I would have to be taken out. It was the resource room but we called it the retard room. We went to do our homework and get extra help. We had to do this. We had to do that. Nothing went on there. We talked, we fooled around, we were yelling at teachers, stuff like that. We got in trouble. It was fun, but there was nothing to learn. When it was reading time, I went and hung out with another kid. We had to type and play that Mario game and stuff like that. Not much reading. Lots of typing. But I still don't know how to type. In seventh grade my social studies teacher told me I wasn't going to go any place in this world if I didn't know how to type.

Unless I ask for help I don't want anybody to help me. The teachers in the resource room always did the homework for me so I refused to go because I wasn't learning anything. But I had to go anyway. In fifth grade I was slacking off because everybody was doing the work for me. I finally got to the point where I didn't want to go because I thought I was such a retard and I thought they thought I couldn't do my own work. I refused to let anyone help me unless I absolutely needed it. Even today I don't let anyone help me. Unless I ask for it. Like if I am having problems with something then I would ask for that help. All they have to do is outline what the work is supposed to be like. Explain it to me and then don't do all of my problems. If they explain it to me then I can do it myself.

I used to avoid everything that had to do with reading. I don't want to be a teacher because it involves reading. Out loud. In English, if the teacher asks me to read a part I'll pass. I won't do it. Because I have never been able to read out loud and even if some people are reading worse than me I won't do it. I can't read English off the paper, you know what I mean? I need to remember the word. Like I can't read every word. I can't sound out every word because it doesn't always come together. In English class the teacher asked us to read something off our paper. But that's okay, because I was reading words that I was writing down. If I write something I can read it. I know what the words look like so I can read it. It is when somebody else writes something I can't. I have very high standards for myself. I have to be good. If I don't do good then I shut down and I don't do it.

I'm in reading workshop this year, and I'm the only one in my class who likes to read. I don't really like to read, I just like the book I am reading. It's not like I read a lot. But I get myself into a book. If I can pick out a book that I like, I sit down and read it. It is basically just turning pages but your mind is in the book. Like with The Outsiders, I was in the book because of the way the author explained it. The first page grabbed me. I felt like I was there. If I like a book I remember everything about it. I don't do anything extra. Nothing. I just read it. It sticks in my head. We have a sign in reading workshop that good readers are supposed to do this or that but you can't do all that as a reader at the same time. It's impossible. Unless you might be doing that without knowing it. You can't read and ask yourself questions and do all this stuff and then read. If you do that you're out of the book. I used to try to do that when I was a little kid because that was what I was told to do. It got me so mixed up. That is why *it made me sick to read. Like I wanted to do that with* The Little Mermaid *book, and I would sit down at night and read it. But I never ended up finishing it. I started and I got to the third page and I couldn't read any more. I was looking at the pictures and the words and going over in my mind what was happening. I just couldn't do it.*

I dislike reading when I have to read stupid books like Deathwatch. *My English teacher picked it out and it doesn't make any sense at all. She thinks I am almost done but I haven't read very much of it. I probably won't finish it because I am not interested in it. I have been trying. I sit down and I actually know I have to read it. I have to finish the work. Then I keep on going and I get so bored I am ready to cry. I read it in school during reading workshop and study hall. I am not wasting my time out of school reading that worthless book. I don't like textbooks either. They are evil. Our science teacher makes us read the book when he doesn't want to deal with us, at least that's what I think. He gives us time to read to ourselves in class. All I ever do is look at the pictures. I don't want to read about something like the distillation of wood. But it's not that bad in geo-political studies. The teacher has us read answers from the textbook. It's only like twelve words. It's not that hard to read out loud when there are no big words. For me a good reader is someone who can read out loud fluently. I can do it a little bit now. Except when I can't pronounce certain words.*

I've never liked school. I would rather be home sleeping. I went because it was a thing I had to do. I had no choice and I had to go to it. But I don't mind it as much now that I have started having classes that I like with my friends in them and stuff. As for reading, I just read. I guess some parts were a pain, but I never really thought about it. I have never pictured it as fun. Soccer is fun. It is not bad; it is probably good. I haven't figured it out as part of my life. It is like walking; it's just something that you do. So far I just did it. It has never really dawned on me that I am a reader. I need to think about that for a while. And I need to think about how reading is going to fit into my life. I just don't know.

Alexis's View of Reading

Before Alexis went to school, she loved being read to on her mother's lap, the first reading experience for many preschoolers. Like most of the students in this study, she delighted in listening to her mother read aloud her favorite picture books, hearing them over and over as parent and child sat together in the comfort of family and home. As she and her mother shared this special time together, Alexis began to see reading as an enjoyable social activity, one that fueled her imagination and connected with her feelings page after page and story after story. Mermaids came to life, handsome princes fell in love with beautiful princesses, lost bunnies found new homes. The repeated words became so familiar she could "read" the books herself. Reading for this preschooler, then, was a pleasurable process, one she looked forward to learning more about as her formal schooling began.

But Alexis's view of reading was dramatically altered as her kindergarten year unfolded. Extracted from "the context of illustrations, friendly voices, physical contact, movement, and leisure for imagination" (Atwell-Vasey 1998, p. 118), reading was no longer about stories; it was about unlocking words. It was about memorizing twenty-six letters in the alphabet and all the sounds that went with them. It was about reading aloud words that made her stumble, words that she hadn't been able to memorize as she did in her reading at home. It was about going faster and faster and feeling totally out of control. It was about feeling stupid. No longer could Alexis think about a princess being saved by a handsome prince; instead she had to concentrate on combining *b* with *a* and *t* to make *bat*. And she couldn't do this very well. If this is what reading was all about, she didn't like it. Indeed, there was no point to doing it at all. And she didn't.

Alexis's changing view of reading as a young child mirrors those of her reading workshop classmates. Of the twenty-two students I interviewed, nineteen had been read to at home as preschoolers. All nineteen of these children had come to school loving books and excited at the prospect of learning how to read for themselves. But all were caught off guard by the harsh reality of doing it. Paul's words as he looks back on his early reading experiences echo Alexis's:

> When I was little my mom read me books and stuff. I like it. It is easier to do it yourself and it is funner too. You actually feel like you are in the book. But when I went into the first-grade room, we sort of had to read so I was totally, "Oh, man, I don't want to do this at all." We had to pronounce letters and words like *cat*. I just saw what I had to read and I was like, "I hate this." My head hurt when I read. I just didn't want to do it.

Learning to read was harder than any of these students had imagined, as the focus shifted from a rewarding process of shared discovery to a frustrating procedure of isolated drill. In the ensuing struggle to read, then, their love for reading diminished.

Only three of the reading workshop students had not been read to as children: Jasmine, whose family of five was in crisis when her mother died while Jasmine was in preschool; Sergio, who grew up in a family of first-generation Portuguese immigrants; and Mick, whose parents focused their attention on an older sister who suffered from severe mental and physical handicaps. Interestingly, none of these students had a positive feeling about reading when they went to school for the first time. Lacking the pleasurable memories of being read to on someone's lap, they plunged into the skill and drill environment and were immediately turned off by it. Jasmine speaks of hating reading from the start: "It was boring in first grade, just sitting there in class and having to sit there and listen. . . . The teacher was helping us sound out the word and everybody would say it at the same time. It was frustrating, having to be there and listen to it and not feeling like doing it." When Sergio talks of hating his early reading experience, he uses the adjective "boring" to describe it as well. He goes on, "It is no fun to just sit there and read for a long time. . . . You would read, then stop. First grade they would teach you to read. You are starting to learn how to sound out the words. You really wouldn't read." Mick's view of reading as a first grader is clear and concise; to him it was "another one of those cases where it is pointless to me." And why wouldn't it be? If most of what a beginning reader experiences is decoding, if meaning becomes subservient to word identification in the classroom, then what would the point be to a six-year-old child?

Alexis's View of Herself

It doesn't take long to find out how Alexis feels about herself as a reader and a student. In our very first interview she lays it on the line: "I'm not very good at [reading]." "I didn't feel good about myself" in school. It takes even less time to extrapolate from her comments how Alexis feels about herself as a person; she is a failure. It shouldn't be surprising that Alexis feels this way. After all, she has struggled with reading—and school—from kindergarten on; at the age of six she failed first grade. In our schools success in reading is a prerequisite for success in school; students who can't read can't succeed. Only recently in public schools have we begun to look at and value other ways of knowing, but in Alexis's case it seems that little has come along that she can excel in as a person. She points out that even her lack of typing ability, a subject no doubt studied to make learning easier for her, is looked at by some as a deficiency that will hold her back in life.

Since her second year of first grade Alexis has been pulled from her "normal" classroom and sent to the "retard" room where "nothing really goes on," except perhaps troublemaking, for Alexis and her "unnormal" friends. It's as though this hand-picked group of children is incapable of learning. Peers have made fun of her, even teachers have occasionally let it slip that she simply isn't of the same intellectual level as most of the other children in school. Singled out by virtue of her academic struggles, Alexis has had aides assigned just to her to be sure she gets her work done, aides who have followed her "everywhere, out to recess, to the bathroom, everywhere." Her refusal to go to the resource room or to accept help underlines her anger at how she is perceived by the school as a reader and a student; in her mind only people who are stupid need to have their work done by somebody else.

That Alexis is anything but stupid can be seen in a psychological evaluation done at the end of second grade. The evaluator points out that Alexis scores solidly average or above average in intelligence and that her frustration with reading may stem from a specific learning disability. Both as a young child and an adolescent, though, it is clear that Alexis, like most of her struggling peers, believes that her problem with reading is a problem with her intellect. She sees herself as a failure, and much of what has happened over the past ten years in school has only served to reinforce that belief.

Very few of the reading workshop students would be classified as of below average intelligence, yet in every instance these students see themselves as somehow inferior to their classmates. During their years in school, some have been designated special ed, some are Title I students, others have escaped a formal label. However, simply being—and being seen as—a struggling reader is all the label each of them needs; that alone is enough to frustrate these adolescents as they view themselves as failures. Like

Alexis, Carol sees herself as stupid: "Things never click in my head. I have gotten low grades forever." When asked to describe his reading history, Mark describes himself as "not real smart." "How do you know that?" I ask. "I know I'm not smart because I couldn't do a lot of stuff in school. I always had trouble. I just didn't understand it." Eric's view of himself, though, transcends even Alexis's and Carol's "stupid" and Mark's "not real smart": "In the classroom I feel like a ghost. I don't know most of the stuff they are throwing at me, like the words. I feel invisible." Four months after this interview, Eric, a ninth grader who had been waging a battle with reading since first grade, gave up the fight. He dropped out of school. He had just turned sixteen.

The Beginnings of the Struggle

For most children the struggle with reading begins when they take their first tentative steps through the doors of the first-grade classroom. In Alexis's case it started much earlier when her mother, sensing that her preschool child would need extra help in learning, sent her to a private preschool and kindergarten. Though the action was well intentioned, the message was painfully clear to this thoughtful four-year-old: something about her made her mother think she was going to have trouble in school. "I went to the private school because my mom went to the public kindergarten and they couldn't help me out like I needed because from kindergarten to fourth grade they were packed." So Alexis started her formal education in a school whose low teacher-student ratio would afford her the individual attention she seemed to warrant. But even that was not enough. "I went to a private kindergarten and we did more, and my friends went to a public kindergarten and they did less, but they were still smarter than me. They could read better than me, they could write better than me, they could speak better than me. The teacher listened to me because she was interested in what I was going to say, but I couldn't get my words out."

At the age of four, then, Alexis viewed herself in a new light; the struggle with reading had begun. The child who had seen herself as a reader was no longer quite so sure. She discovered early on that she couldn't read out loud like the teacher expected her to; she quickly tired of the work. Kindergarten was "too hard"; to her it felt like third grade. She was in over her head and she knew it. In her frustration she chose to turn herself off to reading and school. Where once she had felt self-assured and competent, she now felt only a lack of confidence and failure.

Once the downward spiral begins for young readers like Alexis, there seems to be nothing to stop it. A bad start spells nothing but disaster. Once a struggling reader, always a struggling reader. Once the kindergarten teacher places a child in the low reading group, she is doomed to stay there forever, regardless of what she does. Once the label has been given, a child begins to look at herself in a different light. And so does the school. Instruction changes, behavior changes, relationships among peers change, treatment by adults changes. As Christy remembers it, "I had a tough, rough beginning in reading. It seemed like I was out a week, the week that they started reading or something. When I came back it seemed like everyone else knew how to read really good. But I didn't. And I didn't know what to do."

Problems Encountered in the Struggle

What kinds of roadblocks do these struggling readers encounter in their painful years of schooling?

Big Words

Alexis points out the initial one, "words that don't always come together." Although single-syllable words do not seem to pose a problem for most of these students, it is when the text moves to "bigger ones" that decoding becomes a dilemma. Sounding out a three-letter word may be doable for these emergent readers, but once the letters multiply the task becomes overwhelming. Students who can unlock *cat* are stuck when they are faced with *elephant*. It's not the meaning that gets them down; after all, most first graders can recognize an elephant as well as a cat. Rather, assigning meaning to the letter arrangements on the page stymies these students. Indeed, the inability to recognize and pronounce multisyllabic words is a problem that surfaces early in their reading careers and never goes away. For whatever reason, these students are unable to break the reading code; the tyranny of the "big word" is a common chord sounded as they detail their early and present struggles. Listen to their chorus:

> KRISTIN: I don't remember first grade too good but I always had trouble sounding out big words and pronouncing them. I am still not very good at it.
> KEITH: I know I will always stumble on words. I always have. It happens all the time. It has happened pretty much the whole time I have been reading.
> KAYLA: I come to a big word. I want to ask but I sit there and try to sound it out. Sometimes I will just sit there for hours trying to figure out what the word is instead of asking. I think I am embarrassed to say I don't know.

As a student progresses through the grades, more and more big words are included in the texts the children are required to read. Because these readers lack the ability to decode automatically, quickly, fluently, and efficiently, big words become an obstacle impossible to overcome.

Big Books

As the big words multiply, it's harder and harder for these students to keep up with their work. Big words lead to big books, the logical next stumbling block for struggling readers. The tension increases, and so does their frustration. The challenge of longer and thicker books is overwhelming and downright scary.

PAUL: We went from little *Cat in the Hat* books to *Matilda* books and stuff like that. The words got bigger and longer. Instead of five words on a page, it came to twenty words on a page. It was like a chapter book. Wow! See all the words. I have to read all this? I only read slow. It would take me ten years to do a book.

CODY: Reading a lot of words is hard. It is like I am sitting down here and I have to climb Mt. Washington. It is a big mountain. If it is a little hill, like Pat's Peak, then I can do it. Not a mountain, just a little hill. Or even better, like walking from the cafeteria to the soccer field. Then I can do it.

BOB: The thing that is bad is scary big books. I tried one. I got through a couple of pages and it took five days. They take longer. I have to keep going through it because I am not sure of what I read because there is so much on one page. So much information and I can't keep up with it.

Big books for these students are a nightmare that won't go away. First, *Matilda* makes Paul and his classmates nervous; finally, it is the reading demands of a ninth-grade curriculum. Old hands at this kind of frustration, though, more often than not these adolescents are resigned to the fact that they can't possibly succeed. Kim has fashioned a handy response to this recurring dilemma; she simply doesn't do the work: "If I get a big book I just have the attitude that I can't do it. And I don't."

Reading Aloud

If first big words and then big books present obstacles for these young readers, imagine having to go public, to exhibit this struggle in front of your more successful classmates. This is just what happens each time a floundering reader is asked to read aloud in the classroom. Alexis vividly remembers the embarrassment of stumbling over words as her fellow first and second graders sat front row center. So do Patti and Kristin:

PATTI: In the earlier grades when I had a hard time with the words, the teachers would make you read out loud. I didn't like that at all. If I didn't know a word, I would stumble over it. And you know when you stumble over a word, everybody is staring at you. Then a kid might try to help you and the teacher would tell them to be quiet.

KRISTIN: I can't read out loud. Because I get all nervous and everything. When I am reading out loud to the class, I always mess up and stutter. I hate standing in front of a group of people and then messing up on reading. I read it all wrong.

Extremely conscious of her trouble pronouncing words, even now Alexis refuses to place herself in this demeaning situation. It is only when she is confident that the words to be read will flow easily that she agrees to read aloud in class.

Over the years, reading workshop students have found ways to deal with this painful dilemma. Carol taught herself to read one paragraph ahead, so that when the teacher called on her she would be ready. "I will read the first paragraph as she is talking. And then while somebody is reading the first paragraph, I will read the next one." By seventh grade Cody had this sort of preparation strategy down to a science. "Here's what I'm doing. I count out how many kids are in there and figure out what paragraph it is and I would read it over and over and over until I could read it." When I asked students what they thought the teacher's purpose was for asking them to read aloud, none of them really seemed very sure. Kristin thought that maybe it was a way for teachers to get students to pay attention. "Or maybe they thought kids would get more out of it." Patti guessed that it was a way to help students who were having a hard time with words. "But if that was it," she confided, "it wasn't good at all."

Accelerating Expectations

The fourth problem that seems to be a common thread in the stories these reading workshop students tell is the change in expectations that occurs when moving from one level of instruction to another. For Alexis the imminence of a big change came early, between first and second grade. Her teacher warned her of what was to come, and she knew enough to be worried. "Every year your teacher says it is so much different going to the next grade, so much more work. So I was afraid to go to the next grade. I had been in first grade for so long, but I still didn't want to go to second grade." As she had feared, her workload increased when she reached second grade; so did her frustration. By the end of that year she had been coded learning disabled.

Depending on the student, a leap like this may show up at different points in the curriculum, but the reaction is inevitably the same: as a student's abilities fail to keep pace with classroom demands, his discomfiture builds.

> SERGIO: The biggest jump I remember was going from second grade to third grade. The books got bigger. The length. Even books for physical science. Humongous. And hard.
>
> CODY: In fourth grade we had pillows to sit on. It was fun. Nice and comfortable. We would just sit there and read. Then in fifth grade you are just sitting [at your desk] reading a chapter or you read your book, chapter sixteen, by Monday. You are taking notes down. You are taking tests. It is not as fun.
>
> BOB: In fifth grade they expected a lot more. They expected you to read a lot. They would tell you to bring home the text every day. So much you had to read. I just couldn't keep up with everything. All the subjects. I would bring it home and have to read the social studies book, science, reading. I was just getting things confused more and more.

That these students feel confused shouldn't be a surprise; after all, each step up the educational ladder leaves them farther and farther behind. And yet they keep stumbling on. Sergio lays some of the blame on teachers who fail to prepare students for what lies ahead. "This year is tough. I think in eighth grade they should have prepared us for what it was going to be like in ninth grade. What the reading is going to be like. In eighth grade there were one-hundred-page books. Now they give us bigger books, stuff to read on your own. They should have tried to help you out."

But by this time in the educational careers of these struggling readers there seems to be no way for classroom teachers to truly "help out" these students. They have fallen so far behind in their reading abilities that the intensive reading instruction they so desperately need is rarely offered. Instead, well-meaning educators help the students complete assigned work. They never catch up, but they do move on.

Trying to Get Help at School

Alexis has decided never to accept help unless she asks for it herself. She has found the help offered to her in the past to be worthless or demeaning (often both). Her reading workshop peers may have ventured down alternative avenues of assistance, but the results of this intervention are in essence no different from hers. Time after time, these students have found themselves at the same dead end of learning. They continue to struggle with reading; they continue to see themselves as failures. What kind of assistance has been offered in school over the years? Each student has his own tale to tell of help gone awry.

Help From the Classroom Teacher

It would seem logical that the first place for a child to go for help is the classroom teacher. After all, she is the one who should know the needs of her students best. And indeed, there are many teachers who offer that kind of support. Mick remembers Mrs. Love, who would come and sit beside him if he didn't understand something:

> While the rest of the class was doing something she would explain it, the words I didn't understand. First she would explain what certain things were and then she would ask me if I understood and then she would show me different ways of understanding things. Sometimes I would get it and sometimes I would still be in a blur. But then I basically told her I understood so we could move on to something else.

In his desire to keep up with his classmates, Mick would negate the help offered by pretending it had solved his problem. "I wouldn't stick with it and learn it. Getting the subject done and over with was fine with me."

Eric, on the other hand, had a first-grade teacher who was anything but helpful, one whose memory has been indelibly stamped on his fragile psyche. When he didn't participate in class because he didn't understand what to do, her reaction was frightening. "Every time you didn't read, she would get on your case. She would yell at you, 'Why didn't you read?' in a mean voice. So we would make up an excuse or something." Kayla had a similar experience with one of her first teachers. In her mind the teacher didn't care when Kayla struggled with reading. "I don't think [my teachers] really cared. I would ask for help so they would help me only a little and then they would just leave. They wanted to . . . get on with the books, do what they have to do." Instead of asking for help, Kayla decided to pretend to do her work. As a result, she never did learn what was being taught.

Like Eric and Kayla, Bob decided to play it safe when it came to asking for reading help. "I have learned not to raise my hand a lot in school. I am afraid to get something bad and make fun of myself." In his early reading experience, if you made a mistake you were sent to the corner. "If you couldn't like say the word they were trying to help you with, they would send you in the corner for a couple of minutes. Then you would come back and see if you could do it again." When I inquired how he thought that being in the corner would help him learn the troublesome word, he frowned as he replied, "I don't know. I just know I hated it. I used to be in the corner all the time."

Classroom Aides

Many of the reading workshop students have had experience with teacher aides. Usually untrained paraprofessionals, these helpers are an integral part of many classrooms these struggling readers have known. Aaron shares Alexis's negative feeling about aides when he describes them as ladies who "just sit there. They get paid for it. They are supposed to come around and make sure you get what you are learning and that you have no problems, but they are really just sitting in the back of the room. Some of them are good and some of them aren't, but they all sit around."

Jasmine knows the purpose of having aides in the classroom, but she questions their effectiveness: "They were there to help students whenever they needed it. But if you raised your hand for help, the aide wouldn't really get up and help you at all. She would just sit in the corner filling out paperwork or something. Or they were running errands for the teachers and stuff." Mick, on the other hand, held his favorite aide in highest regard. "She was great. The Mom of Newsom, we used to call her. She basically helped out anybody. And to be sure I know her well; I have had extra help my entire life." Knowing Eric's negative experience with his first-grade teacher, it is a relief when I hear that he too remembers aides in a positive light: "I needed help. So they started adding aides and stuff in the room. Most of the kids were slow readers. Not terrible bad, but they couldn't read. It was a lot easier then, because there were more aides and more teachers to help you. When you raised your hand and asked what the word was, they would come over and help you read. They would actually slow down. They would actually sound out the word for me."

Well-meaning aides could sound out the word for Eric; but they weren't trained to help him sound it out for himself, a fact that must have weighed in heavily as this angry and frustrated adolescent made the heartrending choice to throw in the towel on reading, school, and himself.

Pullout Help

When classroom intervention proved insufficient to meet Alexis's needs, she was introduced to the world of pullout help, first as an uncoded student and ultimately as a learning disabled student assigned to the resource room. Not surprisingly her reading workshop classmates are veterans of all sorts of pullout intervention as well. They tell story after story of teachers who gave them worksheets, who read books to them, who helped them with words they didn't know. They talk about day after day and year after year of special help. All too often, though, they talk of kind teachers who rather than help them catch up did little more than water down the work in order for them to be "successful":

> CODY: She took me in her class to give me a different kind of worksheet. Some kids got one worksheet and I got a different one, a little easier. The vocabulary words for me were on the page, and the vocabulary words for them were in the book. I think that was kind of stupid, because they had to read for it and I just had to find it on my paper. I didn't have to read at all. All I had to do was look it up.
>
> MICK: After first grade I started going to her every day. And she helped me out. She would give me work I would understand. If one of our normal teachers gave us work and we didn't understand it, we could go to Mrs. Allman and she would give us something easier that we understood. Although it was basically the same thing, we covered it the easier way because then we would actually understand it.

It is true that these students need support in order to keep up with their peers, but the kindness shown to them in the pullout setting proves to be a two-edged sword. By cutting back on the demands of the classroom, well-meaning teachers send a message that though subtle is nevertheless picked up by their struggling students, the fact that these readers are deemed forever incapable of doing the work of their "normal" peers. They are lifers.

Alexis sees this help as demeaning, and she rails at the assistance offered her. Few of her pulled-out classmates agree with her, however. Some, like Cody, are sharp enough to question privately the simplified work given them, but rarely does a child turn down a proven way to ease the growing burden of her reading life. Instead many struggling readers react as Mick does, slipping effortlessly into learned helplessness as they begin to believe that they are incapable of doing the work assigned to their peers. In most cases it's not that these students are mentally incapable of completing the regular work with the appropriate support. It just begins to seem that way as well-intentioned special educators, through their words and actions, send the inescapable message that these handicapped readers can't make it on their own. Struggling students like Alexis, whose only problem is that they are behind their classmates in their reading achievement, are labeled learning disabled. And in due time most of them learn to be just that.

Special ed, Title I, 504—whatever the name, the aim of this special help is ostensibly the same: to help these students improve as readers. Yet none of these struggling readers talk of "graduating" from the program, of catching up with their peers, of tackling and succeeding at normal classroom activities. Indeed, for these struggling readers there is nothing very special about this special help at all. Once a struggling reader, always a struggling reader. Little wonder, then, that they become the newest crop of lifers.

Parents Step In

With no schoolroom cure in sight for their chronic reading disease, the first place many of these suffering students turn is their family. Parents, grandparents, aunts, and cousins are so concerned with the child's lack of progress that they offer what help they can. These supportive adults take on the role of surrogate teacher, all well intentioned but often with little or no expertise in the teaching of reading. Kayla, Eric, Christian, and Jasmine all talk of adults who read to them, helped with extra worksheets, and sounded out words they were stuck on. Cody's mother went so far as to purchase "a *Hooked on Phonics* type thing, with a record player and a little activity book to follow along with." When this didn't work, though, she tried another tactic. "She started to read with me at home. She was forcing me to. She locked me in my room with her in there and she made me sit down and read to her and she read half and I read half." But clearly for both mother and son the frustration was mounting. "A lot of times I tried to push her out of the way. A bunch of times I threatened to leave and she said 'Okay, I will help you pack.'"

When Cody's mother realized that her assistance was ineffective, she contacted the school, just as Alexis's mother had. Her rationale was sound; she knew that if the school would label him learning disabled, then Cody would be eligible for the reading support he needed and deserved. The process was long and tedious: "It took them a year to get someone in there. The questions where I had difficulty were in the reading part. My weak point was reading." The testing confirmed what Cody, his mother, and his classroom teachers already knew; so Cody started getting special support in reading.

What Cody and his mother didn't know, however, was that this help would not be the desired panacea for his reading struggle, no more than the year of readiness that Mick, Kayla, Eric, and Christian participated in or the repeated grades that Alexis, Paul, and Frank endured. A series of letters Frank's father wrote to Frank's upper elementary and middle school teachers may well speak for all the parents of these struggling readers (Frank had been receiving special services since preschool, but it was clear to everybody that he had made little progress):

2/94 I am writing to express my concern with the level of education that my son Frank is getting. Frank cannot read. The single most important thing Frank needs out of school is the ability to read. . . . Whatever approach to teaching reading Frank is getting now, it is not working, and we need to try something different.

12/95 This is not a game we are playing. This is my son's life, and his future, we are talking about. I see no need to saddle him with this sort of coding for the rest of his life. If I had to do it all over again I would not have had him coded to begin with.

Avoidance

When all of the well-meaning help, both at school and at home, fails to alleviate their reading woes, these struggling readers simply want to ease their pain. All come up with their own strategies to avoid reading, an activity they shy away from at all costs because they are not able to do it well. In addition to watching the movie or asking a friend, favorite techniques of many readers both good and bad, the most popular avoidance strategy used by these students is pretending. They sit quietly at their desks and pretend to read when an assignment is given. Christy knows that the key to having this ruse work is to look the part. "We would have reading time and everybody else would be reading, but I would just be sitting around trying to look busy. I would get my folder out and pretend I was reading the book, but then I would just wait until it was over." One of the most important components of this strategy is to appear to keep up with the class; that way the teacher has no reason to think you are struggling. "Be sure to have your book open," suggests Cody. And "just keep moving on, just pretending that you know," adds Kayla.

Patti has learned to be a good listener during class discussions. The more you listen, the less you have to read. "We have conversations in class. When we have a conversation, it talks about everything in the story that's going on. So if you listen to that, most of the time you get what's going on in the book and you don't have to read it." Mark has a word of advice if you are asked to participate in the discussion: "I would just make up stuff and go along because I don't want to read it. Just guess nice. I get away with it."

Many students complete a small part of the reading, having figured out exactly what they need to read to get by. Cody, for instance, knows that textbook questions generally follow the order of the text. "I found out that trick about it. They would always go in sequence. The first question is in the first three pages. That's where you have to look. Don't read the whole chapter." When reading a novel, both Mark and Sergio know the importance of reading the back of the book. If you do that, they say, you already know what's going to happen. In addition, Sergio reads "the first and last chapter and middle chapter. . . . I know tricks like that now." "Does this always work?" I ask. He chuckles. "Sometimes I would get away with it but not all the time. I did the summary word by word. The teacher would look at the back of the book. She said, 'That is pretty good. Where did you get it?' I said I made it up. She said, 'I don't think so.'"

Even when the reading assignment is over, there is more avoiding to do. What if the teacher decides to give a quiz? Kim knows what to do at the culmination of a reading assignment as well: "The teacher says that if kids want to talk about it, then we don't have to take a quiz. So I just make up stuff and tell her. Instead she lets us do a project on it, but that is easy. I pick the easiest one. All you have to do is get a shoe box and make it look like the book. Anybody can do that."

The sad thing here is that if we believe that children become better readers by reading, then these reading workshop students, who will do anything to get out of doing just that, don't have a prayer. With few or no reading experiences they have little or no opportunity to improve. The less they improve the farther behind they fall. It's not that they don't want to succeed as readers; in my twenty years of working with at-risk adolescents I have yet to meet one who said to me, "Mrs. Mueller, I like not being able to read. I like being unsuccessful in school." But I have had many say to me, "What is the point of all this anyway? I have been trying and trying for years and years, but still nothing good happens with my reading." Mired in a quagmire of failure over which they have little or no control, they seem to have no way out. They're lifers.

Chapter 2

From Love to Hate: Educational Practices That Turn Kids Off to Reading

Each year a very small proportion of children reaching compulsory attendance school age comprise a population requiring special clinical help. These are the children burdened with neurological and emotional disabilities that precipitate reading failure if and when early diagnosis does not lead to appropriate adjustment of instructional practices and learning expectancies. However, by far the larger number of children who become reading failures with varying degrees of disability are the result of pedagogical shortcomings. These children are indeed the unfortunate victims of a society that knows better.

—R. Stauffer, J. Abrams, and J. Pikulski
Diagnosis, Correction, and Prevention of Reading Disabilities

Last fall I was working in my office with Theresa, a junior who had struggled with reading all through school. I told her of my on-going interviews with the ninth-grade reading workshop students, of the reading histories they were sharing with me. "Oh, I wish you would interview me," she said. "I would have so much to tell. Like the time in first grade when I was going out to recess. I was putting on my jacket. The teachers were talking. I heard one of them say, 'It's too bad that Theresa is having so much trouble with reading. If only her mother would take her to the library and read with her at home.' When I heard that, it made me so mad. You see, Mrs. Mueller, my mother always took me to the library. She read with me every night. That wasn't my problem. School was."

Too often in education today, when talking about reading failure, we point an accusing finger at the home environment, as if a family setting devoid of print is the primary culprit in every student's reading struggle. And for some students this may be true. In the case of these reading workshop students, however, it is clear that their reading problems do not begin in the home. Most come to school excited about reading; indeed, like Alexis, many see themselves as readers already. Rather, it is what happens when they arrive at school that precipitates and escalates their struggle. Love for the written word turns to frustration and in many cases to hate as these young children are introduced to formal reading instruction. Kayla, shy and vulnerable as she shares her reading journey with me, is nevertheless able to pinpoint the roadblocks she faced while learning to read. It's a literacy pathway she likes, then hates, and finally loves, when she manages to rise above her school experiences and become an enthusiastic "reborn" reader. Although interspersed with "I guess" and "I don't have a clue," her hesitant words tell us that she comprehends far more about her struggle with reading than she is willing to admit.

I was frustrated with reading for a long, long, long time. I hated it. But not always. Before first grade I sort of liked reading. I had a stack of books when I was little. I loved to look at the pictures. My mom would sit down and read the stories to me. She helped me learn little words. In preschool and kindergarten I was doing great. They only gave me words with two letters in them and I knew them. It was really easy until I got to first grade. Then in first grade something happened. They gave harder words and I couldn't do them. I didn't do a very good job in reading. School just kept going and I just went along with it. It got worse and worse.

I don't have a clue how they taught us to read. I just know I couldn't do it. I couldn't read the words. There was no one telling me what the words were, teaching me the words and how to spell them and stuff. The teachers wrote words up on the board and then they asked who would know them and if you didn't they would help you. They made us sound them out first. Then they would sound them out the way they should be but they didn't tell us the word. Like they would do el–e–phant. We would have to say what it was. That was the help. But that didn't work. I don't know why, it just wasn't enough for me. I needed to know what the word was in order to sound it out.

It got even harder when I moved all over the place. Maybe they had already passed the stuff that I was just getting to. I was at a school that gave easy words and then I was at a different school where I never had seen the words before. Anyway, I am slow and it seemed like everybody else in the class kind of knew the words and stuff and the teachers just thought I knew them. Well, I think they had an idea I was in trouble, but I don't think they really cared. I would ask for help, so they would help me only a little and then they would just leave. They wanted to do their work I guess, just get on with the books, do what they have to do. I was little and I just went on. I kept moving ahead, just pretending I knew. But now it hurts to think about it.

When I was learning to read I wasn't put in a special class like I am now. I was with the whole class. We all did the same thing together. Like we all had to read this book and then we had to tell what the whole story was about. I just couldn't do it. I didn't comprehend what the book was saying. It was hard. I would ask and the teacher would say, "Don't worry about it. I will tell you later." And she never ended up telling me later. So I would just pretend I could do it and try to do the work she gave me. Nobody even noticed. We had questions to answer and most of the time I just guessed because I didn't know the answer. Sometimes I was lucky though. The teacher would happen to pick out the pages I read. But not very often.

By fifth or sixth grade I really hated reading. We had to read like three hundred plus pages in like five weeks. I just can't read that fast. In this big fat book I would be on the third page and everybody else would be on chapter seven. They started asking us to read out loud and I just skipped over the words. I couldn't deal with the big words or anything. I don't know what I did after three pages; I don't even know how I took a test. I had no clue of what was going on. I kept on pretending I guess; I didn't think anybody would help. No one else had helped me so far, and I was just used to doing it myself.

When I went to seventh grade we took a test to see where we were and I was in a third-grade reading level. They put me in a class with five other people that had the same problem. We were in there one period every day. They taught me how to sound out the words better. They would cover up like half of the word and say it to me and then do the same with the ending. I still have hard times with some words now. I sound them out and most of them I get, but there's a lot of big words that I still don't even know. Sometimes I will just sit there for hours trying to figure out what the word is instead of asking. I don't ask all day. I don't know why, I am embarrassed I think.

After I got better at words I started reading outside of school. My brother was in fifth grade and reading a sixth-grade book. He read better than me. I wanted to learn how to read, but I didn't like being made to read in school. After school I didn't have much to do. I got on the bus and read. I read when I got home. I don't know why. I just know that I started picking up books and reading them. I think it was because I had a lot of time to read. I didn't have to. I wasn't made to read. I picked out books that I wanted to read, not books that some teacher assigned to me. I found that I liked reading, that I could read by myself. I basically was learning how to read myself. And I was still listening to my mom. She was still reading to me. My mom would read to me and then my brother. Then we would take turns reading aloud. I liked that because I knew that no one would make fun of me. My mom would correct me on the words that I got wrong and I was not as nervous as at school.

If you ask me when I really learned how to read, I will say ninth grade. I like how we read a half hour every day. That helps me. I have read almost five books in two months. Since I have been able to read the words, I just know I can read better. The hard part is that there are still words that I get stuck on, words that scare me. The easy part is that I can read by myself. I know how to read. If I have a really good book, one that I just fit right into, I can read for a long time. Like in Animal Farm, the animals came alive for me. I could understand them talking and stuff. I could imagine what was going on. Some of the books I just fit right into the story. Instead of another person, I put my name in that book and I could fit myself into it. Now that I am in high school, reading is like the best thing I could ever do.

If I were giving advice to teachers I would tell them to take more time and make sure the little kids understand the big words. I would tell them to be sure to ask if anybody needs help and to help the little kids that need it. They didn't do that for me. They just moved on. If I have kids some day, I will read to them like my mom did to me. She helped me to learn. She helped me to read. She showed me not to be afraid to ask about the big words. Maybe a teacher can be like a mother. But only if you're lucky.

Ineffective Instruction

Time and again Kayla's words are echoed by her peers as they talk about the reading roadblocks they have faced in their classrooms over the years. These roadblocks are not peculiar to this group of students; they are dubious educational practices that are common denominators in many classrooms in our country, practices that despite valid research refuting their worth, have nevertheless remained mainstays of our educational system. Many students, indeed most, manage to rise above these roadblocks, but the at-risk population does not. Fragile learners who need the best the educational establishment has to offer are the unknowing victims of a system that remains unresponsive to their needs. As the reading workshop students shared their stories, it became clear that no one classroom or teacher shouldered the blame for their dilemma; rather, it was the composite of their experiences that slowly and inexorably shepherded these readers from love to hate as each of them took on the inescapable label of lifer.

Methods That Don't Work

When Kayla arrived in first grade, she was eager to learn how to read. She "was doing great" on easy "little words," frequently encountering single-syllable words that she was able to memorize and recognize by sight; she was ready for something more. Somehow, though, she got shortchanged by the instruction she was exposed to. Her teacher's approach to beginning reading emphasized synthetic phonics training; in lesson after lesson students were expected to match isolated letters to sounds in order to read them. If *m* says *muh*, *a* says *aah*, and *n* says *nuh*, then *m–a–n* must say *man*. But not for Kayla. In all likelihood she lacked the linguistic awareness researchers see as a prerequisite to success in such an instructional approach. As Adams (1995) points out, in order to decode words beginning readers need to be aware of the phonemes that make up a spoken word; they also need to exhibit mastery of letter-to-sound correspondences (p. 70). For whatever reason Kayla was without this crucial knowledge, a fact her teacher failed to recognize. Burdened by such a deficit, this young reader was unable to make sense of this method of instruction right from the start; she simply didn't understand what was going on. She didn't do "a very good job in reading;" things got "worse and worse." Exacerbating the problem, her teacher didn't seem to notice the depth of Kayla's struggle. Or if the teacher did, she didn't know what else to do. She just kept on teaching Kayla to sound out words, thinking no doubt that with enough drill her problem student would one day "get it." When Kayla finally got up the courage to ask for extra help, even that assistance didn't work; it was simply more of the same. The instructional method had let Kayla down. She was lost.

Kayla is not alone. Frustration held court in my office as these reading workshop students poured out their negative experiences with trying to learn how to read by sounding out words, a method of reading instruction that had never met their needs but that they had been subjected to in classroom after classroom by teacher after teacher. Just as Alexis talked of her battle with words that "didn't come together," every one of these adolescents recalled their early phonics skirmishes. Jasmine remembered her first-grade teacher "writing words on the board and sounding them out with us." She "started off easy with the little words and then we worked our way up to bigger and harder words." Paul's teacher did likewise: "She would write on the board the letters *at* and ask, 'What does it sound like?' We would go, '*Ah–t, at.*' Then we would write it down on a piece of paper. So when we said *cat* we would look at the *c*, the *a*, the *t*, and go '*Ca–ah–t, cat.*'" A bemused Mick spoke of the phonetic rules he was expected to memorize, incomprehensible rules that meant nothing to him, rules that only served to cement his growing dislike of reading. "Reading has always been so frustrating for me. Everything was so confusing to me. You were learning how to say words and all of those *r*-controlled words like *er*, *ur*, and *ir*. I didn't really understand a lot about it."

Patti's teacher took this method of reading instruction a bit farther. Moving beyond letter-sound matches and the rules that ostensibly governed this puzzling activity, this teacher taught her young students how to break unknown words into syllables. Students who had yet to grasp the sound-symbol relationship necessary to divide a simple word into its component phonemes were being asked to analyze the sound structure of multisyllable words. When I asked Patti how long this approach to reading instruction went on, she replied with a groan, "Forever." Bob, who struggled with decoding in school, was rewarded by being told to practice at home. As he remembers it, "They gave you little sections of cards and stuff, like a pack of cards. They would tell you to bring them home and sound them out with your mom and stuff." "Did this help?" I ask. "Oh, I never really did it. I didn't like it any better at home."

All of these students point to decoding as the primary focus of their early reading instruction; in fact for many of them phonics became synonymous with reading. Yet for most it was an extremely ineffective method of learning. Indeed, for all the time spent, there appeared to be very little learning going on. Although a 1967 federal government study (Bond and Dykstra 1967) found that a "combination approach" to beginning reading worked better than any single approach, more than twenty years later these children were struggling to learn to read in classrooms where only one method, phonics, held sway. And if they didn't "get it" the first time around, their dubious reward was a lot more of the same. It's not that some children can't benefit from this instructional approach; there are many proficient readers who can point to this sort of synthetic decoding instruction as a useful part of their reading histories. It's just that for this group of young readers it wasn't a good match. Indeed, Adams (1995) points out that for at-risk children especially, "phonological awareness, letter recognition facility, familiarity with spelling patterns, spelling-sound relationships, and individual words must be developed in concert with real reading and writing and with deliberate reflection on the forms, functions, and meanings of texts" (p. 422).

Unaware of what research could have told them, teachers using phonics and phonics alone precipitated nothing but failure for these disillusioned readers. Too often, it seems, teachers fail to notice that an instructional method isn't working with some of their students. Even when a child's call for help points out the ineffectiveness of the process, some teachers simply don't get the message. They don't learn from what their pupils have to say. Not only do they fail to know the research, they also fail to know their students—and themselves. Moreover, many of these educators lack the expertise or the professional support to help them figure out what else to do when a teaching method isn't successful with some of their children. They forge ahead in their teaching, with the curriculum rather than the child driving the instruction.

Instruction That Doesn't Teach

Instruction itself, not just the method of instruction, can be ineffective as well. As I heard Kayla and her peers describe their classroom experiences over the years it was not only the learning that was missing; often the teaching was missing as well. Duffy and Roehler talk of classrooms where there is little evidence of instruction of any kind, where teachers tell students what to do, monitor students to be sure they are on task, direct recitation lessons, and provide corrective feedback when necessary (quoted in Tharp and Gallimore 1988, p. 16). I was reminded of that description as I listened to the reading workshop students recall classrooms in which the instructional emphasis was on telling rather than teaching. Many of them echoed Kayla's memories of endless recitations and corrective feedback sessions. Bob describes his early reading instruction this way: "She wanted us to sound out words. She would hold up a card to make like *oo* or something. She would say it and then she would tell us to repeat it."

Eric's memory goes beyond the discomfort of rote recitation when he poignantly describes his experiences with a first-grade teacher who didn't teach:

> The teacher told us to read, but she didn't really want to explain how to do it. She didn't teach us really. We had these little books. They had like two or three words on each page. She would tell you to take out your book for reading time and go sit anywhere you want in the room. So I am sitting there by myself. What am I supposed to do? She never showed us what to do; she just said, "Read. Try to understand most of the words that are in there." Most of us didn't know how to read them so we just looked at the pictures and stuff.

"And where was your teacher during all this?" I ask. His response is unsettling though not unexpected. "Sitting at her desk. Sometimes she would walk about and see what you were doing. See how far you were in the book."

Of course not every teacher falls into this category, and when students are lucky enough to have effective instruction they remember such teachers fondly. Mick tells about a teacher whose instruction gave him the support he needed as he worked to improve his reading. Her teaching style was participatory as she modeled what she wanted her students to do, discussed how to do it, gave them support as they tried to do it themselves, then carefully removed that support as they learned to work independently:

What we would do is she would show us how to do it. She did it herself on the board. We would talk about it for a little bit, but we wouldn't cover too much. When I didn't understand the teacher would come over to me. While the rest of the class was doing something she would explain it again, the things I didn't understand. First she would explain what certain things were and then she would ask me if I understood. Then if I needed it she would show me different ways of understanding. I would read a paragraph and then she would start asking questions to be sure I understood. We just moved from there.

This teacher was using Bruner's (1986) handover method of instruction, when an adult intervenes and gradually provides less assistance to a learner. Neither "hands off" nor "handout," this method of instruction demands active engagement on the part of both teacher and learner. As Atwell (1998) describes it in the second edition of *In the Middle*, "[The student] watches me, I watch her, I do it for her, she tries it, we talk, I lend a hand when I see she needs help. We get our hands dirty together until she gets it and doesn't need me to intervene anymore" (p. 20). If this is effective instruction, then clearly there was little of it going on as these reading workshop students struggled through the years with what in retrospect was teaching that didn't teach.

Sierra knew what she was missing. Listen as she capably describes what she considers a good teacher to be:

A good teacher teaches you something and doesn't keep on going if you don't understand it. He doesn't just go by it and say, "Forget about it, learn it on your own" or "Here is a worksheet, go do it." A good teacher explains it to you and helps you when you are wrong and lets you know why you are going to need to know this in the future. He makes sure you know how to do it.

More often than not, though, the students remember teachers who, as Cody says, "just told you how to sound out the words and then expected you to read. All they were doing was telling you to read and do questions." The tragedy is that although Sierra and her peers knew good teaching when they saw it, they were powerless to avoid those who couldn't or wouldn't teach.

One Size Does Not Fit All

Unlike Alexis, who suffered from the effects of the pullout method of instruction for slow learners, Kayla received most of her reading instruction in a regular classroom, with all students participating in the same lessons at the same time. Whether drilling on the sound of short *a* or picking out the main idea in a story, Kayla's individual needs were virtually ignored as her teachers employed a one-size-fits-all approach to reading instruction. Such an educational model had been adopted by schools in reaction to the mechanistic "sorting machine" mentality that peaked in the 1970s and 1980s, a time when beginning readers were grouped by fixed ability levels in order to master a reading curriculum centered on a complex hierarchy of specific skills. As a direct result of this model of instruction, low-level students fell farther and farther behind as "slow it down and make it more concrete" teaching assured that they would never catch up (Allington and Walmsley 1995, p. 4). Even those, like Alexis, who were placed in pullout programs never seemed to catch up, in part because of the assumption that "low ability" was a fixed and permanent condition. After large-scale evaluations produced data suggesting that these special programs were not so special after all (pp. 23–24), many schools began to dismantle reading groups and pullout programs, offering instead classroom models that touted uniform instruction, uniform materials, and uniform expectations (Roller 1996, p. 9). In doing so, however, they ignored the natural variability that exists among learners; and struggling readers like Kayla, their educational needs once more not met by the conventional curriculum, were no better off than before. Just as Alexis was penalized by a model of instruction that didn't work for her, Kayla was too.

As a result of this generic instruction, Kayla usually found herself behind, rarely understanding what was going on as more advanced readers basked in the limelight of successful learning experiences. Sometimes she was brave enough to ask for help, but she soon discovered that good help was rarely forthcoming. She began to wonder if her teachers even cared about her struggle. Not wanting to appear slower than her classmates, she began to pretend that she understood what was going on, a coping strategy that only caused her to fall farther and farther behind. The farther behind she got, the more she came to dislike the root of her pain and suffering. She "really hated reading." By seventh grade, when she took a test that revealed she was reading at the third-grade level, Kayla, tired of living a lie, was almost relieved to be singled out for small-group remedial instruction.

Like Kayla, Eric remembers struggling to make sense of group learning activities. Even during a kindergarten read-aloud he began to feel the frustration of being left behind. Used to a mother who engaged him in conversation as they turned the pages of a picture book together, Eric found that sharing a story read by the teacher with his kindergarten classmates wasn't nearly as rewarding. "She would read the book really fast and not let you ask any questions. If you didn't get something you would raise your hand and she would say, 'Wait a minute.' Then she would usually forget. Or I would." Lacking the interaction and comfortable pacing he was used to with his mother, he felt lost in this unfamiliar storytelling experience. "I didn't really understand what she was reading. The other kids were somehow paying attention, so they must be getting it, right? But not me. All the stuff that was going on in most of these books happened so fast that I couldn't remember it." The same thing happened when as a class they read a "little five-word book" together:

> The teacher would always be ahead. She was always ahead of me. And she wouldn't sound anything out for us. If you don't know something raise your hand. That's how

you learn. But she didn't call on me. The other kids understood what they were reading. But not me. So then I just sat back and listened. I listened to what they were saying, so I knew what they were doing. But I still didn't really understand. Finally I started to block out the stuff they were saying because it got really boring.

The boredom—and frustration—that Eric felt as a six-year-old grew stronger as little books he couldn't read evolved into chapter books, novels, and ninth-grade history textbooks. Perhaps it was this very boredom that drove Eric to give up on all reading—and himself—ten years later.

We have already heard how the one-size-fits-all instructional practice of reading aloud in front of classmates is seen as a big problem for these struggling readers. Indeed, it's a traditional whole-class activity that stokes up unhappy memories in the minds of proficient readers as well. Although defined by Harris and Hodges (1995) as the "outmoded practice of calling on students to read orally one after the other" (p. 222), Opitz and Rasinski (1998) note that round-robin reading is a classroom strategy that has managed to thrive despite its negative label. Whether it has persisted because of tradition, as a method of classroom management, as a means of reading assessment, as a way to save time, or simply because teachers don't know what else to do (p. 84), it's a detrimental reading practice that has dogged these at-risk readers from grade school to the high school classroom. I not only saw the pain associated with round-robin reading in action as I shadowed reading workshop students through a typical day of freshman classes but also heard about it over and over as one student after another described the kind of oral reading that goes on at Daniel Webster. As Jasmine describes it, "In history class Mr. Collins would start off reading the first paragraph and then he would call on someone. Then after they read a couple of paragraphs he would call on someone else. We'd go around the room."

In the context of generic instruction, round-robin reading can probably be considered one of the most harmful components of group learning. By providing students with a misguided sense of reading as a word-perfect activity, by causing unnecessary subvocalization, by hampering listening comprehension, and by instigating inattentive behavior that can lead to discipline problems, it poses many problems for all students caught up in the circle of stop-and-go recitation (Opitz and Rasinski 1998, pp. 6–7). The damage to struggling readers is more far reaching. Not only are these children required to perform far above their individual reading level, but also the pendulum swings inexorably toward hatred of reading as, word by stumbling word, they are humiliated in front of their peers. Asking these struggling adolescents to read sections of text "cold" in front of the entire class only serves to underline their deficiencies.

So too does the seatwork they are often expected to complete independently as a follow-up to a group lesson they have failed to understand. Even as the work is assigned, these students have the sinking feeling that here is something else they can't do. Their more competent classmates will do well perhaps, but not them. Paul remembers how getting this sort of an assignment felt:

The teacher would write these things on the board. It would be like, "Read this and do these questions." I would go back to my seat and there I was, all by myself, and I didn't know what to do. So I would just sit there and wait and everyone else would be finished and I would still have to read the whole thing for homework.

Kayla admits that she just pretended to do the work, knowing all the time that without having understood the reading she was destined to fail unless luck intervened. Teacher comments on her report card often pointed to a "problem with poor or inconsistent effort." It is plausible to think that the results of her pretending may have been misconstrued by teachers whose generic instruction didn't meet her needs. It is surely plausible to accept that this uniform approach to instruction, touted as a solution to problems that arose from segregating readers by ability and achievement, has instead spawned new problems for Kayla and her reading workshop peers.

Choice Makes the Reader

In *Variability Not Disability* (1996) Roller talks of the importance of choice in effective reading instruction, particularly with struggling readers. If we believe as Roller does that meeting children's individual needs in the context of a regular classroom setting is the key to developing successful readers, choice allows such accommodation. Just as early language learning is highly successful because children pursue their own topics a majority of the time (G. Wells 1986), choice in the reading classroom gives a diverse range of students the opportunity to rub shoulders with material they can learn from. They want to read. They read. They become better readers by reading.

This simple concept is not new. Almost twenty years ago *Becoming a Nation of Readers* (Anderson et al. 1985) pointed out that being able to choose what they read independently positively affects students' fluency. Books by Atwell (1987), Krogness (1995), Rief (1992), and Allen (1995), to mention just a few, all point to the importance of giving students an opportunity to read on a level where they can meet success—and improve—as a reader. Yet none of Kayla's teachers seem to have gotten this message. Instead they gave uniform assignments to the whole class, books Kayla was incapable of reading on her own. It wasn't until her ninth-grade reading workshop that she remembers being given any kind of choice of reading materials in school; up to this point she was expected to march lockstep through texts that were invariably well above her ability.

When Allington and Walmsley (1995) point out that "all children are entitled to the same literacy experiences, materials and expectations" (p. 28), they surely do not mean to suggest that all children, regardless of ability, must be reading on the same page at the same time. Yet for Kayla that is exactly what happened. As the years passed and the difficulty of the class texts increased, her frustration grew. How different her reading history might have been if her teachers had been familiar with research that tells us that readers will show little or no improvement when they are asked to read material that is too difficult for them. How different it might have been for this at-risk reader if she had been given the opportunity to choose her own books at her own level. It is little wonder then that Kayla failed to grow as a reader. Little wonder that her positive feelings for reading diminished as day after day and year after year she faced words she could not unlock, pages she could not understand.

Assigned Reading

Many of the reading workshop students talk about the burden of assigned reading and of their changing opinion of reading itself. Starting in first grade, these students remember having to suffer through books that they could neither read nor understand, either individually or as members of the group. They talk of being forced to read, of plodding slowly through the book, trying without success to keep up with those around them. Children who previously saw reading as an enjoyable activity now talk of it with growing disdain, perhaps surprised to discover that it is something they cannot do. "Well, I really hate reading now," says a rather vehement Kim. "But when I was little I liked it. I liked it because I knew how to do it." David talks of struggling with "just plain dull books," books the teacher made students read as a group. Mick, Carol, Patti, and Jasmine all speak of having to get through "boring book" after "boring book." Kim's words are particularly biting as she describes her feelings about assigned reading. "They didn't let us pick our own books. They gave us like stupid books to read. When they said read, I wouldn't read. I would just open the dumb book and look around and do nothing. Real dumb and stupid, that's what it was." As she sputters out her words, she glares at me, as if daring this reading specialist to defend her turf. Not getting a rise out of me she continues: "And then they would say, 'You've got to go home tonight and read these pages now and read those pages tomorrow and then we will have a test on it.'"

It's more than the reading that turns these students off; it's the difficult and time-consuming work that goes with it, work that takes away any lingering joy there might have been in reading while emphasizing a struggling reader's deficiencies. Cody sees the fun of preschool reading gradually slipping away as teachers ask him to do more and more with his reading:

> I used to love reading. My mom would bring me to the library. We would pick out a few books. I would be sitting there reading. . . . As the years went by you *had* to read. They told you what to read. It started getting on the line of not being fun anymore because we *had* to read in order to get this and in order to get that. You *have* to read in order to get questions done on a chapter or take a test. It wasn't fun.

For reading workshop students the pressure to read frustration-level text is exacerbated by the equally frustrating work that follows. There's hardly an adolescent alive who, if given the opportunity, won't complain about long and boring homework assignments and the reading that precedes it. The difference here, though, is that these struggling readers, over their heads in assigned reading, have something valid to complain about. If they can't read the book, or if it takes forever to read and make sense of the assignment, then any follow-up activity will simply magnify their discomfort. And it does.

Choosing What to Read

On her own Kayla has wandered into the arena of choice—and with remarkable results. She is reading, she is understanding, and for the first time in many years she is seeing herself as a reader. Spurred by instruction that finally helped her come to terms with "scary words" and eager to keep pace with the literacy progress of her younger brother, she takes her first tentative steps into reading what she wants to read. While sitting alone on the school bus, she has time to read and does. Then as a reading workshop student she is encouraged to choose her own books as well, and in two short months she has "learned how to read." Once she sees herself as a reader, she is one.

Unlike Kayla, who discovered the power of choice on her own, Frank and David have needed reading workshop to point up the importance of this educational practice. Among the weakest students in the group, both boys have suffered through years of reading materials written way over their head. Using disdainful phrases like "boring," "not interesting," and "a waste of time" to describe their previous experiences, they nevertheless cannot disguise their frustration at being asked to do something they simply are not capable of doing. Being encouraged to select books he wants to read and can read without the pressure of keeping up with his peers, however, has given each boy a new outlook on reading. We hear their despair about their reading histories slowly giving way to a glimmer of hope for the future:

> DAVID: I never got to choose my own books. By eighth grade I hated reading. I didn't like the books that I got because they weren't interesting. They were boring. Now I am starting to like reading. But sometimes I fall back to hate when I don't get it. Easy books make me love it; real hard challenging ones make me hate it.
> FRANK: Choosing books is helping me with my reading. Because now I read the book. That's new. It's not boring. It's interesting. We get to read a half hour by ourselves. I like that because we don't get told what to do. If you are slower than the rest of the group you don't get told you have to read this many pages. I read the pages pretty fast. I don't know why. It is just easy. I know how to read better.

Sergio doesn't think about reading from Kayla's perspective or from David's and Frank's, but like his classmates he knows the difference that can come with reading what one chooses. Comparing assigned reading to choosing for himself, he says:

> Reading is boring when you are told to read certain things. You don't really want to read. If your teacher says to pick your own book, something you want to read, I think

it is more interesting because you find something that you are going to be interested in. Not what the teacher thinks might be interesting. She already knows what the book is about, so we have to read it and know all the stuff she wants us to know. But if we read something we really like and we really want to know about it, it is more interesting. And then you don't mind reading it. And you do.

Perhaps Sergio wants to be sure the reading consultant sitting across from him really understands the difference choice can make for a reader when he adds:

I don't hate all reading now. I hate reading when I'm being told to read. I hate it and I won't do it. Well, I might do it but I will read it and forget it. I won't care about it. If it is a pick-your-own-book and you make sure you like it, I will probably read it. And I will probably like it too.

Although some students confess to getting interested in an assigned book on occasion ("I had to read it and then I got interested in it," admits Alexis about *Lyddie*, a novel assigned by her fifth-grade teacher), more often than not it is in and through a book chosen by herself that a struggling student becomes a reader. Choice can mean the difference between participation and avoidance as boredom gives way to interest and students read because they want to. Reading an interesting book written at an appropriate level—and reading it at one's own pace—leads to engagement and understanding. It also leads to a sense of accomplishment as children begin to see themselves in a different light, as accomplished self-directed students rather than practiced failures.

Choice, though, isn't something that happens naturally for these struggling readers. As Roller (1996) points out, many of them choose books they do not want to read or cannot read—sometimes both (p. 43). Mick admits as much when he states, "I am not really good at choosing books. I don't know why. A lot of the time I choose a book with not many pages in it and then I start reading it. But I won't get through the first chapter and I think, this book is junk. So I put it away."

Keith knows he isn't good at picking out books either. With little experience under his belt, he is required to choose books in his reading workshop, more often than not with poor results. "We have to choose our own books. Mrs. T. makes sure I pick one out. So I look at the cover and the back. Then if I don't like it after about a week I pick out a different one. I do this all the time."

Both boys know that judging a book by its length and cover doesn't usually work, but they seem unable to use any other strategies. Keith, however, has found a workable way out of the dilemma. He is currently rereading *The Adventures of Tom Sawyer*, a book he admits to having read three or four times in past years. And why not? By now he sees the book as an old friend ("I like pretty much everything—the characters, the setting, the situations"), on the shelf to rescue him from the discomfort of yet another bad choice.

Jasmine understands the problems many of her classmates are having with choosing books they can and will read from start to finish. In her mind, "They don't know where to start. They don't know to read the back of the book, read a couple of pages, stick with the book until you get hooked, until you get to a part where it connects with you. Not just read a page or two and find it boring and put it back on the shelf and not read it." She used to be like Mick and Keith, picking and then abandoning book after "boring" book. Then over the years, by practicing the techniques a reading teacher showed her, she has learned to choose books wisely. "When I was younger I wasn't too good at it. But as time went on and I got to pick my own books and I became interested in something that I actually liked, then that has made me better about wanting to read." The ability to choose books she wants to read has clearly affected her desire to read, an important step on the road to reading competence.

"Assigned" Choice

When I asked the reading workshop students to tell me about the times they had been given the opportunity to choose their own reading materials, most, like Kayla, said they had never been given the chance to pick their own books. And for some that may have been true. Because allowing students to choose which books to read isn't a formal practice in many elementary and middle schools, a particular student might never have experienced this liberating phenomenon. But I also knew of classes and years in which choice had been a component of the curriculum, albeit a minor one, in the schools from which these students came. All Newsom students, for instance, take a one-semester reading workshop in seventh grade; in this same school, Mrs. O'Brien, a beloved teacher whom some of the reading workshop students had been lucky enough to have, always includes a unit of self-chosen reading as part of her fourth-grade curriculum. In addition, I knew that both nearby towns with elementary schools had at one time or another instituted a sustained silent reading (SSR) period or something like it.

At first I was tempted to believe that these readers' failure to mention these experiences was simply an oversight; their memory of them had been overshadowed by all the assigned reading they had struggled with. But I also knew that what has been omitted in an interview can sometimes be as important as what has been included. So I pondered what I had not heard. And I thought about what I knew of these readers and of choosing one's own reading in general. I thought back on Gonzalez's description of her classroom SSR as a "battle zone" (Allen and Gonzalez 1998), then reflected on how this young teacher's experience related to what I had seen of Daniel Webster's weekly half hour reading break. A time set aside for pleasure reading, reading break was more often than not a time when students like these did everything in their power to get out of this "assigned" choice. They might go to the nurse, take a suddenly very important trip to the guidance counselor, wander the halls on their way to the bathroom on the far side of the building. Or they might pull out a book that had been stowed in their backpack for the past six weeks, slam it to their desk and then fall asleep on the unturned pages. I thought of Mrs. T.'s reading workshop, where after three months of being given the opportunity to choose a book for independent reading, students like Mick and Keith continued to resist that task. I thought of the discomfort I felt when sitting in on a reading workshop's silent reading session, trying my best to enjoy *Animal Dreams* as Paul squeaked his sneaker in wide circles on the floor and Kim shifted noisily from one end of the couch to the other.

Then it dawned on me. For many of these struggling readers, choice isn't choice at all. It's no better than an assignment. The very act of reading is so abhorrent to them that an assigned choice is the only choice they will make. And they won't do it willingly. Not until these struggling readers move beyond their histories of reading failure, not until they free themselves as Kayla has done, will choice be a valid and unencumbered option for them. For some it is painfully clear that this day may never come.

Reading That Emphasizes Decoding Over Understanding

Kayla's frustration with reading began when she got to first grade. Until then reading was an enjoyable social process she participated in with her mother, as together they looked at pictures and shared stories—an "act of communion, grounded in love and relation" (Atwell-Vasey 1998, p. x). As a part of this reading experience Kayla remembered learning little words, and she felt "great" about her progress. But in first grade something changed. Learning to read was very different from what her preschool experiences had taught her about reading. Words rather than meaning became the focus of reading instruction as she struggled without success to sound out and spell harder and harder words. Reading was something she was expected to do on her own, not something she shared with others. Understanding, once the emphasis of her reading experiences, became subservient to decoding and was ultimately lost as she fell farther and farther behind her classmates in the skill-and-drill atmosphere in which she found herself. For Kayla, reading had been transformed into a process of unlocking words rather than making sense of stories, a common thread woven through the reading histories of each and every student I interviewed.

It's a thread that appears again and again as researchers look at what has gone wrong with reading instruction for at-risk readers in our country. Cunningham and Allington (1994), in describing failed classrooms, talk of reading programs in which the reading and understanding of real books takes a back seat to the skill and drill that is part and parcel of phonics and/or basal instruction. They note that children in these programs are expected to read—and construct meaning—only when they have finished their seat work or when they are at home (p. 14). A year later Allington joins with Walmsley (1995) in calling for the rethinking of literacy programs in America. Both researchers see a preponderance of schools in which arbitrary skills sequences, rather than reading and writing, drive instruction, schools where poor readers experience a curriculum short in understanding and long in word recognition (p. 8, p. 28). Dionisio (1991), a middle school remedial reading teacher, touches close to home when she describes middle school readers who, like Kayla and the rest of the Daniel Webster reading workshop students, have relied so long on drilled strategies that they have lost the notion of reading as making meaning (p. 9). At-risk readers, it seems, are expected to struggle through the nonsense of meaningless worksheets, the surest way to make learning to read impossible, the surest way to develop and sustain a group of "lifers" (Smith 1997, p. vii). Small wonder that our reading workshop classes are bursting at the seams.

Too Much Decoding

That reading is all about unlocking words can be seen in the responses reading workshop students have given over the years to my request to "tell me about a good reader that you know." Their answers vary—"Mrs. T.," "my mother," "the girl who sits next to me in English class"—but the portraits are always the same: "A good reader is somebody who reads huge books and does it every day." "They can sound out words and split them into different syllables." "They never have to ask for help." "A good reader is able to read out loud fluently." Nowhere in these descriptions is any mention made of understanding; nowhere is a good reader seen as one who gets meaning from print. This shouldn't surprise us; when telling about their first years of reading instruction, these students recall class time spent on identifying words rather than on comprehending text.

Like many reading workshop students, Sierra was introduced to formal reading instruction when she went to kindergarten. Her mother had read to her as a preschooler after dinner each night, but kindergarten was where she began to learn how to read. For her this meant learning "the facts of reading," that is, "sounding out words and putting words together." In Sierra's mind, learning to read is quite straightforward. "At first you learn the alphabet and learn what the sounds are. Then you put sounds together to make words. Then you can read word after word." Unlike Sierra, Jasmine had little preschool reading experience, but her memories of learning to read are strikingly similar, even though one child lived in New Hampshire and the other first in Mississippi and then in Florida. For Jasmine learning how to read was about "pronouncing all the words." Starting in kindergarten,

> teachers put a couple of words on the board and helped us sound them out. They would sound them out with us. That is how I remember learning to read, by sounding them out. Oh, and by learning the letters of the alphabet. Then as time went on they would give you the little tiny books and you were reading out loud in the classroom. That is pretty much how I started reading. We did this from kindergarten to first and second grade.

Eric, Mick, and Christian all attended kindergarten too; but due to "a short attention span" (Mick and Christian), "attention-getting behavior" (Mick), and "low language skills" (Eric), each was assigned to a year in a readiness program, a gift of time meant to support them in their slower-than-anticipated academic development. Remembering little about their kindergarten experiences, each boy instead points to his year in readiness class as his introduction to formal reading instruction. As Eric recalls, "Readiness was to help you with your reading. They boosted your reading grade up by saying out different parts of speech and words and stuff." Mick remembers the emphasis on word attack as well:

> Well, we used to sit at the table and every month they would give us this packet and it was about this tiger, this bear, this parrot, and this rhino, and they were best friends and everything. There were pictures and there were words, and there was something showing us how to pronounce them. Like there would be a word and then in parentheses like in a dictionary it would tell you how to pronounce it.

Although Christian thinks that he learned to read in first grade, he sees readiness as a head start. "Well, that was probably my starting point. They basically taught you on your nouns and how to spell words." Along with this, he remembers being given books and being told to "read this. They would sit with you and they would point to a word and tell you to read the sentence and sound it out if you didn't know what it was." Rather than an extra boost, the boys' readiness experiences may have simply prepared them for more of the same in first grade, the place where Kayla had come face to face with her word-attack nemesis for the first time.

Although all the students interviewed experienced decoding instruction as an introduction to reading, some wondered if this was really what reading was all about. After telling me about all the time spent pronouncing letters and words in first and second grade, Paul, almost as an afterthought, added: "Oh, by third grade we could read normally." "Normal" reading began, it seemed to him, only after this sort of reading was over and done with. Like Paul, Sergio is not sure if reading was what he was doing when he thinks back on his early reading instruction. "First grade they would try to teach you to read. You are starting to learn to sound out the words. If we needed help with the words, the teacher would help us. You would read, then stop. You really wouldn't read." Cody is more definitive in giving his opinions of his kindergarten and first-grade reading lessons, times when "you go around to all these different places where there are tape recorders and listen to sounds for *t*." For him this reading instruction wasn't reading at all. "In kindergarten and first grade we were just learning the words. We never really read. They just taught us the sounds of the letters and we were supposed to put them in sentences." When I asked him how this type of instruction worked for him, this loquacious teenager seemed at a sudden loss of words. Then he said with a sigh: "Not very good. Before, when my older sister was in first grade, she was trying to teach me how to read because she was having so much fun with it. She had a different teacher in first grade and she learned how to read. I didn't." Although he wasn't sure of the difference between his sister's first-grade instruction and his, he did know one important thing. "She liked it. But for me it wasn't fun. She learned to read in first grade, but I didn't learn until second grade when we finally picked up on how to read. In second grade is when we started to really do reading."

Unlike Cody's sister, who was learning how to read in first grade, these reading workshop students were learning how to unlock words. Seen as a prerequisite to reading, decoding skills needed to be worked on and mastered before "real reading" could begin. Although Paul, Sergio, and Cody showed some understanding that there was more to reading than sounding out words, their inability to master the code precluded their getting to the real thing. Skill lesson followed skill lesson, worksheet followed worksheet, and still they struggled. "By fifth or sixth grade I really hated reading," says Kayla. No wonder.

Too Little Comprehension

With all the emphasis on decoding in reading programs, it comes as no surprise that comprehension instruction is given too little time in many elementary and middle school classrooms, particularly with our at-risk readers. As Allington and Cunningham (1996) note, children who are placed in high-ability reading groups have more opportunities to read, and their instruction is often more focused on comprehension. While children in lower-achievement groups are mired in the basics of isolated skill and drill and oral round-robin reading, their more competent peers participate in higher-level reading activities that facilitate the development of independent comprehending readers. The achieving student focuses on understanding; the struggling reader works on oral reading accuracy (p. 17). In a class like Kayla's, where group instruction is the norm, struggling readers have all they can do to recognize the unknown words in the text assigned to them; comprehension is usually the farthest thing from their mind. When understanding is called for, more often than not it is a process that is "caught rather than taught" (Pearson and Johnson, 1978).

That comprehension was not a high priority for these students became clear in the course of my interviewing. As the reading workshop students shared their reading histories with me, I heard very little mention of comprehension. In fact only once during my first round of interviews did I hear a student allude to understanding as an integral part of the reading process. As Jasmine told of learning to read with tiny books, she also touched on a comprehension task she was expected to perform. After having students read the books aloud in class, "the teachers would have questions on them about what happened in the book." My reading consultant curiosity finally got the better of me, so during the eighth taping session, with only four students remaining to meet for the first time, I finally asked. First Mark and then Sergio shared the now familiar story of how teachers had instructed them to read by telling them how to sound out words. "Did they ever talk to you about understanding what you read?" I asked, my voice no doubt tinged with a trace of dismay at what I had not been hearing. "I don't really know," replied Sergio. "They would give us three questions, and you would have to try and figure it out. You would have to go back and understand what we were reading."

Like Galda, Cullinan, and Strickland (quoted in Harris and Hodges 1995, p. 207), I define reading as "transacting with a text to create meaning," "bringing meaning to a text in order to create meaning from it." For me, then, meaning making—or comprehension—is the primary focus of the reading process, the very heart of reading. It is clear that both Jasmine and Sergio—and their teachers—are looking at comprehension in a very different light from the one I use, as simply remembering what is read rather than truly making sense of text. Nevertheless, even this limited view of comprehension, and the teaching that goes along with it, gets shortchanged when these adolescents talk about their experiences with learning to read. Understanding, it seems, is expected from them rather than taught to them; in truth, more often than not comprehension is used as an assessment tool to measure a strategy that most students have to pick up on their own. As Christian recalls, even in the early grades testing was the primary function of comprehension: "They would read the book out loud and they would say questions out loud, and you would have to write them on a piece of paper. They wouldn't give you a paper with the questions on it. All you would have to write was the answer."

For reading workshop students, of course, their inability to do this is yet another roadblock in their perilous reading journey. And it's not that these readers don't know when they don't understand or remember; like Kayla, who just couldn't "tell what the whole story was about," they are all too aware of this deficiency but feel powerless to do anything about it. As Cody explains it, "I have trouble comprehending what I am reading. Like if I read a bunch of pages, I can't really remember all that much about it. I just don't get it. I don't understand it." When I asked how he knew he wasn't understanding, he had a ready reply: "Because at the end of the chapter we have questions. Between chapter one and two we have questions. I can't answer them. I have to go back and read the whole thing over and over. And then we have open notebook tests. I fail every single one of them." Sergio too admits that comprehension is a struggle for him, that he "can read a whole book and the only thing that I can remember is the end. Unless I read the whole book in less than an hour, then I will forget it. I am not very good at remembering."

During the second round of interviews I asked the students if anybody had ever taught them how to understand what they were reading. Bob recalled learning about comprehension as a first grader:

Well, there were worksheets on the book you picked, a different worksheet for each book. The books were small. After you read it the worksheet would be like two or three questions, questions about what happened to the ball or something. You would write down what happened so you would understand the book.

Sierra didn't remember getting comprehension instruction until her eighth-grade study skills class. Even then it would be a stretch to label her teacher's lessons as instruction. "He taught us about remembering what you read and being able to understand it. He would show us movies and have quizzes after. Or tell us stories and have quizzes on that after. Then a big quiz or test at the end." Christian's brush with comprehension instruction was even more revealing: "Teach us about understanding what we read? Oh, yeah, they would tell me if I *didn't* understand it. Then I would read it over and over until I got it in my head."

If there was one way that teachers taught these students to comprehend, it was, as Christian suggested, to tell them to "read it over and over again. Read it until you understand it. " In most cases, however, this strategy proved about as effective for these struggling readers as the teacher's admonition to "just sound it out" when they came upon an unknown word. Reading and rereading text written at a student's frustration level usually leads to just one thing for the reader, more frustration. Sergio remembers having to go back every time he was asked to answer a comprehension question. "I would read it, but I could never remember it. Then the teacher would help me read it over again or whatever." "Did this help you?" I ask. "Not really. But I just studied at home and after a while I started remembering." Sergio and Cody also tell of learning to write things down, of taking down what Cody describes as "the important stuff." "Like now," says Sergio, "when I read a book I like to write little notes down. I am a little bit better about remembering when I read a book. But still not that good."

Sometimes it was the teacher herself rather than the method of instruction that worked to help these students improve their comprehension skills. After a shaky start in first grade, Christy had a second-grade teacher who in her words "really helped me a lot with understanding." As she remembers it,

> I was slower than everyone else and always behind and I couldn't comprehend the book. She told me not to rush myself. I would get kind of nervous because I was behind and I would try to read the book faster. But actually I was going slow because I had to go back and read the book over. So she told me to slow down, to go at my own pace and not care that anybody was ahead of me. And just try and understand the book.

"So the comprehension part, did that improve?" I ask. "Yeah, it did a little bit," she responds. And then she adds in a quieter voice, "But not really." "Did your teacher have any other suggestions?" I continue. "Not that I can remember."

Looking at the learning experiences of these reading workshop students, it's no wonder that for many of them comprehension remains some mystical process that can't be taught. In Kristin's opinion, "I don't think someone could really teach you that." Kayla echoes this thought when she says, "It's something I have learned to do by myself. When I was little my mom used to ask me questions about the book. Then maybe I began to ask questions myself. I developed into it." And Cody, when reflecting on his lackluster comprehension instruction, doesn't seem to put much faith in the efforts of his teachers either. "I think you get it as you grow up."

Ineffectual Teacher-Student Connections

In Kayla's school experiences, nobody has lived up to her mother's expertise as a teacher. She hasn't been "lucky" enough to have a classroom teacher who has shown her mother's attributes of sensitive caring, patient supporting, unflagging encouragement, and quiet understanding. Nor has any classroom matched the comfort and safety of her living room, a place where to this day Kayla feels valued, involved, and empowered as a reader and learner. Although we know that all children can benefit from being an integral part of a responsive community of learners, it seems that at-risk students are impacted the most when they miss out on such a positive teacher-student relationship. Palmer (1998) points out that "good teachers possess a capacity for connectedness. They are able to weave a complex web of connection among themselves, their subjects, and their students so that students can learn to weave a world for themselves" (p. 11). In most of the classrooms they've been a part of, frustrated reading workshop students have felt a sense of alienation as teachers, often without knowing it, have failed to develop that classroom connectedness that empowers all students to learn and grow.

Disconnectedness

A dropout on his sixteenth birthday, Eric is the first of these students to live up to the future the at-risk label foreshadows; likewise he is one of the first to sense the disconnectedness between himself, his teachers, and the classroom curriculum. As early as readiness he remembers "bad experiences" with learning, times when "the teachers didn't really want to explain how to read." His first-grade teacher, a "weird lady with white hair," "was always ahead of us. She wouldn't sound anything out for us." There seems to have been no sensitivity to or understanding of Eric's language needs, no effective support or encouragement as this "ghost" of a reader, all but invisible in the classroom, slipped farther and farther into his nightmare of failure. And things didn't get any better. Estranged year after year from teachers who "go way ahead even when you raise your hand and ask them to slow down," teachers who "go to the next chapter when you are still writing things down," Eric never was able to feel that sense of connection so vital to successful learning. He was never able to experience success in classrooms whose curricula precluded any meaningful involvement on his part.

It is interesting that nine years later Eric finally meets teachers who seem more in touch with him and his needs. Only two months into his freshman year he tells of a teacher who has encouraged him to read his text out loud, having realized that for Eric "out loud is better than in your head because in your head you lose whatever you are reading." And for the first time he is working with another teacher who "goes slow. He doesn't jump ahead like some teachers, like going to the next chapter so quick." Unlike his earlier teachers, here at last are two who understand his needs and who reach out to support and encourage him in his struggle to learn. By now, however, it is too late.

When students think of teachers they haven't been able to connect with, more often than not they remember teachers who, like most of Kayla and Eric's teachers, failed to give them help when it was needed. David recalls one teacher who "never really helped. Like she wanted me to do a math problem. I told her I didn't get it and she said 'Do the math problem.' I kept on telling her 'I don't get it,' but she kept on saying 'Do it.' That made me mad." Kristin describes a particularly annoying teacher who told her to "'do that by yourself. You know how to do that.' We had to do everything on our own. If we had questions we had to ask somebody else in the class. He never gave us any help. He was weird." Christian tells of the meanest teacher he's ever had, one who "yelled too much, was really old (like seventy) and was always in a bad mood. And she never was there to help us." Christy also recalls a teacher who would not help, but her memory brings into focus other aspects of the disconnection that can occur between a powerful teacher and a vulnerable child. She says her first-grade teacher "never really liked me." "Why didn't she like you?" I ask.

> I don't think she liked me because she never really helped me out. Every time I would ask her something on any subject she always had a negative attitude towards me. She would use a really mean voice and sound like she didn't care. And that year a kid kept on bugging me. She just told him to say sorry to me, but she never really stopped it.

A teacher's voice and demeanor, her daily moods, the way she addresses a young child's simple request and responds to a plea for help, all have a subtle but lasting impact on the development of a meaningful teacher-student relationship.

Connectedness

It is somehow comforting that Christy, a student who was so impacted by a teacher who failed to forge a connection with her as a shy and quiet first grader, was also blessed to know one who did quite the opposite. Christy's vivid description of Mrs. Ruman inspires me to hope that every struggling reader has the opportunity to learn from this kind of teacher.

> She was my second-grade teacher. She'd sit me aside from the others. She helped me a lot on understanding and she'd help me personally too. Sometimes we'd sit at her desk—I can still remember that her hands always smelled like grapefruit. She'd have that for snack. Sometimes I'd see her peel it. Or we'd be sitting at a table and she would ask every student if they had trouble, if they understood what they were reading. At that time, I wasn't shy and I told her that I was having trouble and I needed help. Sometimes it was the reading. Sometimes she'd tell me I needed spaces in my writing.

Sergio is also fortunate to have memories of this sort of teacher. Looking back on his third-grade year he paints a vivid portrait of Mrs. Lassiter, his favorite teacher:

> She was a good teacher. If I needed any help, if I needed anything, she would give me a hand. If I got in trouble or something she would be like a good friend. If I needed to talk to her about anything, I could talk to her. She gave me confidence. She told me I could do it and not to worry. "You are just having trouble with the

word; I know you can do it." There were three reading groups. I was in number three, the worst. She said not to worry about it. "First and second doesn't mean anything. Just because you are younger and slower doesn't mean anything." She motivated me. She gave me confidence in myself. "Just give yourself a little while and you will be doing better than anyone else."

Mick points out the importance of teachers who are fair in their dealings with students. These teachers

understand kids. They know it. Like Mrs. Wilson, she is like the Mom of Newsom. Everybody knows her. Everybody loves her because she understands what we say. A lot of the teachers always say, "That is not true." But not her. She always listens to both sides of the story and then she will listen to reason.

Kindness, fairness, offering help, giving encouragement—these are teacher attributes that reading workshop students point to as valued in interview after interview:

ALEXIS: She was nice. She didn't yell at me.
BOB: She encouraged me. "You can do this. It is not that hard. I will help you with the first couple of questions. Then I know you can do it yourself."
KRISTIN: She was nice to everyone and she was fair. Some teachers are wicked unfair and favor certain kids. I don't like that. She liked us all.
DAVID: She helped me out whenever I needed help and stuff. I would read a book and I would ask for help and she would help me with the word. She did this with everybody.

Paul also appreciated teachers who let students see their human side, who connected with their students on a personal level:

I like teachers who don't really fool around but once in a while they make you laugh and joke around and help you with your work. I don't like teachers that just say, "Do your homework; it is due tomorrow. Now get to work." In some classes teachers talk to you. They ask, "What did you do this weekend?" They still get the work done. They do the exact same thing as the teachers that tell you to get your homework done, but they make it more fun. Not really talking loud but letting us whisper to our friends who are sitting right next to us.

When thinking of teachers they had found success with as learners, Sierra and Kim both pointed to individuals who, like Paul's teacher, were able to make learning fun. Sierra told of playing games to learn, hands-on activities where "you are actually doing something with what you need to learn. Then you may remember the game that taught you how to do it." She also saw the importance of projects as a follow-up to reading: "It's fun and they will help you understand the book more."

As Kim recalled, one of her favorite teachers "used to love Indians. So on fun days we always had this festival out back and people dressed up like Indians and stuff. I remember for Christmas she gave everyone four pencils with our names on them in this little pouch. She was so nice. She helped us all."

Along with seeing an effective teacher as a kind and caring person to connect with, Cody's memories of his favorite teacher include the comfortable reading environment she set up for her students:

> We would always get pillows to sit on and put our heads on. My friends and I would make a humongous couch. For the four of us. These things were like four or five feet long, about five inches up from the floor. She brought those in for us to have a comfortable place to read. She thought that would make us all read better because we would be comfortable. If you are not comfortable you are squirming and you are not concentrating on the book, like shifting around. Then you can't get into your book. You can't read it.

"Did this work for you?" I ask. "Yeah. It was like a bed. It was nice and comfortable." Cody paused for a moment, then returned to the reality of most middle and high school classrooms. "But now we are just sitting at desks reading a chapter and taking notes down. It is just not as fun."

These descriptions, so unlike the picture of Christy's unfeeling first-grade teacher, bring to mind Kayla's mother, sitting in the warmth and comfort of a safe place and giving her child the caring, personalized support every learner deserves and needs. These descriptions reveal teachers who can make a crucial difference in the lives of children, children who through no fault of their own seem destined to wage a never-ending battle with reading, a battle that some of them, like Eric, are bound to lose. These descriptions reveal teachers who, for this group of "unlucky" reading workshop students, have been too few and far between.

Chapter 3

Journeys Not Taken: Going Nowhere in Your Reading

[We] spent many hours observing and scrutinizing the work of elementary students identified for Chapter One services. The profiles of many of these children—thirty percent or more—troubled us. These were children who successfully read words from word lists on comprehension inventories. They were able to decode words accurately with acceptable pronunciation. Some even read fluently. Yet after they read, many were unable to tell us what the passages meant. These children didn't know when they were comprehending. They didn't know when they were not comprehending. Many didn't know what they were supposed to comprehend when they read. Others didn't seem to know that text is supposed to mean something. . . . Increasingly we became aware of a growing group of students who could decode words, but couldn't really understand what they read.

—ELLIN KEENE AND SUSAN ZIMMERMAN
Mosaic of Thought

I am observing a fifth-grade reading class. In order to help students visualize what's going on in Gary Paulsen's *Hatchet*, the teacher has suggested to her twenty-three students that each of them sketch a picture of what they see in their mind as she reads this adventure story aloud to them. She has handed out large pieces of paper and colored pencils to each child. As she begins to read, the students first listen intently, then pick up their pencils and begin to draw. Quickly their papers are filled with lean-tos, trees, birds; a young boy sitting alone on a large rock, a crashed plane burrowed into the field next to him. Colorful images blossom on desks around the room as the teacher continues to pull her students into Paulsen's fictitious world. Over in the corner, I notice a sullen boy sitting motionless and silent, staring into space. He has yet to pick up a pencil. As his classmates continue to embellish their pictures, I approach his desk. "Where is this story taking you?" I ask in a discreet whisper. "Nowhere," he grumbles to me. "Nowhere at all."

43

One of the biggest problems we face in working with struggling adolescent read-ers is their total disengagement from text. Many have learned to unlock unknown words successfully. Some are capable of flying through a page of text fluently. Yet by and large these students read passively, believing that understanding is something that simply happens in the course of reading, though usually not for them. Unaware of the mind journeys on which reading can take them (Keene and Zimmerman 1997, p. 28), of the reader's world there for the taking, they see reading as a dead end, a pointless process that goes nowhere.

Mick, a tall, lanky, ADD adolescent with a sharp tongue and a quick wit, has struggled with the mechanics of reading all his life; only recently has he begun to real-ize that there may be more to reading than unlocking words and filling in the blanks. Daring to venture away from his long-held what's-the-point stance, his words paint a portrait of a young man wrestling with the ambivalence he feels about reading.

You'll probably find that talking to students about reading is confusing. The answers you get depend on who you talk to, the type of kid. I am the type of kid who hates reading. I don't like it because it is boring to me. I feel there is no point to it, but I know it is going to be with me for the rest of my life so I am dealing with it. When I was little, back then before I went to school, I didn't read. Oh, there was the occasional time with Pop walking in, reading a book, and then leaving. But I never really sat down and read with anybody else, unless you count the one time my dad read me a book. I only remember that one time. He read me Abby YoYo or something; I can't remember the exact title. It was this book about this big giant guy that comes in. He was a giant and all these people were afraid of him. Then this kid starts singing this song about Abby YoYo, and Abby YoYo and the kid become friends. I liked that book. I thought it was cool, because I was a giant back then too. I wasn't really, but in my mind I was.

I don't remember much about reading in kindergarten. The only time the teachers would read to us then would be during nap time. Story time during nap time. Why are people read-ing stories when you are supposed to be sleeping? I just sat there and looked at the pictures. Or the other kids and I would fall asleep. Of course I needed that time to nap. It was called nap time. It was one of those cases where reading seemed pointless to me.

Then came readiness. I was getting ready to go to school and first grade, and two weeks before first grade I got this phone call. The two-week phone call, we called it. The school called and said, "Oh, your son's not capable of going to first grade. He needs to go to readi-ness because we feel he is not prepared." My parents weren't too happy, but I didn't know anything about it. I was just in school. Readiness was awesome, I thought, at least until we started doing work. At first all we did was finger paint. Then it started getting confusing, when we were basically starting to read. Doing all the vowels and everything was easy. It was hard when you started getting into bigger words. It never made sense to me.

I didn't really like first grade that much. In first grade we had to stick with the same vowel and letter stuff until everybody understood it. It was just more of the same. That's when reading really started to get boring. It just wasn't as interesting as everybody had made it out to be to me. Kids would get going, get these books and they'd be reading and saying how much they liked these books and everything. I would get this book and I'd read the first couple of pages of it. I'd figure it was pretty boring because I really couldn't see anything in my head like I could see on the TV screen. I figured why read when you can just go home and watch everything on TV. I guess I thought to myself that it is better to see a picture in front of my eyes rather than just words. People made reading out to be something you are going to need in life. But back then I figured I wasn't going to need it in life. What was the point? I could watch TV instead.

By second grade my reading was pretty bad. I just didn't care for it. I didn't like the idea of actually taking up time to do it. Most kids would be on the second-grade reading level, and I would probably still be under the first-grade reading level and all that. I'd hear about how some of my friends would even be on the fifth-grade reading level, and here I would still be shuffling through picture books. Everybody else would like be on these thick stories with over one hundred pages in them, and I figured one hundred pages was way too much for me to read. I figured if I couldn't do it, why do it at all? I felt I had better things to do. I remember liking the field trips though, like the Rocky Shore trip. We went to the ocean and we got to dig around in the rocks. We got to make our own tee-shirts with sponge paints. It was awesome. Just the idea of going some place during school hours and seeing something new. That is different from sitting in school and reading words. I don't think that trip had anything to do with reading and writing. I think it had something to do with getting away from it.

I have had extra help in reading my entire life. I was basically one of those kids that always needed help. I guess you could say that I was lazy a lot, and I just didn't understand anything. The problem I had was every time I read, I would be thinking of something totally different. My head would be full of something I had done before. I would still be reading the words but the words wouldn't be processing. I would be concentrating so much on what I was thinking before that my mind wouldn't keep up with the words. I didn't understand what I read; it just didn't cross me. After first grade I started going to Mrs. Curtis every day. She helped out. She would give me work I understood. Some of the other work teachers gave me was like, huh? I just didn't understand it. Everything was so confusing to me. So they took me to her and she pumped some sense into me. I went to her until seventh grade.

When I really started reading, reading by choice, was in middle school. I'm not sure why. I just decided to read for myself. In seventh grade everybody had reading workshop. Up to then we weren't reading much. But in that class we had to read all the time, just read. Then we would talk. Like we read Banner in the Sky. It was about some kid who was climbing a mountain that his father climbed in some Austrian country. Mrs. Love would draw a mountain, and we would do this game to see who was the first one to the top of the mountain. She would ask questions about the book and what happened, then we would all talk and explain what we understood about the book. After we talked, we got to move up the mountain. I had two other teachers trying to help me that year too, ones I got along better with than any of my other teachers. Basically what they said was "Why don't you just read and see what happens? See how you feel." And then when I said, "I still don't want to read!" they said, "Well, you have to." So I thought I might just as well try. It wasn't by choice; but I actually started thinking about things longer, thinking about the events and people in the story. I don't know how. I just started doing it. It might have been through school or I might have just decided to figure things out on my own. I might have gotten there through imagination.

Now when I read I can picture the event happening in my head. Probably not the way the story is making it out to be, but I have a picture in my head of what I am reading and what it seems like. It is one of those things that happen when you really don't know it. You do it but you don't realize it. In English class we just got done reading Of Mice and Men. It's about two best friends. There was a part at the end where one of the friends killed a woman. The book was saying how he was shaking her around and all of a sudden her neck snapped. I could see what he was doing to her. In my head I could picture that happening to her. Now when I read I always have a picture in my head, even if it is not about the book. It may be of something else. If the book is boring another picture will come into my head. Then I will be reading, I will be looking at the words but not really reading. I know when the book starts to lag because my mind starts to go to other things. For me a book is boring when it doesn't get to the point, if it just sits there and describes boring situations. It gets interesting when it has you sitting on the edge of your seat and getting all psyched up, ready for what happens next. I'll start reading a book, and if I can picture things in my head about it then it will usually trip my trigger. If I feel it is pretty boring, then I'll just put it down.

Books are getting better I guess. The last couple of books I have read seem pretty interesting. Like that Deathwatch book I thought was pretty good. It started off and really had me thinking, thinking through the entire book, like what was going to happen next or what something really looks like. I don't know why, maybe it's maturity. It's one of those things you really can't explain. You know how sometimes you feel like an adult? Like when your parents leave for a while and you have the house to yourself? You feel like you are the boss. You feel like, yeah, I'm running the place now. Sometimes then I just pick up a book and I say to myself, hey, I'm reading! That's a good feeling. But it doesn't happen that much.

Most of the time reading is a pretty passive thing. Nothing really goes on. Nothing. Well, maybe you're doing something, but it's just not interesting. You are just sitting there and reading words. You are looking at a bunch of letters and paragraphs and sentences. You just read. It is pretty basic. It's boring. It's different for these people that actually like to read. They get a kick out of it. Like some of these nerdy kids. They really get into it. They like to read, read, read. I really don't know how people get into reading anyway. That's what I'm still wondering. How can someone sit around for hours and read words all day? I couldn't do that. I am the type of person that has to keep moving around. Some people, like my mom, she can sit there for forty-eight hours and read a book. I could probably sit there for an hour and read a book, but I would have to stop every twenty minutes and move around and do something else.

All little kids want to learn to read. It's just that when you get there it's not that great. I would probably be reading all the time if I liked it. But why do something that you don't like, that hasn't been fun from the beginning? I know reading is important. I have already accepted that. You need reading to do basically anything. You get a letter in the mail, you look for a job and have to read job applications. You read something every five seconds, you can't help it. You see a word and you read it. Even if you don't really mean to do it, you are doing it. It just happens. It is not something like it is a pain in my ass to try to get rid of because I am not trying to get rid of it. I am going to learn more about it, but I am not going to put aside everything and just work on reading for the rest of my life. I'm still not sure how reading will fit into my life. I won't know until I get there.

The Roots of Mick's Ambivalence

Reading is an enigma for Mick. When he closes his final interview by telling me how confused I will be as I listen to the stories of twenty-two reading workshop students, how "different kids will tell you different things about reading," my researcher's intuition tells me to keep a close watch on how confusing dealing with his reading history has been for him. And I am right. On the one hand, Mick knows the importance of reading; after all, from the early grades people have been telling him that it is "something you are going to need in life." It's something you have to do all the time, something you need "to do basically anything." On the other hand, though, through most of his academic career, reading has seemed pointless, an activity that has taken up much of his time but has never really made sense to him. Indeed, for this adolescent, reading by and large has been pure drudgery, a never-ending struggle to master words and text that have had little or no connection to him or his life. *I've spent all this time on it. What's in it for me?* he seems to be asking. He has other questions as well. Why is it that his mother, not to mention those "nerdy" kids he has to deal with in school, can sit and read for hour after hour while he can barely get through a couple of pages without being bored? What's going on for them and not for him? And what is there about reading that can make you feel so grown up and in charge of your life? Just what has he been missing all these years?

It is only in the past few years that books have "gotten better," that novels like *Of Mice and Men* and *Deathwatch* have begun to interest him as he has begun to visualize characters and events in his head. It is only recently that Mick has been hooked by a book, actively engaged in making sense of text. But even that new development is a puzzlement. Where do these pictures come from? What exactly happens in order for a reader to take these mind journeys? And why do most books still lead to dead ends for him? To understand the roots of Mick's ambivalence, of the mixed feelings he has towards reading, it is important to look at his early reading experiences.

Reading at Home

According to Butler and Clay, "the most valuable preschool preparation for school learning is to love books, and to know that there is a world of interesting ideas in them" (quoted in Clay 1991, p. 29). Children who are read to at home discover the excitement of venturing into the reader's world, a magical place where characters and settings come alive through the interaction of mind and text, a place where everyday lives and ideas are forever expanding. Early on, they experience for themselves a love of story that motivates them to want to learn how to read. They think to themselves, *If reading is so interesting I want to be able to do it all by myself.*

Most of the reading workshop students have once harbored such a thought; and like Alexis and Kayla, they poignantly recall the joy reading held for them as preschoolers, short-lived perhaps but there nonetheless. Aaron and Carol talk of the fun they had listening to stories told by parents and grandparents. "I liked it a lot," Aaron tells me in his matter-of-fact way. "I liked all the stories my parents read to me."

"My grandfather and grandmother, they'd always sit down and read with me," reminisces Carol. "It was so nice. I think reading with my family really helped me out a lot." Kristin remembers when she, her brother, and her mother would get involved in a story: "My mom used to go to the library and get us books that had just the pictures. We used to sit there and make up our own story. Then my mom always used to read them out loud to us. We got into them together."

For some students, such positive memories are harder to come by, overshadowed perhaps by more recent chapters in their reading histories. But once retrieved, they are cherished. Although Christy initially tells me that reading has never interested her, she changes her mind as she recalls the mental journeys books took her on during story time with her mother: "I remember my mother reading short stories, like fairy tales, to me when I was little. I always asked her to read one certain one, I think it was *Snow White*. She used to become the character. She would act out the voices and everything. It was so fun to listen to."

Mick, on the other hand, has always hated reading. He is one of the few students in this group who came to school without the early reading experiences that form the basis for a child's initial love of reading. Growing up in a home where a disabled older sister's needs took precedence over his, he had rarely known the comfort that comes from climbing into a parent's lap and together entering the world of a story. Only once does he remember "getting into a book" with his dad, of transacting with text (Rosenblatt 1978) as he connected with a picture-book character who came alive in his imagination. And the memory of that "cool" giant is not enough to sustain this sociable kindergartner, labeled "very fidgety" during preschool, as he comes to see story time as an unwelcome usurper of nap time. Simply sitting quietly in a circle and looking at pictures—for that's all it was to him—was no treat at all for an active preschooler like Mick; such an activity was distasteful and pointless. With no mind journeys to spirit him away, Mick would have preferred to catch up on his sleep!

Reading at School

Mick came to school, then, with no initial love of reading; he only knew that it was something "important" to learn. Like many of his classmates, however, Mick's first taste of reading instruction came in the form of isolated phonics instruction; and from the start it certainly wasn't "fun." As he remembers it, learning the sounds of vowels and consonants wasn't too hard; it was only when he had to put them together to make words that he ran into difficulty. Indeed, even after two and a half years of repetitious drill his report card duly noted that Mick "has no idea why letters make the sounds they do." Not surprisingly he recalls such instruction as "boring" and "confusing," "senseless" learning that held less and less importance for him the longer it went on. And it went on for quite a while. After two and a half years of frustration he was referred for special ed testing, with a notation that his reading progress up until then had been "slow despite daily forty-five-minute remedial reading sessions." Coded learning disabled at the end of his second-grade year, he spent the next year taking reading and spelling in the resource room. It was more of the same, albeit easier work that he had more time and support to understand. This extra help went on until seventh grade.

The emphasis of his resource room reading instruction was decoding and comprehension; and his report card stated that he made excellent progress his third-grade year, reading "grade-level passages with few mistakes and with all comprehension questions correct." The report card said nothing of Mick's growing dislike for reading; it said nothing of the pointlessness that reading held for this third grader. And despite his success, remedial instruction went on in some form for the next four years. In Mick's words, it seemed as though he had been getting this sort of help "my entire life." Such academic support took a toll. Lacking the love of reading to buffer him from the pain of having to "stick with the same vowel and letter stuff until everybody understood it," his initial disenchantment with reading flourished with every syllabication rule memorized and main idea lesson completed. Reading may have been important, but this struggling student couldn't understand why. What importance could it have if he were not actively engaged in making meaning, if there were no connection between what he read and what he knew?

As Mick understood it, his job as a reader—and a dreary one at that—was to extract meaning from the text, not make meaning for himself. And why not? All through his schooling the instructional emphasis had been on decoding words and answering questions to which somebody else already knew the answers. No creative engagement was asked for or expected. What learning he remembered had very little to do with reading. When he recalls the excitement of going to Rocky Shores in the second grade, he has no memory of reading about oceans and rocks before and after the field trip. "We talked about it a lot," he told me. "But I don't remember reading anything at all. Maybe we did, but it just didn't click with me." Instead he tells of digging around in the rocks and making awesome tee-shirts with sponge paints. Rather than an extension of a mind journey started in the classroom, Mick saw the trip as an opportunity to get away from reading and writing, a welcome detour from a part of school he had always hated.

What's the Point?

Wilhelm (1997) describes an engaged reader as "an active meaning maker, one who connects personally to what is read, who spends pleasurable and stirring time with stories, and who might judge or resist the text and its author" (p. 15). Without engagement like this, reading has no meaning or purpose, so it should be no surprise that Mick and his classmates, passive readers all, describe their reading histories as pointless and a waste of time. Like Mick, Keith is blunt in his assessment of reading: "I don't like it. I don't enjoy it. There is no point of it." Eric is almost as concise: "Reading is just a waste of time. Some people just don't like opening a book and reading pages. They say it is wasting time, and I say the same thing." Cody, perhaps more mindful of my feelings than his peers, thoughtfully cushions his judgment about avid readers: "I don't mean to offend you or anything, but I really do not understand those people who love to read. I feel there are so many other good things you could be doing. Go outside and do something. Why would you stay inside on a nice, good day and read a book?" Paul, on the other hand, is not averse to attacking the whole reading workshop curriculum I have developed: "It's stupid. Pointless. I don't know why they have it in the school."

When I invite the students to delve into what's behind their comments, to think about the negative baggage they carry with regard to reading, their words reveal just what it is Paul doesn't understand about reading workshop. Their voices explain why a corrective reading program is a necessary part of our high school curriculum. In story after story a frighteningly similar cycle of reading dysfunction comes into focus: these are students who, in viewing reading as decoding from the very start of their educational careers, have failed to become actively engaged in reading as sense making. Not only that, Wilhelm's "pleasurable and stirring time with stories," which causes many an enthralled reader to "stay inside on a nice, good day," is off-limits to them, at most a distant memory from their preschool experiences.

Unengaged, Passive Readers

As Mick well knows, some of his first- and second-grade peers became competent and avid readers while he struggled to unlock words. For whatever reason they thrived on an instructional program that emphasized the skill and drill of decoding and treated comprehension as dependent on native intelligence and experience rather than classroom instruction (Samuels and Farstrup 1992, p. 146). Without knowing it these fortunate children had journeyed into the magic of the reader's world, active readers engaged in making sense of text. But not Mick. Still "shuffling through picture books" as his classmates zipped through a hundred or more pages, he was amazed by their rapid progress in a reading curriculum he couldn't fathom. Although he sees himself as lazy, Mick's problem with reading went beyond a suspect work ethic; here was a child who had to put so much effort into word identification that he failed to have any energy left for understanding. Here was a child whose instruction had emphasized surface structures— graphophonic, lexical, and syntactic—at the expense of the deeper structures on which meaning is based (Keene and Zimmerman 1997, p. 220). Not only that, engagement with text did not come naturally for this active little boy; and until seventh grade there was no one there to teach him how to transact with and make sense of the books he read. No wonder he preferred the colorful and changing pictures of TV to the black-and-white monotony of text.

Most of his reading workshop peers look at reading in the same light. When asked to describe reading as either an active or passive process, Stan and Cody weigh in with Mick. "You are not really doing anything," explains Stan. "You are just sitting there reading." Cody agrees. "You are just sitting there looking at a bunch of words. Grouping them together to get them to make sense. You are sitting there doing nothing." Paul compares the active process of chess with the passive process of reading:

In chess you have to think about what the other player is going to do and you try to stop that before he does it. In reading there is nothing going on. I don't pay attention to the book. I will be reading and thinking about something else. What I will do after school. What homework is going to be. It's weird. Then I will read a page and go back and think to myself, what was that page about? Then I will have to read the whole thing over again. So I get backtracked all the time.

Eric understands the pitfalls of passive reading too, particularly when he knows he has to understand and remember something for a test. "Reading isn't active for me when I have to do it for a final or something. I have to just sit down and read it and remember it and I get really mad because I don't even remember what I read."

These students, then, know that passive reading is worthless reading, as words and ideas go in one ear and out the other. Some of the lucky ones, like Sergio, have had times when they have read actively, when they have been engaged in making sense of their reading; and they know the difference active reading can make for them.

If reading is passive you sit there and think about something else. You don't pay attention to it. You don't really care. If it's passive I could read the whole book and I probably won't remember one word, not even one sentence. I would read it in my mind, I would hear it and say it but I couldn't understand it. If I was active, then I would be thinking of the book and I would be into it.

Fascinated by his description of both types of reading, I encourage Sergio to tell me more: "So when is it active and when is it passive?" His reply should not surprise us: "I think active is if I like the book and I want to read the book. I actually put myself through it and it is something I enjoy reading. Passive is something terrible to read. I really hate that when somebody picks a book for me and tells me a certain kind of book that we have to read. That is just passing time."

Passing time—how much of these readers' histories have been spent doing just that? What might happen if these struggling readers were given more time and support to read books of their choice, books that caused their passive stance to give way to active engagement? Would they begin to see themselves as readers, with the competence and confidence to tackle whatever reading assignment came their way? I reflect on Mick's recent experiences with *Deathwatch* and *Of Mice and Men*. I think of Jasmine's description of "getting into" a book. "How I get into it is when there are funny parts, I laugh. I picture things in my own mind. I think like if that has happened to you or what might happen to you if it did." It is clear that Jasmine, like Sergio and Mick, has had a taste of where a journey of the mind can take her. How do we help these students take repeat journeys into the reader's world, a world from which they have been outcasts for so long?

Boredom

Once a student sees reading as decoding rather than understanding, once reading becomes a passive process devoid of meaning, boredom sets in. Without engagement, reading becomes dull and pointless—and frustrating as well, as struggling students are asked to cover more and more, knowing all the time that there is less and less in it for them. Whatever interest reading may have once held for these students is quickly extinguished. For Mick, such a negative feeling has saddled his perceptions from his earliest recollections of reading; and even now, with his memories of *Deathwatch* and *Of Mice and Men* still fresh, he does not dare to let go of the stance he has held for so many years: reading is boring. And he is not alone; virtually every student used this adjective when talking of reading. It's a descriptor with varied shades of meaning.

BORING = LACK OF INTEREST

For most of these adolescents, the word boring relates directly to their lack of interest in and engagement with the materials they are studying. School is boring, geography is boring, *Animal Farm* is boring. Interestingly enough, these are students who, like Mick and Sergio, have on occasion connected with a book they have liked, who have tasted what it means to be hooked on a book. And they know such mental journeys don't happen nearly enough, though they are unsure why. Kristin explains:

> You know how sometimes you can pick out a book and start reading it and it is boring? And you can pick up another book and it is really good and you keep on reading it? Some books just aren't interesting. They are boring to read. Other books are a good story. *Of Mice and Men*, I didn't like it. I don't know what made it boring; it just wasn't interesting.

Patti thinks it has something to do with the way the book is written. She doesn't like too much detail in her reading, and she looks forward to a climax in the story. "I like it when you don't really know what is going to happen. Good is a book that has a lot of action, like an adventure to see what happens next. A bad book would be a quiet one with no climax whatever."

Christian knows that the subject matter is the key for him: "It is boring when I don't like the book, if it is not a subject that I like." Cody agrees: "If it is a book I like reading, it is interesting, because it talks about things that I like; but if it is something I don't like, it is boring." Always wanting to make sure I understand his words, this garrulous young man continues, "It is boring when a book I am reading . . . if I am reading a love book or something, a love story, a woman wants to marry or something, it is boring." Bob also realizes that the topic is the key to how he reacts to a book. "The topic can make it boring. If I read about basketball or some kind of sport, I like sounding out the words. That is cool."

Too often in their reading histories these students have been assigned texts, and for many this lack of choice is the kiss of death. Reading is going to be a struggle, so why make any effort at all when someone else picks the book for you, when it's something you care nothing about? As Sergio explains it, "Reading is boring when I am being told to read and they tell me what books I have to read. You don't really want to read. The teacher wants you to read what she thinks might be interesting. She wants to know what the book is about, so we have to read it and we have to know all the stuff." On the other hand, "If she says to pick your own book, something you want to read, I think that is more interesting because you find something that you are going to be interested in. If we read something we really like and we really want to know about it, it is more interesting. Then you don't mind reading it."

For some it hasn't always been this way. Jasmine didn't mind being assigned reading when she first began to read: "Then you were just first learning, and it was really neat because you could actually read something. But now it's boring because you don't have a choice. You're not in touch with the book you are reading. You are assigned it. You have to do it for school."

Cody remembers the novelty of learning to read as well, a novelty that gradually wears off as he is continually assigned books that don't engage him as a reader. When he first began school, he says, "I wanted to read. It was something new. Okay, if you get a toy, you really want to play with that toy, right? It is the only thing you want to play with. But after a while you get bored with it. It's the same for reading." Especially when time after time and class after class you're expected to read "a love book or something."

BORING = LACK OF SUCCESS

All students have to contend with assigned books they cannot relate to; this sort of boredom is not reserved for struggling readers. However, for struggling readers the boredom has an additional element. Not only are they expected to read books with which they cannot connect, they are often required to read text written well above their instructional levels; comprehension is either elusive or lost. Such a mismatch results in the kind of boredom stemming from being asked year after year to do something you are not capable of doing. Struggling to describe her present dislike of reading, Carol ponders the meaning of the word *boring*. "Right now reading is boring. How can I say this? It doesn't interest me to pick up a book and read for two or three chapters, to just pick up a book and read it out of the blue." When I ask her to elaborate, she continues:

> Maybe I think a book's boring so I don't want to pick it up and read it, but yet I might think it's boring because I can't understand it when I read it. The information, what I read, is just a bunch of words or sentences or paragraphs. Okay, I can take a book and read the first page, but I won't necessarily understand it; and then going from chapter to chapter I won't remember what happened in the past chapters. What happened in the beginning of the book? It doesn't really make sense to me.

Her classmates readily agree that assigned reading, almost always over their head, almost always without meaning, leads to boredom. In Sergio's view "things that are boring are things I don't understand. Things that don't make any sense. Then I really don't care." David divides his reading into interesting books that he likes and boring books that he hates. The definers that he uses are telling: "Easy books make me love it; real hard challenging books make me hate it." Alexis tells of trying to read *Deathwatch*, an assigned text that makes no sense to her, a book that gets her so bored that she is ready to cry. Eric, who from his first day in school to his last never knew the luxury of keeping up with his classmates, talks of the boredom that comes with being behind in his reading from first grade on: "If we don't catch up in our reading, in the book that [our first-grade teacher] gives us, we get behind and we have to read more to catch up. That gets kind of boring after a while." For this struggling student, the long stories that were read to him were boring, most of the books that he looked at on the bookshelf in the library were boring, and even the authors of the books he was assigned fell victim to his long-held frustration with reading. "Most of the people that write them, I don't really like either. The way they write the books." No wonder that for Eric reading is "mostly boring because it is a waste of time to me."

Stan had an easier introduction to school reading than Eric, but the end result, a depressing and uncontrollable journey into boredom, has been the same. When he first started school, Stan liked reading. He fondly remembers sitting on the floor and listening to Mrs. Cox read. "We didn't have to do everything ourselves." His report card pointed to "good progress in all areas"; according to Mrs. Cox, "Stan seems to enjoy reading." In his memory second grade was okay too, although his teacher ominously noted, "Stan tends to guess on words if he doesn't know them. Reading out loud would help him a lot." In third grade, as if in answer to this suggestion, came the pain of round-robin reading. "We each read a page and then we switched. We had to read out loud. I read too much so I didn't like it." Although his report card noted that he was able to read on grade level at this time, his effort and achievement began to drop. By fourth grade he was "not using his time wisely, choosing instead to sit idly or talk to his peers." "A good reader," in Stan's mind, had become "someone who could read the words." He couldn't. No wonder that for this young boy reading "got boring. Not very fun. You just sit there and look at words. It is not very fun for me." Looking at words in the absence of meaning—and stumbling over them in the presence of his peers—is a memory he has not been able to shake. "We did it all the time," he recalls. I am not surprised, then, when Stan looks up at me and quietly says, "I would rather be skate boarding than reading."

Aaron differs from most of his peers in that throughout our interviews he rarely admits to having trouble with reading. Indeed, he insists to the end that reading has never given him a problem, that "I can read just great." The reason he is in reading workshop, he tells me over and over, is that the substitute teacher gave him the wrong test booklet. Nevertheless, his cumulative file shows otherwise. His report cards contain a preponderance of 70s and an occasional low 80 in reading throughout elementary school, and his standardized test results consistently list comprehension scores at least 30 percentile points below vocabulary scores. Indeed, in his midyear reading workshop self-evaluation Aaron ventures closer to the truth when he writes, "My comprehension skills are very bad." Perhaps that is why he points to "big books" as the impetus for his boredom with reading. Like many of his classmates, being able to decipher words is not enough for him to make sense of his required reading. The "bigger" the books get, the more he has to struggle with understanding; the greater the struggle the more his boredom grows. "Books are not very interesting," he tells me. "They are so long. There is too much in it. It goes in depth too much and it gets boring." When I ask what he means by boring, he continues, "They kind of lose the whole point. It doesn't teach you much. You really don't get much out of it." When I ask Aaron whether his boredom might be synonymous with his confusion about what he is reading, he quickly resumes his tried-and-true stance: "I just don't like reading. I would rather be doing other stuff. Books seem like they are going nowhere."

Boring = Lack of Activity/Lack of Attention

Of the twenty-two reading workshop students in this study, seven of them have been tested at some time in their educational careers for either attention deficit disorder or attention deficit hyperactive disorder. Still others have received report card comments that describe them as "easily distractible," "inattentive," or "lacking in self-control," though for some we cannot rule out that such behavior may in fact have been a manifestation of their reading struggles. It is not surprising, then, that like Aaron, they would rather be "doing other stuff." If reading instruction means being expected to sit quietly at a desk doing repetitious worksheets or going through the motions of reading incomprehensible texts, if there is nothing going on for either body or mind, it is understandable how these active and/or inattentive children can come to look at reading as boring. For them it is surely "not very fun." Most, to be certain, would prefer "to be outside doing other things."

According to his teachers Mick was fidgety from the start, loud and active and exhibiting poor self-control. As he remembers it, when he tried to read he found it difficult to concentrate; his head was always full of the wrong thing. He would be "reading the words but the words wouldn't be processing." Even after going on medication in second grade, he could not focus on his reading. "They gave me that Ritalin stuff and the teacher said there wasn't anything different. They came to the conclusion that I was always going to be hyperactive."

Christian is another readiness graduate who has yet to move beyond the "short attention span" label that prompted the school to place him in the readiness class so many years ago. Tested for an attention disorder but never coded ("They thought I had like ADD and stuff, but I got tested for it and they said I didn't"), he has nonetheless always struggled with the concentration that reading demands. Indeed, for most of his reading history he has been reading without comprehending, a fact he is just now beginning to understand. "It's hard for me to read," he says. "When I read it is not clicking in my head. I don't absorb it to know what I read." Small wonder that he has never really liked reading, preferring instead to play with his friends or go to a softball game with his grandfather. "It wasn't fun to read at all," he admits to me.

Lest we think that only boys struggle with the boredom that springs from inattention and/or hyperactivity, listen to what Carol and Kim have to say. Carol, who unlike many of her peers only began to struggle with reading in third grade when comprehension rather than words became the focus of reading instruction, thinks that one of her problems with reading comprehension is that she can't "sit still long enough to read my assignments. I don't think I was that way as a little kid, but now that I'm older

I can't sit still." Sitting still may be difficult for Carol; sitting still to focus on something she does not understand makes it even more so. Kim, a student who according to her records has never been tested for ADHD but who in my classroom observations rarely stayed on task for more than ten minutes, hates the enforced inactivity of reading. In fact, she notices a big difference in classes where teachers work to dispel the regimen of "just plain reading." In her mind her reading improved in a class where she could "get up and do stuff instead of just sit there and read. . . . [The teacher] would give you little projects to do. You got to pick whatever you wanted to do it on. On Fridays he would bring us doughnuts. We got to go to the police station. All kinds of stuff."

It is difficult enough for an active child with no attention deficit to attend to an instructional program that focuses on the tedium of repetitive and uninterrupted seat-work interspersed with generic group work, so for students like Mick, Christian, Carol, and Kim it can be downright intolerable—or in Paul's scathingly succinct words "totally boring."

A Glimpse Into the Reader's World

For years now, Mick has labeled reading as pointless and boring. Yet, because he has always been told that reading is important in life, there has existed an ambivalence that has prompted him to stick with it, to learn more about reading in spite of the meaningless words, sentences, and paragraphs he has had to struggle with throughout the grades. And in the past few years such determination has begun to pay off. Although Mick is at a loss to understand why, in middle school he started to look at reading in a different way. He began "thinking longer," bringing sense making into the reading equation for the first time. For this reader, then, meaning starts to gain precedence over decoding. He begins to "really read." Blessed with a nurturing relationship that developed between him and his special education teacher and aide, fortunate to be in a seventh-grade reading workshop where students were given the time, choice, and response so necessary to developing readers (Hansen 1987), Mick begins to engage with the text. Without really knowing why, he takes his first tentative steps in an all-important mental journey toward understanding. For the first time since pre-school, he enters the reader's world, and almost despite himself, he likes what he sees.

Pearson et al. (1992) propose that visualization is but one of the cognitive processes proficient readers use to engage with and make sense of text. Keene and Zimmerman (1997) outline six others that together create the mosaic of thought that leads to comprehension (pp. 22–23). Nevertheless, it is the riveting glimpse into the world of Lenny and George in *Of Mice and Men* that sets off a construction of meaning ("trips my trigger") that overcomes the boredom that has saddled him for so long in his reading. First and foremost, then, it is visualization that lures this struggling reader toward books.

Other reading workshop students have had similar experiences. Both Alexis and Kayla touch upon their ability to "get into" the reader's world through visualization. David tells me that he now makes pictures in his mind "all of the time," pictures that help him remember a good story long after he closes the book. Jasmine gets more specific as she outlines the way she takes a mind journey: "I kind of picture in my head the setting of the book and what the character is doing. Like if she moves to pick up something, I can kind of follow that certain picture in my head of a person picking up a certain object or something." It is Kristin, though, the daughter of an English teacher and an artist, who is best able to paint a word picture of the power of visualization:

> I can't make a picture in my mind of all books. Some just kind of jump out. You get a picture in your head of what the character looks like and what the setting looks like. You get a view. When I read *The Shining*, I could actually picture things. I actually saw the hotel and the people. Everything seemed so clear when I read it. When I was reading it I saw all kinds of pictures. I think if I see the book more clearly, I understand it more. I like the book more because I know what is happening.

Interested in Kristin's description of visualization, I probe for more information: "How did you learn to do this? Did anyone ever teach you to do it, or is it something that you figured out for yourself?" After pausing to think, she replies with a shrug, "It's just something that happened. I don't know. It's happened all along." Her confusion at how she came to visualize mirrors Stan's, who realizes that visualization is "doing something in your mind but not doing anything. I don't know. It's weird. I just started doing it when I was young." Christy is one of the few students who recalls anyone talking to her about making pictures in her mind. "I remember sitting down in a little part of the room and my teacher would be in this chair and she would read us a book. She wouldn't show us the pictures. She told us to imagine it because that is what grown-ups do." "Did she show you how to do it?" I ask. "No," Christy replies. "She just said to imagine." "Well, could you do it?" I ask, wondering all the while what it might have been like as a first grader to listen to picture books being read without seeing the pictures. "For *James and the Giant Peach* I could imagine it. But not for much else."

Without being shown how to embark on a mind journey through visualization, Christy hit a stone wall in her attempt to enter the reader's world. And more often than not, so do most of her classmates. Even though some reading workshop students know what might trigger pictures in their minds—both Patti and Eric point to the author's use of detail as the key ingredient in their mental journeys, Christian points to interest in the book—more often than not they do not know how to activate such a voyage on their own. Lacking the ability to think about their thinking, they are powerless to jump-start their trip. Mick is all too aware of what happens in that case; the boredom of reading returns as his mind vacates the reader's world and "starts to go to other things." Once again he is going nowhere in his reading.

Destination: The Reader's World

More thoughtful about his reading than many of his peers, Mick exhibits a changing consciousness whereby he has moved from looking at reading as decoding to seeing it as sense making. His deliberate decision to give reading a try, along with some serendipitous teaching and mentoring, has given him a new taste of reading that he admits to almost savoring. A "good feeling" that "doesn't happen that much," this new outlook nevertheless constitutes a foot in the door to a magical world to which he has long been denied access.

It's a world where stories come alive for the reader, where the point of reading need not be argued as students immerse themselves in Technicolor meaning that transcends the black-and-white pages of the book. Whether engaged in the story through either Bruner's (1986) landscape of action or his landscape of consciousness, visitors to the reader's world establish contact with the characters as they construct the story landscape. Decoding words and making verbal sense of text take a back seat to the reader's transaction with the author's words. Liberated through a "pretty good book" from "sitting on the bench during the big game, completely bored, without even realizing [he] hadn't participated in the action"(Wilhelm 1997, p. 87), Mick shakes, if only for a brief moment, his deeply ingrained what's-the-point stance toward reading. Listen to him talk about reading *Deathwatch*:

> It really did it for me. A lot of people didn't like it. It was good for me. I enjoyed it a lot. I was grabbed by the entire idea about a guy trying to find water and food with another guy chasing after him trying to kill him. And then by how the author describes many situations, like how he almost gets water but the guy that is trying to kill him ruins the path, trashes the water and so on. Or he tells about how this family's car moved down into the side of the road out in the desert. They decided to leave the car in the middle of the day, and the sun was beating down on them and you just knew they were going to die of dehydration. And there was a part in the book where they said the mother wiped lipstick all over her children's faces to keep the sun rays off of them. I can picture that really good in my head.

Mick's visit to the reader's world is matched by only a few of his peers. But through their words, and his, we can gain some sense of what is possible for these nascent adolescent readers. Kayla, for instance, talks about "fitting myself into the book." And in our last interview Alexis talks excitedly of the mind journey *The Outsiders* had taken her on. Grabbing a copy of the book from my bookshelf, she recites the whole story from memory, telling me proudly that she knows the entire book by heart. "So what makes this book so good?" I ask. At that point she opens to the first page and begins reciting the text: "The first page, it says, 'When I stepped out in the sunlight. . . .'" "So you were right there in the book?" I query when she stops reading and looks up at me. "Yes. And what really interests me is the way she did it again at the end." Turning to the last page, this struggling reader again begins to read, "'When I stepped out. . . .'" "Wow," I say. "That is really remarkable. How do you remember so much?" Alexis's reply, along with her oral reading performance, should make all of us rethink her struggling reader label. "When I read it, if I like it, it will stay in my head. If you read a book, if you are really into it, you are the book. You can see in your mind what is going on in the book."

Just as Kristin was able to describe visualization, she is able to portray the creativity necessary to venture into the reader's world:

> Reading is kind of like watching a movie but you get more of a picture. It's weird. Because when reading a book and then seeing a movie, you might picture everything so differently. When you see a movie [after reading a book] you say, that person doesn't look like that. When you read, you can picture everything so clearly. You kind of make up your own story as you are reading. You make up what the characters look like or what you think the environment around looks like. It feels like you are actually there and the things are happening. It changes the book. It might make the book better.

Bob's words encapsule the feelings that a mental journey engenders for him and his peers: "Everything comes to a halt and you can see what is going on in the book. You know how you go to sleep and time flies? It is like that when I am reading. Everything around me just kind of stops but it's actually moving pretty fast. I just key into the book, like the plot and the people."

"Any kind of reading?" I ask. "I think it depends on the type of book. If it is stuff you like, you can get into it. Like *My Side of the Mountain*, I will feel like I am in it. If it is a real sappy book, you just sit there."

Mind Journeys Aren't Easy

Just "sitting there" is the bane of these unengaged readers, some of whom are fortunate enough to know what it's like to be a part of the reader's world, but none of whom understand how to precipitate such a mental journey on a regular basis. According to Keene and Zimmerman (1997), thoughtful, active, and proficient readers are metacognitive; that is, they think about their own thinking during reading and in doing so, they deepen and enhance their own understanding of text. In addition to creating images to draw themselves into the reader's world, good readers activate prior knowledge, determine importance, ask questions, draw inferences, synthesize, and use a variety of fix-up strategies to repair comprehension when it breaks down (pp. 21–23). Most of us engage in these cognitive strategies without even realizing we are doing it; and with effort we are able to make sense of a wide variety of texts, even those that don't immediately interest us. But not these reading workshop students. Having been schooled in classrooms in which students are expected to understand without actually being taught how to do so, they are the unlucky ones who for whatever reason do not "catch on" to comprehension. They are the unlucky ones who, in putting word attack ahead of sense making, have lost sight of the whole point of reading. Over the past few years Mick has been thinking more about his reading, and such effort has begun to pay off; but even so he is at a loss to describe why reading engagement occurs for him. Indeed, he describes a mind journey as "one of those things that happens when you really don't know it." Lacking Clay's (1991) self-extending system of literacy expertise (p. 317) and unable to choose books that mesh with his interests and his instructional level, Mick must rely on the luck of the draw to become engaged in a book. It doesn't happen very often.

As part of our last interview, I ask Mick to tell me what goes on in his head as he is reading. "Nothing too much," he tells me. "At least not in *my* head. Not like all those kids that actually like to read." Having just listened to his vivid description of the pictures that *Deathwatch* evoked for him, I am initially baffled by his response. After thinking about his words though, I readily connect them to his ongoing ambivalence toward reading, to how important it must be for him not be grouped with the "nerds." His reply also reminds me of his total lack of self-knowledge, of how a struggling reader's mind can operate without his even knowing it. I probe a little more. "I'm going to list things that people sometimes do in their minds when they are reading. See if you do any of these things, okay?" As I describe Keene and Zimmerman's seven cognitive strategies, he offers quick nos to three of them—determining importance, asking questions, and synthesizing. He allows that he sometimes uses prior knowledge ("I was just reading a magazine about trucks in reading workshop. I was thinking about when I bought my first truck and I was trying to repair it"), infers every once in a while ("like when I knew that guy in *Deathwatch* was going to get killed"), and employs the tried-and-true fix-up strategy of reading something over again when he doesn't understand what he has read ("Sometimes it works. Sometimes it doesn't"). When I ask about visualization, Mick tells me of the pictures that are always in his head, even those that aren't about the book, and of his frustration when the ones triggered by the book fall victim to boredom. The pictures inspired by the book vanish, and this struggling reader, not in touch with the thought processes going on in his own head, is powerless to retrieve them. All he knows is that his mental journey screeches to a halt; without understanding why, he's no longer "really reading."

Prior Knowledge: A Helpful Tool

Students who use prior knowledge see it as an important tool in helping them become engaged in their reading. By connecting with something they already know, these readers are able to make better sense of what they are reading. Bob, for instance, tells me how he used his prior knowledge to connect with his favorite book, *My Side of the Mountain*. He liked the book because he and his dad had done something like what happened in the book.

> Once my dad and I went biking. There is this trail from Eastville that goes all the way up to Canada. We would stop on the side of the road and camp out. When we got to Canada there was this tree and I got an idea. When my dad went fishing, I built a shelter. He came back and we spent a week there. Just like in the book.

Kristin connects her reading with her own life experiences too. "If I am reading a book about something that has happened in my family, I think, Oh, I remember when such and such happened to my mom." Like Kristin, Carol reads books that connect with how my family has been, what's happened to one of them or what's happened to me. [I do this] instead of just plain reading it and trying to understand it and being done with it. I think that might be why I can't connect to wars and stuff, because it's never happened to me. It's never happened to my immediate family.

But without fully knowing, she is able to take the use of prior knowledge a step farther than Bob and Kristin as she also realizes that information doesn't have to be firsthand in order to connect the known with the new. Along with text-to-self connections, Carol can make text-to-text or text-to-world connections (Keene and Zimmerman 1997, pp. 57–60) when she reads: "If I have heard about it on the news, like that Oklahoma shooting in the schools, then I will read it [in the newspaper] and sort of understand it because I have heard about it before. Some article that has never been on TV or on radio before, I am going to go, huh?"

That these students grasp the usefulness of such a strategy is obvious. "It is easier to comprehend when you know something about it," says Cody. "If you already know something, you can actually get further in the book," adds Eric. Kristin continues to exhibit her understanding of the power of metacognition when she says, "If you are reading a book and if you connect it with something that has happened to you, you get a better idea of what happened because if it is something that has happened to you, you know what it was like."

Questioning: Helpful but Infrequent

The students who see the importance of visualization and the use of prior knowledge in their reading are generally the same ones who ask questions as they read, but not always. Mick, for one, is quick to say no when I inquire whether he asks questions of himself while he is reading. So does Alexis.

But when engaged by his reading Bob is always asking, *What will happen next? What will they do?* Kayla also admits to asking questions of herself as she reads, though "not to anybody else. Like I wonder why she is going to do that. And why won't the father help him?" Jasmine occasionally poses the same I wonder why questions in her head, although she states that she is more apt to raise her hand and depend on the teacher rather than herself when her reading doesn't make sense. Carol, who throughout our interviews has shown the most frustration with her inability to comprehend ("I think I have a learning disability," she tells me. "When I read I don't understand"), doesn't recall visualizing as she reads; but along with using prior knowledge she also asks questions of herself when trying to make sense of a text. As she describes it,

in *It Happened to Nancy* the main character has a kidney problem. And she pees in her pants a lot. And when I was reading it, I was like well, can a kidney infection really do something to your bladder? Can that really happen? And then I talk to myself about it, and if I can't really think of the answer, I'll ask a teacher or my parents or something like that.

And it shouldn't surprise us that Kristin, clearly the most thoughtful of these struggling readers, questions herself as she reads, that "sometimes I will be reading and I wonder what this person is going to do or how this person feels."

Fix-Up Strategies: A Limited Repertoire

To Keene and Zimmerman (1997), fix-up strategies include a variety of methods used to repair comprehension when it breaks down. According to them, proficient readers choose appropriate fix-up strategies from one of Rumelhart's (1977) six language systems to best solve a particular problem that comes up in reading (p. 23). Such problem-solving strategies might be skipping a particularly difficult word, using context, rereading, or sounding out an unknown word. Not unexpectedly these struggling readers have very few effective fix-up strategies to rely on. Two boys, Mark and Bob, tell of skipping over the difficult word. "Then," Mark continues, "after a couple of spaces go by I maybe will know what it means." Patti speaks of using a dictionary or "asking people what that little phrase might mean." Four students mention rereading as an aid to comprehension, although, like Mick, Carol doesn't seem sold on the effectiveness of this particular strategy. "I can try and reread it and reread it and reread it and reread it to try and comprehend it, but to me that gets really annoying." "But does it work?" I ask. "No, except sometimes if I've been rereading enough." Interestingly, when asked to think of fix-up strategies they call on when reading, not one of the twenty-two students mentions sounding out words as a viable problem solver. This omission lends further credence to the idea that for these students word identification is a part of reading that has little or nothing to do with the puzzle that is comprehension.

Inferring, Synthesizing, and Determining Importance: Leading Nowhere

I suspect that all of these reading workshop students have at one time or another been exposed to the Barnell-Loft school of reading comprehension (as a reading consultant I admit to still storing one of these ubiquitous kits on a dusty shelf in my office), that as part of their reading histories they have spent class after class droning through multiple-choice exercises taken from leveled workbooks entitled *Drawing Conclusions* and *Choosing the Main Idea*. It seems that such drill, however, has had very little effect on their use of the cognitive strategies that most closely align with these skills: drawing inferences, synthesizing what has been read, and determining the most important ideas and themes in a text.

I get very little positive response when I ask students if they ever infer or synthesize as they read. Even after explaining such thinking strategies in words the students may have heard in the past ("You know how sometimes teachers ask you to read between the lines? That's another way to describe inferring." "Do you ever try to pull everything together, to retell your reading in your mind in order to understand it better? That's synthesizing"), I more often than not meet with a blank stare and a rather disinterested no. Only Bob and Kristin refer to inferring as they speak of predicting what might come next in a novel. And no one claims to be able to synthesize, although both Kayla and Patti admit to going over in their mind what they have read to make sense of it, particularly if the book is "a little bit difficult."

I have slightly better luck when inquiring about their use of the cognitive strategy of determining importance. At least this is a strategy more of these adolescents recognize, albeit with limited enthusiasm. Reflecting a distinct distaste for such a task, Patti quickly responds, "Not unless I have to." "No, I just read it," replies Eric. "I try to just keep going and then maybe do it after I'm done, like if there's a question at the end of the chapter." "I write everything down in my notes," David states proudly. One of the few diligent students in this group, he allows that "that's how I remember what's important."

These responses reflect the way many if not most high school students approach the reading of textbooks, by anticipating and searching for answers to those inevitable end-of-chapter questions, questions that ask students to retrieve and retain specific information rather than think about and make sense of what they have read, questions that can often be answered correctly without having read the text. Such an ability surely doesn't allow these students to decide what the piece is about by first deciding what ideas and themes are most important to each of them. Such an approach to reading isn't the mind journey Keene and Zimmerman (1997) have in mind when they describe determining importance in text as making instantaneous decisions about what is important on the word, sentence, and text levels and defending those personal positions in meaningful classroom discussions (p. 94).

Finding Their Way

Within this group of readers, Kristin may be seen as the poster child of metacognition; indeed, she "sometimes" uses six of the seven cognitive strategies. In responding to my list of cognitive strategies, determining importance elicited her only all-encompassing no. What she doesn't do, though, is employ these strategies on assigned reading. Those books become the "boring" ones, the ones whose stories don't "hook" her. When she compares her feelings for *Of Mice and Men* ("very boring") and *The Shining* ("very interesting"), she is adamant about how differently the two novels affect her. But other than sketching out the two plots for me, she is unable to point out what makes one novel boring and the other interesting: "*Of Mice and Men*, I didn't like any of it. I don't know what made it boring, it just wasn't interesting. *The Shining*—I liked the plot, where they were and everything. The hotel and the people and stuff. . . . I liked the way the author wrote about them and what they did." It doesn't seem to strike her that her stance differs depending on whether the book is assigned or chosen, and that as her stance changes, so does her understanding. While reading *The Shining* for instance, she reads slowly and carefully, thinking about plot and character all the while. She is in the reader's world. "It feels like you are actually there and the things are happening." With *Of Mice and Men*, on the other hand, she reads quickly to finish her assignment. "I don't really concentrate, and I am just reading it because

I know what pages I have to read. I am just reading and not really thinking about it." No mind journey here, just a tedious trip through page after meaningless page, with the goal of passing a chapter quiz based on memory rather than understanding.

As a student who takes a metacognitive pleasure in her reading, Kristin stands head and shoulders over most of her reading workshop peers. Without having ever given any real thought to it, she has somehow stumbled into the reader's world. Although lacking the self-regulation needed to duplicate a mental journey at will, nevertheless she has been able to rise above her reading history and develop the cognitive strategies that initiate and sustain such a trip. Her peers have not been so fortunate. Some, like Mick, already use a few of the cognitive strategies, but the entire mosaic of thought that proficient readers create in their mind is not there for the taking. Still others have never given a single thought to reflecting while reading. Paul, for instance, never "pays attention to the book." Nothing goes on in his head when he is reading. "Nothing at all. [I] will just grab a book and start reading it. . . . Just turn the pages." Even when he goes back and "reads the whole thing over and over again," he comes out with nothing, "Zero." No wonder he is so frustrated with reading; no wonder he angrily dismisses it as being "stupid" and "pointless." With no thinking going on, he has no chance of setting out on a journey of the mind. Just turning pages leads to only one place for this reader, a dead end.

For many years, Mick viewed reading as Paul still does, as decoding rather than sense making. But his fortuitous mind journeys of the past few years have begun to shake his what's-the-point stance toward reading. Aided by the juxtaposition of school, imagination, effort, and maturity, this thoughtful adolescent has come to understand the rewards that reading has to offer, rewards that far transcend the functional use of literacy he has always accepted as important. *What's in it for me?* has been answered for the moment. Nevertheless, despite this all-important discovery, he continues to be lost. Because he is still not in touch with what triggers his ventures into the reader's world, he is ambivalent about the part reading can play in his life. Only when Mick becomes a self-regulated constructor of meaning (Samuels and Farstrup 1992, p. 172) will he be able to figure out the possibilities that reading holds for him in the years ahead.

Chapter 4

What These Lifers Teach Us

My students . . . taught me as much as I taught them, and their strongest lesson was a frightening one: adolescents who have not been successful—have failed—in traditional classrooms are at risk. Unless we find ways to engage them, they will shut down. If we continue to focus only on identifying deficits and devising sterile remedies, these students will surely use their energy and talent for unproductive purposes— or not at all.

—Mary Krogness
Just Teach Me, Mrs. K.

A few weeks ago I was meeting with a group of high school teachers enrolled in a graduate course. We were discussing the first chapters of *From the Other Side of the Desk* (1991), a book in which Linda Cleary examines what has gone wrong in writing instruction for forty eleventh-grade writers. Based on qualitative research similar to mine, Cleary's book is a compelling forum in which these students' voices are being heard for the very first time. At least I thought so until the other teachers in the group began ringing in with their responses to Cleary's work. "Who are these sixteen-year-old 'experts' that they can tell us we aren't letting them write in a 'fun' way!" asked an obviously miffed English teacher. "Isn't this work a little outdated?" wondered another skeptic. "This doesn't sound like *my* classroom," she added defensively. The history teacher in the group jumped on the data Cleary had gathered through her in-depth interviews: "This is nothing but anecdotal evidence that can be molded to serve the needs of her own educational agenda. I am hesitant as an educator to accept any of the changes proposed by her strictly on the value of her evidence."

Qualitative research invites such criticism, as readers with personal agendas assign their own meaning to the ideas presented by the author. Nevertheless, I hope the knowledge I have gained from these students, the conclusions I have drawn from what they have shared with me, and the changes such insights suggest will be viewed as more than words and ideas molded to fit the needs of my own educational agenda. As a reading consultant concerned with what I already knew of the at-risk adolescent reader, I set out to capture the student perspective of this all-too-common dilemma. Where researchers and educators had weighed in, I wanted to add the insight of the students themselves. Emerging theories gleaned from analyzing their inner voices, in combination with what I already knew, have led me to create a portrait of these adolescents and what has gone wrong for them as readers. If we allow ourselves to learn from their voices, if what they have taught us can become the impetus for change in our educational approach to readers and reading instruction, then their words will have served them—and us—well.

Seeing Is Believing

What have I learned from these twenty-two reading workshop students? Just as Rist (1970) did thirty years ago, I have come to know these adolescents as lifers. Since arriving at school as enthusiastic six-year-olds excited about learning, they have been locked in a losing battle with reading that has affected not only their academic progress but their self-image as well. As their view of reading changes, from a pleasurable social activity to an unrewarding and dreaded chore, so does their view of themselves. To this day Alexis sees herself as stupid and a failure, even as she fights to camouflage this perception created through her own words. To this day she and her peers are haunted by decoding unknown multisyllable words, reading texts beyond their ability, publicizing their struggle in group sharing activities, and meeting unattainable classroom expectations. Is there any escape for these lifers? Some, like Mick and Kayla, seem resigned to their fate, avoiding assigned reading at all costs while continuing to accept whatever help is offered for their deficiencies, help that never seems to make them a better reader but at least keeps their academic head above water. Some, like Alexis, have sworn off the assistance offered, angrily railing against their lot in life but powerless to change it. Others, like Eric, have simply given up the fight, unsuccessful and unhappy readers who have chosen the only way they know to escape their lifer status.

What forces have conspired to create and perpetuate this group of lifers? Researchers like Johnston and Winograd (1985) and Kos (1991) have always pointed to a myriad of factors that impact a reader's progress: the learner, the teacher, the home and school environments, all play a part. And indeed they do; we cannot discount the struggling reader who does not accept and use our support, the disruptive family environment that makes learning all but impossible for its youngest members, the overcrowded and underfunded classrooms that challenge even the most effective teachers in their efforts to make a difference for their neediest students. However, what these reading workshop students' voices illuminate most clearly is the impact certain widespread educational practices have had on them over the years, practices that researchers have pointed to as flawed but that nevertheless continue to be used in many classrooms today.

That the six tenets of conventional wisdom exposed by Allington and Walmsley (1995) as faulty are detrimental to struggling readers is clear when we come to know students like Kayla, students whose achievement and egos have been battered through the grades by ineffective instruction, a one-size-fits-all approach to learning and materials, and a mechanistic view of reading instruction that substitutes word-attack skills for making meaning. Going beyond the faulty pedagogy, Kayla and her peers also point a finger at teachers who for whatever reason have failed to develop and nurture a sense of trust, comfort, and caring in their classroom. Without that meaningful human connection, one that empowers students to learn and grow, these most-vulnerable children can do neither.

Mick's words powerfully point out another common theme: in our ongoing and unsuccessful attempts to teach these at-risk students to read, the very point of reading has been lost for them. Although most of these children came to school having learned to love books through pleasurable preschool experiences, that love was quickly lost as primary-grade teachers—and those that followed them—focused on unlocking words rather than understanding text. Just as we would show little enthusiasm for participating in a book club discussion that emphasized vocabulary recognition rather than meaning ("On page 55 of *Cold Mountain* can you divide *concentric* into syllables and use it in a sentence and then give a synonym?"), these readers soon lose interest in reading when it becomes apparent that it is more about guessing the correct vowel than wondering what the giant is going to do next. And it isn't just pointless and boring; it's hard, so hard that if you can't get it right the first time, you probably won't do any better the next time around, even if a kind teacher sits next to you and helps you with the answers. Mick and his peers know that there's nothing engaging about struggling to sound out words you can't decode; they know that there's nothing active about answering a short-answer question about a series of paragraphs you don't have a prayer of reading. Occasionally, something wonderful happens—a book like *Of Mice and Men* captures the mind of a turned-off reader like Mick, for example—but more often than not this serendipitous venture into the reader's world is an isolated event, hard to understand and even harder to duplicate. What is there about reading that causes some people to "stay inside on a nice, good day and read a book"? Most of these twenty-two reading workshop students don't have a clue. And those who do have found the answer on their own.

If/Then Conclusions

Reading failure is an all-too-familiar problem. For years researchers have been talking about the whys and hows of the painfully complicated struggle some students wage in the name of learning to read. This study has brought the struggling readers' voices into sharp focus. As we listen to the understanding woven throughout their stories, common threads emerge that may help us tackle the task of eradicating the lifer category from our schools once and for all. If we look at reading failure as a puzzle to solve, then perhaps these students' stories are a missing piece, an impetus for rethinking and revising our approach to literacy instruction.

Learning from Alexis

If Alexis and her reading workshop peers are lifers, unable to learn within an educational system that quickly separates winners from losers who are doomed to failure despite all the intervention we offer along the way, then:

- We need to rethink our view of reading and reading instruction in our schools, placing less emphasis on skill lessons keyed to hierarchical scope-and-sequence charts and more emphasis on authentic reading activities that incorporate the strategies good readers use. Reading is not just decoding in order to access and communicate knowledge; it is the act of accessing and communicating knowledge itself (Allington and Walmsley 1995, p. 31). We need to be sure that in asking students to attend to the business of school we do not require them to forfeit their engagement with text. All children, especially those who struggle from the start, must have many opportunities to know the pleasure of getting caught up in a well-crafted story.
- We need to rethink the way we view beginning readers, taking into account the wide range of differences found in a typical first-grade classroom. We need to remember that all children can learn but that some will need accelerated instruction to keep them moving and learning with their peers.
- We need to educate the vast majority of our children in heterogeneous settings devoid of deadly and static achievement groups, making sure we know each student's individual needs and attend to these needs reliably and consistently. By getting away from categorizing and labeling children, we can help each student develop a positive self-image in a learning environment in which all are motivated to strive for reasonable and attainable goals.
- We need to rethink the kinds of intervention we use with our at-risk readers. The traditional learning disability position that reading failure is permanent and untreatable (Spear-Swerling and Sternberg 1996) needs to be challenged and debated. Slowed-down instruction must be replaced by accelerated opportunities to learn. Pullout programs that result in fragmented experiences must be rethought, as must the practices of readiness, retention, and social promotion. Children who require extra support need to be taught by qualified professionals rather than untrained aides.
- We need to continue offering reading instruction and support through middle and high school to those adolescents who can benefit from it. Some students will always need some kind of scaffolding in order to be successful. With appropriate support they will continue to grow as self-extending readers.

Learning from Kayla

If Kayla's plaintive words, in concert with those of others who echo hers, focus on the harm done to struggling readers by poorly prepared and unresponsive teachers using ineffective instructional methods and practices, then:

- We need to review teacher preparation programs. New teachers must not only understand what constitutes effective literacy instruction but also be able to implement differentiated teaching methods that meet the needs and multiple intelligences of a wide range of learners. The importance of nurturing and sustaining a warm student-teacher relationship that fosters learning in the comfort of a welcoming classroom community cannot be overemphasized, particularly when working with our most vulnerable students.

- Staff development efforts must be revisited and redesigned when appropriate. All teachers, from those struggling through their first year of teaching to those with twenty-plus years of experience under their belts, need opportunities to expand their knowledge and the support to incorporate new ideas and methods into their classroom.

- We need to emphasize the importance of ongoing classroom assessment and evaluation. For instruction to be effective, teachers must know their students, and students must come to know themselves. Teachers need to be aware of the changing needs of each and every child, recognizing and honoring requests for help as a valid part of each student's development as an independent learner. Assessment and evaluation need to drive instruction, not vice versa.

- We need to look at the importance of choice in reading instruction. A literacy curriculum that offers choice affords a wide range of children the opportunity to learn by reading interesting books on a level commensurate with their own abilities. It affords struggling readers the chance to experience for themselves the joy and excitement of becoming passionately engrossed in a "good read."

- We need to recapture and reemphasize the notion of reading as making meaning. For struggling students in particular, comprehension must be seen as something to be taught rather than caught. These children need to realize that understanding is the primary goal of reading.

Learning from Mick

If Mick and his classmates have come to see reading as pointless, a skills-driven and repetitive process that leads to nothing but boredom and a sense of failure and is to be avoided at all costs, then:

- We must rethink the way we approach comprehension instruction, emphasizing the thinking strategies that proficient readers use to make meaning. If from the very beginning of formal instruction students learn to make sense rather than memorize, the point of reading will never be lost.

- We need to give struggling readers plenty of time to read books at their instructional and independent reading level, books they have chosen themselves. As their fluency improves, they can devote more of their efforts to taking the mind journeys proficient readers embark on as a matter of course.

- We must rethink what goes on in the name of reading intervention. For students to see any point to remediation, instruction must be in agreement with what educators know about the reading process and how children learn best. If extra work does not lead to improvement, what's the point of doing it at all?
- Learned helplessness needs to be eradicated from our schools. Instead of being told that they are incapable of working on their own, struggling students must be supported as they learn and practice the strategies of an independent reader. If we believe that all children can learn along with their peers, we need to be sure that struggling readers are given this all-important message as well.

Can We Make a Difference?

If we have learned from the voices of these reading workshop students, if we want to do our part to rid our schools of lifers and make literacy a reality for every child, we need to make changes in the instructional practices currently dominating our classrooms from kindergarten through grade twelve. To advocate for such educational change is not to shoulder full blame for the dilemma of struggling readers. To agree that we need to rethink some of our teaching procedures is not to dismiss the roles that unwilling learners, negative home influences, and unresponsive administrative bureaucracies play in perpetuating this educational predicament. But if we reflect on, learn from, and act on our own classroom missteps, we cannot help taking a major stride toward eradicating lifers from our schools once and for all.

I have spelled out for you many of the ifs and thens that these students' voices lead us to consider, ideas that if implemented have the power to rewrite the stories these at-risk readers have shared. These conclusions are by no means new and earthshaking; not surprisingly, these adolescents' words and understanding validate much of what researchers have been saying about reading failure for the past thirty years. The suggestions based on what these students have taught us align closely with many of the principles driving the educational reform initiatives of the 1990s (Cunningham and Allington 1994; Allington and Cunningham 1996; Allington and Walmsley 1995). They also parallel ideas included in recently published reports that deal with the qualities of exemplary literacy instruction. (IRA and NAEYC 1998; Pressley et al. 1998).

What is new here is the lens through which this knowledge is viewed: the words and stories of the lifers themselves. This new perspective, I believe, cannot be ignored. Flesh-and- blood adolescents have breathed life into a portrait of academic failure at the age of sixteen, failure so tenacious that any hope of escaping from its grasp has all but been eradicated. Their voices bring color and immediacy to the mournful literacy histories that have brought them to this dismal place. It may be simple enough to read what the experts have to say about what's going wrong in our classrooms and what we should be doing about it, to nod our heads in silent agreement while writing up that same old lesson plan for tomorrow's class. But how easy will it be to turn a deaf ear to Alexis's bristling anger, to Kayla's resigned sadness, to Mick's cocky ambivalence?

Have we heard enough? If so, what can we do to make a difference for these lifers? Allington and Walmsley (1995) remind us that there is no quick fix for our literacy dilemma, no silver bullet or one-size-fits-all recipe that can guarantee success for all learners. Contrary to what some people in the field of education might want us to believe, effective literacy programs cannot be bundled into child- and teacher-proof curriculum packets and distributed throughout a building for all to use, one lesson plan at a time. Rather, meaningful change must come from concerned educators who see a wrong and set about to right it, teachers who are willing to read about, reflect on, discuss, and experiment with innovative ideas in order to make a difference for their students.

This is not a task to be taken lightly. Change is difficult. Change is slow. Change takes time, effort, and unwavering commitment. It can be frightening, requiring us to take a risk, to leave behind something that we are comfortable with for the threatening shadows of the unknown. It can be confrontational, as new beliefs and concepts clash with old ones. It can be frustrating, as fresh ideas don't pan out and untested methods backfire. But meaningful change, evolutionary rather than revolutionary, can occur. It can occur for one struggling reader, one classroom of lifers, one day, one week, one semester at a time. And when it does, it surely makes a difference.

Part 2

A Revised Curriculum and Re-visioned Readers

The common denominator among [lifers] is that they have become their own worst enemies. They have acquired a view that the world is populated by two kinds of people: those who can read and those who cannot, those who can learn and those who cannot. . . . The key to helping [lifers] is to help them revalue themselves as language learners and users, and revalue the reading process as an interactive, constructive language process. They must set aside the pathological view of themselves, cast off the labels, and operate to construct meaning through written language using the strengths they have built and used in making sense of oral language or sign. To do that, they need support and help.

—KENNETH GOODMAN
Retrospective Miscue Analysis: Revaluing Readers and Reading

We have spent the last five years at Daniel Webster Regional High School dealing with change. Wishing to free our at-risk readers from the "culture of failure" (McDermott and Varenne 1995), we have discarded the traditional remedial model that has let down so many in the past. Relying on much of the understanding highlighted in part 1 of this book, we have worked for substantive change in our corrective reading program, both in the curriculum we use and in the readers we teach. Our goal is twofold; not only do we want these struggling adolescents to improve their abilities to unlock and make sense of text, but we also hope to transform the manner in which they look at reading and themselves. To this end we have read, reflected, discussed, and experimented. We have invented, refined, expanded, discarded, and begun again. We have celebrated our successes and learned from our failures. Supported by an administration that believes every student has the right to develop as an independent learner capable of a successful future, we have created a comprehensive grade 9–12 curriculum for at-risk readers* that we think can stand as a model for concerned educators who want to do the same. This curriculum includes:

- Year 1: Reading Workshop I (reading at grade level 5–7) or Reading Rebound (reading below grade level 5).
- Year 2: Reading Workshop II.
- Years 3 and 4: Literacy Workshop Electives (Literacy Tutoring, Independent Learning Seminar, Oral History, The Play's the Thing, Real-Life Writing, The Reading-Writing Experience, Breakfast Club/Lunch Bunch).

The chapters in part 2 discuss these curricular units in detail. It is our hope that others can use this model as a starting point for their own change, as classroom by classroom and school by school we strive to make a difference for the lifers we know.

---

*The typical at-risk population (in a class of two hundred students) breaks down as forty to fifty students in grade 9, ten to fourteen students in grade 10, five to seven students in grade 11, and three to five students in grade 12.

Chapter 5

Reading Workshop I: Laying the Foundation for Change

Teachers need to find ways to increase at-risk students' motivation to read, to provide time for them to do so, improve their knowledge of reading strategies, promote their thinking about what they are reading, and encourage them to view reading as a useful, joyful activity.

—Sharon Kletzien and Barbara Hushion
"Reading Workshop: Reading, Writing, Thinking"

I am sitting in the principal's office on a crisp March New Hampshire morning, my highlighted copy of the first edition of Atwell's *In the Middle* (1987) balanced precariously on the administrative pile of clutter bridging the table between Bob and me. I am there to report on the results I have just compiled from our latest round of eighth-grade testing, done each spring to give us an idea of the reading abilities of our freshmen-to-be. I share the depressing fact that in an incoming class of 193 students, 48 pupils have scored below the thirtieth percentile in reading. From thirteen years of experience with new ninth graders, I know that these are the students who will struggle to meet success in high school classes. These are the students that I as reading consultant need to support on their arrival next September. These are the lifers.

"So what are we going to do?" Bob asks. "Any thoughts?" Naturally I have a thought, or I wouldn't have made this early morning trip to his office. Bob knows this as well as I do; and supportive administrator that he is, he's ready to listen to my newest ideas for change in our approach to corrective reading instruction. "I want to try something different," I tell him, gesturing at Atwell's book. "Something that I read about in a course I took last fall. It's called reading workshop. It's based on the premise that students learn to read by reading, that at-risk readers need the opportunity to improve their skills by being given the opportunity to choose their own books, the time to read them, and the chance to respond to them in a caring community of learners. I don't want it to be a replacement for English class, a 'low and slow' approach to literature and reading instruction; we all know the message that sort of tracking gives to these vulnerable students. I want us to look at the course not as less but as more, an extra dose of reading for those who need it most. I think it can make a difference for these kids. It can make a difference in the way they look at reading. It can make a difference in the way they look at themselves."

And so Daniel Webster's first reading workshop was born five years ago. The foundation of a corrective reading curriculum that now spans grades nine through twelve, each year the program has supported at-risk adolescents in their often reticent quest to grow as readers. They do. At the end of each school year close to three quarters of the reading workshop students "graduate" from the corrective program, armed with the reading skills to succeed in high school if they put their minds to it.

Most leave the yearlong course with a new outlook on reading and an enhanced view of themselves as readers. Not that this is an easy transition. Despite the rather straightforward goal of giving the students the opportunity to grow as readers by reading, the course has many obstacles to overcome. In addition to combating the attitudes and behavior of the students themselves, a challenge that is part and parcel of working with this group of disaffected adolescents, each year as facilitator of the program I struggle with the realities of teacher assignment, student scheduling, and room and furniture availability in an overcrowded and underfunded school. Nevertheless when September comes, we do what we can to ensure that we can make a difference for our newest crop of ninth-grade lifers. In September and October, life in the reading workshop trenches may look bleak, but if you look very carefully the signs of change are in the air.

Reading Workshop in Action: "Do We Really Have to Read Today?"

Kim's loud voice precedes her down the dimly lit hallway leading to the reading workshop classroom. "Hey, Mrs. T.," she practically shouts as she spies her teacher walking into 158A ahead of her. It is the end of morning break; the bell signaling the beginning of block C is about to ring. "Do we really have to read today? I think we should have a big study hall period because I have lots of homework. What d'ya think Mrs. T.?"

Mrs. T. doesn't respond. It's only her second month as a reading workshop teacher, and she is thinking about the ninety minutes that lie ahead. She writes the day's plans on the board as her seven struggling readers wander in:

9:50–9:55	Check agenda
9:55–10:10	Minilesson—introduce books on tape
10:10–10:25	Reading aloud
	BREAK
10:25–10:55	Silent reading
10:55–11:05	Journal work
11:05–11:20	Book share/homework

Each part of the lesson plan evokes comments from this unruly group of students: "Can I go get my agenda? It's in my locker." "Oh, we did books on tape last year. What a drag." "Reading aloud. I thought you said we could have a movie!" "I'm just gonna take a zero. There's no way I can read today." "Do we have to journal *again*?" "You expect me to talk about a book in front of these jerks?" "I'm gonna fail my health test if I don't get a chance to read over my notes." Kim's booming, "Do I have to wait for break to go pee?" prods her thus far silent teacher to speak sharply. "That's enough, Kim. All of you find places to work and take out your agendas, please." Called to attention by their kindly drill sergeant, this squad of struggling readers reluctantly digs in.

Finding a place to work can be a challenge. Used by four groups of struggling readers a day, this classroom is not conducive to learning. Small and obviously makeshift, the space has been carved out of an industrial arts center that by virtue of a burgeoning student population was recently reassigned to the special education and reading departments. The temporary walls, off-white and dingy, do not reach the original high ceiling. Water-stained and mismatched acoustic tiles try without success to block the sounds coming from other parts of this dreary collection of rooms. Phones ring, doors slam, VCRs blare, clusters of teachers and students converse. Only the daylight filtering through the dirty double window at the back of the room offers a bright spot in this otherwise dismal setting.

The furniture is clearly cast-off, a collection of remnants from classes held here in years past and odds and ends rescued from basements and garage sales by Mrs. T. The only space suitable for study is a round metal table at the center of the room; it is surrounded by two molded-plastic desk chairs interspersed with two high swivel chairs more suited to drafting students than readers. A green wicker couch leans precariously against one wall, soiled cushions askew and legs angled, as if daring one last adolescent body to precipitate its inevitable demise. Mrs. T.'s large metal desk, meant for a regulation-size classroom, takes up more than its share of the room, its peeling gray paint and broken drawer handles a reminder of its age. An unlockable file cabinet abuts the desk, by necessity a haven for supplies rather than confidential records. Two outdated Apple computers flank an equally ancient printer on a narrow folding table below the window in the back of the room, accompanied by drafting stools whose high seats put the keyboards out of reach for most students. As a futile gesture toward comfort in this most uncomfortable room, a few flattened beanbag chairs are piled in a corner under the dusty blackboard filling the front wall. Today there are also two wooden straight chairs in the room, and a square folding table sits next to the door leading to the learning lab (158B). Depending on the day, the seating collection may change. "I'm not sure," Mrs. T. confides, "why our furniture comes and goes."

It's not that students haven't done their best to make the reading workshop room a place of their own, an educational setting where they can feel at home. As if to defy the second-rate feel of the classroom, they have covered the drab walls with posters of their favorite cars and sports figures, crafting colorful collages from outdated magazines and newspapers. This week snow boarders and Chevy Blazers take top billing in this ever-changing exhibit; next month it may be wrestling and rappers.

A poster listing reading workshop expectations, the outcome of a September class discussion, commands a prominent position in the student-made decor, mute testimony to this group's quest for belonging.

And there are books, lots of them. What the room lacks in comfort it makes up for in reading materials. In trying to hook these reluctant readers, Mrs. T. has filled four double-sided book carts with paperback books, all carefully labeled and color-coordinated by topic. Sports are yellow; science fiction and fantasy are green. Teen issues, horror and mystery, poetry and short stories, best-sellers, "real-life" (nonfiction) books, all have their niche in the room's bookshelves. In addition, there are paired books for partner reading, "fastbacks" for quick reads, books on tape for those who like to listen as they read, and a "new and noteworthy" shelf for readers looking for recent additions to the reading workshop library. A periodical rack no longer needed in the media center is filled with outdated magazines, from *Newsweek* to *Rod and Gun*. "Take Time to Read" announces a poster on the door; it is clear that Mrs. T. hopes her students will do just that.

But for this newly hired reading workshop teacher, the third to hold this position in three years, that's a challenge she must struggle with every day. Working with students most of whom feel totally alienated from literacy, she must fight to change their attitude as she helps them develop effective literacy strategies. And with no background in either education or reading instruction, that's a tall order.

> MRS. T.: When I got here this September I didn't really know what I was supposed to do. The first day I had been given this blue three-ring curriculum binder and told to help these freshmen improve their reading. And then for the first three weeks we didn't even have a classroom to go to. That's when I began to wonder if what I was supposed to do was really important. After all, I had a job, kids who struggled with reading, but no place to work with them. By the time I got settled in this room I was getting really nervous. And the kids were off the wall. I took the job because I like kids and I thought it would be a good experience. But I don't really know what to do. I'm not even a teacher.

9:50–9:55: Check Agenda

In response to Mrs. T.'s stern words Patti, Carol, and Jasmine pull their agendas from their backpacks and vie for the two desk chairs at the center table. Carol and Patti win out, so Jasmine heads for the couch, placing her agenda open on her knees as she leans back gingerly. As she goes to put her feet on the back of Carol's chair, Carol bellows, "Cut it out." Bob and Paul, no agendas in sight, perch in the high swivel drafting chairs that easily accommodate their desire for perpetual motion. "I left it on my kitchen table," explains Bob as Mrs. T. approaches him with grade book in hand. Paul chimes in, "I didn't write in my agenda because you didn't ask for it yesterday." "Stop the twirling," demands Patti of the high-flying boys. "You're knocking my chair." Christian sits silently at the computer table, fiddling with the keyboard while he waits for

Mrs. T. to check his agenda. "Where's Kim?" asks Mrs. T. as she moves around the room from student to student.

"Oh, she had to go to the bathroom, remember? And besides, she had to get her agenda in her locker."

MRS. T.: I know I am supposed to be helping these kids develop organizational skills by checking on their agendas. But what am I supposed to do if they say they don't have any homework? And if they don't care even when they do? These are students who tell me they "ruled the roost" as eighth graders, who love to share stories about how they gave their middle school teachers a run for their money. I believe them. So how do you teach kids who pride themselves on being unteachable?

9:55–10:10: *Minilesson Introducing Books on Tape*

Mrs. T. stands at the front of the room, holding up a cassette of *The Outsider*. She plans to spend the next ten minutes introducing her class to books on tape, a silent reading activity that she hopes will appeal to some of these reluctant readers. "How many of you have ever listened to books on tape? Today I want to. . . . " As if on cue, five of her students simultaneously interrupt; only Christian remains silent as his classmates vie for center stage. "Oh, we did it last year." "Hey, Paul, do you remember when Mr. Miller tried to get us to. . . ." "Hey dude, did you know that the shortest book on tape is two hours long?" "Mrs. T., can I have first pick? I know what I want to read." "I hate books on tape. Especially when you have to follow along with the words." After regaining order ("You people need to listen to one another. You're constantly interrupting your classmates"), Mrs. T. goes over the classroom directions for using books on tape, then lets students take turns browsing through the annotated index of available tapes. After a brief glance at the list, Christian is the first to sign up. From his isolated place in the back of the room he seems to be on task. Kim, on the other hand, is not. Having returning from her agenda search empty-handed, she has focused her attention on burrowing into a beanbag chair. Suddenly jarred to attention by the ring of a distant phone, she blurts out: "I hate that friggin' thing, Mrs. T. It gets on my nerves every day."

MRS. T.: Sometimes I just can't get their attention. All it takes is for someone like Kim to set the others off. And then they never want to listen and learn. Those are the lessons that really frustrate me. I know what I want to teach them; I just can't always get it across. I guess I shouldn't be surprised, though. If I were in their places, I wouldn't want to listen either.

10:10–10:25: *Reading Aloud*

By the time the read-aloud begins, students have used their creativity to carve out comfortable spots for themselves. Patti and Carol seem content with their desk chairs.

Bob and Paul have stopped twirling. Christian has moved to the beanbag nest recently vacated by Kim. Kim has taken a place on the still-standing couch with Jasmine; they are positioned back to back, like bookends. From a stool in the front of the room, Mrs. T. starts to read from David Pelzer's autobiography, *A Child Called It*. Only her voice breaks the quiet. Students who up till now have had a hard time waiting their turn to speak listen attentively to every word. Then Paul breaks the spell: "Hey, Bob, you know those kinds of shirts with the button-down collars?" Six sets of classmates' eyes silence him with a collective glare, and Mrs. T. goes on reading. Though Kim's eyes are closed, she laughs when David, the main character in the book, talks about "covering your ass"; even she is hooked by the story.

> MRS. T.: I'm surprised at how well the read-aloud is going. It took us a while to get into it, but once I figured out what kinds of stories the students wanted to listen to (they like Pelzer's writing; I suppose his books really give them a picture in their mind) we were set. I think they need to hear how a real reader sounds. Hearing my voice helps them with that. And what is amazing is now some of them want to read aloud too. I guess when you read aloud you feel like a reader.

10:25–10:55: Silent Reading

The move from reading aloud to silent reading is not smooth. Even after Mrs. T. gives her class a short break ("Get up and walk around, please. Say what you need to say to your friends, because in five minutes we'll be reading silently"), most students find it hard to settle down again when she asks them to get out their independent reading. Adolescents who for the last fifteen minutes have listened quietly find it difficult to return to enforced immobility. As students reluctantly take their books from the red plastic milk carton labeled Reading Workshop Block C, comments and objections fill the air. This group, it seems, can never do anything without putting in their own two cents first. But after a couple of minutes, quiet once more encompasses the room.

Six of the students, having returned to the comfort of their read-aloud spaces, are digging in for the thirty minutes of reading ahead. Mrs. T. has taken out her book and joins Patti and Jasmine at the center table. Even Kim has her book open; only Paul seems unable to settle down. "I said I would take a zero," he repeats for the third time to anyone who will listen. "I have the biggest hangover." At this Mrs. T., obviously used to Paul's defiance, approaches him wordlessly, shepherds him toward a corner chair and hands him a *Hot Rod* magazine. She then returns to her own reading.

Over the next twenty-five minutes the silence is broken only by an occasional whisper and the squeak of Paul's sneakers as he mashes his Nikes against the tile floor while turning the pages of magazine after magazine. "How many more minutes, Mrs. T.?" queries Kim. "Another five minutes and you can get your journals out." But five more minutes are evidently too long for this reluctant reader. Without another word Kim pulls her sweatshirt hood over her head, leans back against her seatmate Jasmine, and closes her eyes. Her reading time is over.

MRS. T.: Silent reading is usually not a problem anymore. Now the kids know it's part of the day and once I can get them to settle down they do it. All except Paul. He has such a hard time sitting still. In a way I don't blame him. He's a kid that needs to get up and walk around, but if I let him he distracts everybody else. The mix of a class like this can make or break a day. You just never know.

10:55–11:05: *Journal Work*

"Okay, get out your journals." The silence ended, students once more move to the milk carton at the back of the room, trading in their book-marked novels for spiral notebooks.

"I don't want to write in my journal today," announces Patti. "I have nothing to say."

"Just write a summary," suggests Jasmine, "then tell what you think."

As students jockey for the few favored spots for writing, Bob proudly announces that he has just finished half of his book. "That's the most I've ever read," he says to no one in particular. Searching for Kim's misplaced notebook, Mrs. T. still manages to give him a thumbs-up.

"I guess I took it home last night," recalls Kim as Mrs. T. comes up empty-handed. Can I get credit if I hand it in late?"

Mrs. T. shakes her head no, then turns her attention to the rest of the class. "Remember what we talked about in last week's minilesson, about things that good readers do? One of the things they do is ask questions as they read. So along with your response, please ask three questions about what you have just read." These not-so-good readers greet her request with moans and groans. Paul voices the frustration some of the others are thinking: "But I never have any questions when I read, Mrs. T."

MRS. T.: I have learned how important it is to get these kids to connect with their reading. And I work to get them to be "in" their books. Sometimes it's hard, but I think those kids who try are going to become better readers by doing it. Even when Patti says she has nothing to write about, she still turns around and does a good job. But the kids who blow it off, they're the ones who will be back in reading workshop again next year.

11:05–11:20: *Book Share/Homework*

When given the choice between talking about their books or doing homework, Kim and Paul quickly pick homework. "Can we go into the learning lab?" asks Kim. "We need to study for our health test. I promise we won't steal anything, we won't let ourselves be tempted by what's in Mr. Dooley's desk, and we won't bother anybody else."

"And I need to type on the new computer," adds Bob.

Minus three of the most disruptive students, the rest of the class gathers around the table with a secretly relieved Mrs. T. Christian, who has been silent through most of the class, seems equally unburdened by his classmates' departure. "Mrs. T.," he says tentatively, "before we talk about stories we're reading, can you read us what I wrote for English class? It's about a rock group, just like the one I'm in. I want to hear how *my* story sounds."

"And then maybe we can talk about Christian's story," suggests Jasmine.

"Why don't you read it yourself, Christian?" asks Mrs. T.

"I'd feel too stupid," he replies almost under his breath. And then in a firmer voice he adds, "I know that you can do a good job." His face flushed with embarrassment, the nervous author hands a crumpled handwritten page to his teacher. Mrs. T. begins to read. Jasmine, Patti, and Carol listen respectfully, unsure readers eager to give support to a classmate willing to take a chance with words. "Two months ago," Mrs. T. thinks to herself, "this never would have happened."

> MRS. T.: The hardest part of this job is classroom management. Without the Kims and Pauls, things would go so much better. But they're part of the job, and I know I have to learn how to deal with them. It's all about trust, don't you think? These kids come to me with a long history of reading failure, of hating reading. If I can get them to trust me, if I can guide them through the year, then perhaps they'll come to believe that reading is not the worst thing in life. They might not like it but they'll know how to do it better. And as a teacher that's all I'm going to ask.

11:30

The bell rings. The block C reading workshop students end their discussion in mid-sentence, hoisting backpacks while chattering about English assignments and cafeteria menus in preparation for the remainder of their school day. "Push your chairs in please. And have a nice day!"

As he reenters the room to grab his books, Bob spies Mrs. T. walking toward her desk. "Will you be at the basketball game tonight? I think I'm gonna play."

"I'll try to be there," she responds. "You know how much I want to see one of my students score the winning basket!" Absently pushing in the chairs that her exiting students have neglected, Mrs. T. is jarred by the loud voice of a newly arriving block E reading workshop student.

"Hey, Mrs. T.," Mick bellows. "Are we gonna have to read again today? I've got so much work to do. Can we have homework time today? What d'ya think, Mrs. T.?"

Course Goal

The goal of Reading Workshop I is the development of a caring community of readers, a classroom that gives each lifer the opportunity to revise his view of reading while re-visioning his view of himself. In other classes the struggling student more often than not sees herself as a failure, but in reading workshop members learn to rejoice in one another's accomplishments. Modeled on Hansen's (1987) writing community, it's a place in which all students are valued for their contributions, where the hierarchies of the haves and the have-nots are replaced by a supportive and democratic environment in which members learn to trust and support one another. In such a community struggling readers can take risks and try new things. When they do, marked improvement in reading achievement can and will occur.

This goal is not easy to attain, as Mrs. T. and other reading workshop instructors can attest. Indeed, it may take an entire semester before recalcitrant students abandon their negative outlook and the obstructive behavior that so often come with the territory. During this time, the Pauls and Kims of the class struggle to maintain the disruptive stance they have long held in response to their feeling of worthlessness; and it is all too easy for a frustrated teacher to surrender her classroom to their educational sabotage.

But the rewards of hanging in there are great. Once the sense of community is established under the guidance of a dedicated teacher, remarkable growth slowly and surely takes place. Just talk to Mrs. T. when June rolls around, when the walls of the school are hung with well-crafted reading collages created by her students as part of their final project, when student self-assessments point to goals met and reading strengths newly discovered, when attitude scales show a ten- or twenty-point jump. "I am so excited with their NRST scores," Mrs. T. confides to me one June day while sitting in my office during our weekly planning meeting. "More than three fourths of the kids have tested out! Even Kim! If you had asked me back in October what I really thought. . . ." As I congratulate her for her well-deserved euphoria, I smile and reflect to myself, "I knew enough not to do that. All you really needed was time. Time and the belief that you could make a difference for these kids. And you did."

Program Effectiveness

That Reading Workshop I is effective can be seen in the results of a 1998 study done by Laura Rogers, a social studies teacher at Daniel Webster. As a masters degree candidate at the University of New Hampshire, she was required to analyze an educational program presently in use at her high school. Because she knew many of the lifers from her freshman geo-political studies course, she set out to evaluate the success of the Reading Workshop I program for these students. In addition to analyzing entrance and exit standardized reading test scores, she administered surveys to participants past and present and interviewed teachers who had been involved with the program in order to ascertain its measurable benefits. The results show that Reading Workshop I is effective not only at substantially increasing the reading levels of most of its participants (average scores have improved by as much as 2.4 grade levels in one year) but also at enhancing the success that students have reading assigned novels and texts in their content area classes.

But there's more going on than increased achievement. There is also a positive change in the way lifers look at reading help. Surveyed students view the reading workshop teacher as a person they can turn to for additional support or tutoring across the curriculum, a valuable human resource that until now has been in short supply for many of these at-risk adolescents. Indeed, after spending two semesters as members of a caring reading community, it appears that lifers who have previously despaired of making any gains in their struggle with the written word are beginning to see themselves as readers—successful readers at that.

Rogers also points out how Daniel Webster's Reading Workshop I class incorporates many of the key characteristics of effective secondary school remedial programs (Bintz 1993; Grant and Metsala 1996). Although I hadn't been aware of this list when I first sat in Bob's office so many years ago, many of these characteristics have become part of our model:

- *The student-to-teacher ratio is 10:1 or less.* We work to keep our classes to a maximum of eight students.
- *Students have an opportunity to see reading modeled by adults and peers.* This happens in a variety of ways, including teacher read-alouds, shared reading, independent reading, and group sharing.
- *Student reading level steadily and consistently increases over time.* Our yearly entrance and exit tests verify this fact.
- *Students are encouraged to focus on reading for pleasure at, not above, grade level.* The reading workshop classroom is stocked with highly interesting, easily read books and other material. Each student is encouraged to read texts of his choice written at his instructional or independent level.
- *There is no stigma attached to the program.* There are no labels in reading workshop; it is simply another freshman elective. Seventy percent of the reading workshop students in Rogers's survey disagree with the statement, "Other students have given me a hard time because I'm in Reading Workshop I.")
- *Students who achieve the target grade level are matriculated out of the program.* At the end of each year, on average, over seventy-five percent of the students score at grade level eight or above on the Nelson Reading Skills Test.)
- *The program is cost-effective.* The program is staffed by instructional aides who are expected to implement an instructional curriculum developed and facilitated by a reading consultant. Their work is constantly supported and monitored; the consultant is always on call, and additional help is given as needed. Although I would prefer reading workshop to be taught by the most highly qualified educators, the use of hourly paraprofessionals allows me to make a difference for a larger group of lifers.

Students and Space

Based on the results of the Nelson Reading Skills Test given to all incoming ninth graders in the spring before their freshman year, students whose composite scores are below grade eight are assigned to a reading workshop class of between five and eight students. This is a requirement, not a suggestion. Too often in the past well-meaning teachers or over-protective parents have removed cooperative skills-deficient middle schoolers from the class, students whose success in ninth grade has subsequently been hampered by their inability to read high school text. Others have attempted to use the class as a convenient "stopping off" place for disruptive students, adolescents for whom behavior rather than reading ability is the issue. In both cases the student—and the reading workshop class—suffer. The simple grade-level prerequisite more often than not precludes these placement errors. Because we believe that lifers need more rather than less reading, and because we do not want to stigmatize these students further by assigning them to remedial English during their first months of high school, reading workshop is not used as a replacement for freshman English. Instead, reading workshop is a "compulsory elective," a class that in tandem with the regular English class gives struggling readers a double dose of literacy work (most enrollees take it in place of a foreign language). Once the assignment has been made in the spring, parents are sent a letter explaining the program (see appendix B). In almost all cases they support the decision.

Because of space constraints, the reading workshop classes meet in a variety of classrooms and teaching spaces, depending on availability. The most ideal setup, which we push for but don't always attain, is a small classroom in the English wing (in other words, no banishment to the special ed corridor). Tables rather than desks fill the room, so that students can read and respond to books around the comfort of Atwell's "dining room table." Beanbag chairs crowd carpeted corners, and a hand-me-down couch or easy chair, complete with end table and lamp, often becomes a favorite spot in which to curl up for silent reading.

Book carts and bookshelves line the walls and are filled with a wide range of adolescent novels, short stories, poetry, picture books, and current magazines appealing to even a reluctant teen reader's interests. Books are grouped by subject, so that would-be readers can more readily find the sports story they are seeking or the mystery written by an author a friend has raved about. The class library is usually expanded twice a year, and fresh selections find a place in the "new and noteworthy" section. In the past few years we have worked to include more nonfiction in our reading workshop collection; it's the genre most widely read in the real world, but too often it receives short shrift in our classrooms (Harvey 1998). It's the sort of writing to which many lifers, particularly boys, are naturally drawn. One shelf holds our budding collection of books on tape, popular texts that struggling readers want to read but that often prove too daunting without the recorded voice guiding listener-readers through the pages. These tapes are often reserved weeks in advance.

An element of the reading workshop classroom that is becoming more and more indispensable is the overhead projector. We know that students learn more effectively when we show rather than tell. A teacher can model a strategy that proficient learners use while projecting the related text. All eyes can focus on the words while she first reads aloud, then thinks aloud about the sentences that have prompted her to visualize a character in her mind or predict what may come next in a story. A visual aid like this is a boon for lifers who for too long have learned to "shut out" the voices of their teachers, believing that most likely there is no learning there for them.

Class Schedule

The yearlong Reading Workshop I meets three times a week, once for fifty minutes and twice for ninety minutes. Following Atwell's (1987) framework, each reading workshop session offers students the time to read, a choice of reading materials, and a variety of opportunities to respond to what they have read. In addition, our model builds in time for these at-risk freshmen to work on their study strategies. A typical ninety-minute lesson plan goes something like this:

8:10–8:15	Student agenda check, daily goal setting
8:15–8:25	Minilesson on a reading or study strategy
8:25–8:55	Silent or paired reading, book chats
8:55–9:15	Journal work or book share
9:15–9:25	Reading aloud
9:25–9:40	Book share or homework, and a progress check

Reading Activities

In the course of a typical week, reading workshop students are given many opportunities to read. At different times class members may gather around the teacher to hear a story read aloud, read independently, or share a book with a classmate. Later in the year, students travel to area day care centers twice a month to share picture books with enthusiastic preschoolers. Or they may read magazine articles aloud to grateful senior citizens in local nursing homes. Choral reading of favorite poems gives pupils the chance to improve their fluency through painless and usually enjoyable repetition; and authentic TV or movie scripts, ordered direct from Hollywood after a closely contested class vote, become vehicles for added practice for these improving readers.

Just as there are varied opportunities to read, there are many chances for these readers to respond to text. In addition to the journal entries that are an extension of independent reading, reading workshop features large-group book shares, during which the members of this community of readers converse about both individual and class reading. Another type of group sharing is the book talk. At the beginning of the year, the teacher chooses a book she suspects will interest her students and gives a three-minute presentation in which she tries to "sell" the book to her struggling and usually reticent readers. She may describe a particularly appealing character, give a short description of the plot, or reveal a dramatic moment sure to hook the most turned-off reader. When done well, the book talk produces a waiting list of students suddenly eager to borrow this "must read" selection. By the end of the year the book talks are handed over to class members, as now eager readers vie for the opportunity to share favorite selections with their peers. There is ample chance for one-on-one sharing as well; in weekly book chats (really informal conferences) teacher and student discuss books and journal entries, set and revise reading goals, and review and reinforce strategies. A highlight of the year are the e-mails reading workshop students exchange with struggling readers in another local-area high school. While reading the same adolescent novel, book buddies from the two schools discuss their favorite characters, debate why the author wrote a particularly poignant chapter, or predict the outcome of the novel.

An important part of each week is the minilesson (Calkins 1994), during which the teacher introduces strategies that can help these lifers improve as readers and learners. At the beginning of the year classroom procedures are covered in these quick but focused ten minutes of explicit instruction; then strategies used by proficient readers and successful students are modeled for the class. Occasionally a series of minilessons deal with a particular topic, for example a bookstore visit that students take at the start of the second semester to pick out new books for the reading workshop library. (For a more complete listing of minilessons, see figure 5–1.)

Study Strategies

Because most reading workshop students find academic success as elusive as reading success, some of our class activities are tailored to meet this deficit. As part of a schoolwide study skills program, all our high school students are required to keep track of homework assignments in school agendas. Since lack of organization is often a precursor to school failure, the reading workshop teacher emphasizes the importance of this organizational tool by conducting daily agenda checks (see appendix C). Is the agenda being used regularly? Is the student learning to manage her time so that homework finds its rightful place in her busy adolescent life? At the same time class members are expected to decide how best to use any in-class homework time, learning to prioritize their workloads in order to meet due dates for content area assignments. At the end of each week teachers assess the progress their students are making in planning and working independently, and this progress—or lack of it—is noted and discussed as part of the weekly book chat. Minilessons address study strategies as well, with the lessons often coinciding with teaching and learning going on concurrently in content area classrooms. Test taking and midterm preparation, previewing a textbook, using graphic organizers, writing current event summaries—the skills covered are ones that reading workshop students will find useful in a number of academic contexts throughout their high school careers.

Setting Expectations

Since incoming at-risk readers are notified of their class placement in the spring, most if not all arrive in September with misinformation and an instant dislike for reading

READING WORKSHOP I: MINILESSONS

Introduction to Reading Workshop
1. Welcome to Reading Workshop—Course Overview
2. Getting to Know Yourself as a Reader: Reading Survey, Attitude Scale
3. Book Selection: How Do You Choose a Book?
4. Student Evaluation—the Reading Workshop Rubric
5. Keeping Track of Our Reading—the Reading Log
6. Setting Daily Goals, Charting Our Progress—the Weekly Progress Sheet
7. Using a Response Journal
   a. Journal Instructions
   b. Journal Rubric
   c. Reinforcement

What Good Readers Do
1. What is a Good Reader? Things to Think About as I Read
2. Reading as an Interaction Between Reader and Text

Before Reading:
3. Activating/Building Background Knowledge–with a novel
4. Activating/Building Background Knowledge–with a textbook
5. Previewing and Predicting
6. Setting a Purpose for Reading
7. Asking Questions
8. ReQuest
9. KWL

During Reading:
10. Monitoring Your Understanding
    a. Visualizing
    b. Using Prior Knowledge
    c. Summarizing
    d. Relating to Purpose
    e. Predicting
    f. Answering Questions/Asking New Ones
11. Using Fix-up Strategies
    a. This Just Doesn't Make Any Sense
    b. Word Analysis: Compare /Contrast Analogy Approach
    c. Use of Context
    d. Text Lookback Checklist

12. Taking Notes
    a Mapping
    b. Outlining
    c. Two-Column Notetaking
13. Underlining
14. Highlighting
15. Use of Flag Words

After Reading:
16. Checking My Purpose—Did I Achieve It?
17. Comprehension—Did I Understand?
18. KWL continued—What I Learned/What I Still Need to Learn
19. Summarizing What I Have Read
    a. Graphic Organizers
    b. Summary Paragraphs

Self- Evaluation: Valuing Myself as a Reader
1. Goal Setting
2. Self-Evaluation

Additional Study Strategies
1. Preparing for the Reading Test
2. Reading Graphs and Charts
3. Skimming for Information
4. Scanning for Information
5. Preparing for Midterms
6. Current Events Summaries

Sharing Our Reading
1. Visiting a Bookstore
    a. Choosing a Book
    b. Book "Tasting"
    c. Creating a Book File
2. Book Buddies
3. Book Posters
4. Good Reader Poster

Figure 5–1.

workshop. And rightfully so. As products of faulty school practices that have turned these adolescents off to anything having to do with reading, these pupils aren't sure what to expect from a course in which reading is the curriculum. If their past experiences have taught them anything, it is the pointlessness of yet another dose of reading instruction; they have good reason to believe that this class is simply going to be more of the same.

To disprove this misconception, the first month of school is spent letting the students know what reading workshop is all about, starting with the simple rationale on which the course is based, that class members can improve as readers by reading and responding to self-selected texts in a supportive community of learners. The various components of the class are presented and discussed, as are course requirements and expectations, including the rubric on which grades will be based (see appendix D). During this introduction to the curriculum students are asked to look at reading in what may well be a new light, as an active process in which the reader himself has the responsibility to bring meaning to the text. Then too, they begin to evaluate themselves as readers, perhaps for the first time ever—their attitudes and interests and the strategies they use. As the course groundwork is being laid during these autumn days, books are selected and begun, and the first hesitant entries are penned in newly acquired journals.

As you have already seen in our bird's-eye view of the block C class, carefully written and executed lesson plans do not necessarily lead to a smooth class session. Setting expectations is not always the same as living up to them, particularly when working with this group of adolescents. Wary of dropping the personas that have served them so well in the past, resistant readers like Kim and Paul strive to hold onto the disruptive status quo even as they take a new look at the written word and their tortured relationship with it. But without even realizing it, class members fall into a routine; a sense of community begins to emerge, and slowly but surely these lifers take their first tentative steps toward revaluing reading and themselves.

Keeping on Track

In a freshman class of close to two hundred pupils, between forty and fifty lifers are placed in six reading workshops, which meet at various times throughout the day. Ideally one person is assigned to teach all classes, but more often than not there are two or more instructors working in the program. In my role as reading specialist I develop the curriculum; then, wearing the hat of reading consultant, I work with the reading workshop teachers to facilitate the successful implementation of the program. I need to ensure the uniformity of structure and practice while supporting each instructor in developing a sense of classroom autonomy.

During the regularly scheduled teacher workshop days of late August, I meet with the instructors and go over the Reading Workshop I curriculum guide. This three-ring binder contains a rationale and overview of the program, suggests daily schedules, and

READING WORKSHOP AGENDA, October 19, 3:00–4:30

1. Update on classes—reading, minilessons, logs and journals, read-alouds, book talks, etc.
2. Beginning-of-year assessments—progress report
3. Minilessons for November
4. Book checkouts—a better way
5. "Inside Scoops" notebook—a way for students to share book responses
6. "Mini-Lessons: Custom-Tailored Teaching" (*Journal of Reading* article)
7. Problems and concerns

Figure 5–2. *Sample Agenda for Teachers Meeting*

provides information about silent reading, reading aloud, group share, book chats, minilessons, book talks, and response journals. An outline of the first month's minilessons and directions for administering beginning-of-the-year assessments are also included. During the first weeks of school I touch base frequently with all teachers but especially with those new to the reading workshop program. I troubleshoot issues running the gamut from student placement and room assignment to classroom management and instructional components. If a teacher is unsure how to do a book talk, I model one for her; if she is struggling with a particularly recalcitrant lifer I offer suggestions based on previous experience.

Starting in late September I hold monthly reading workshop teacher meetings. Agendas (see the sample in figure 5–2) include class updates, minilessons and activities for the coming month, and management and curriculum issues that individual teachers have brought to my attention. During these meetings we brainstorm ideas on how to deal with students who refuse to do journal entries or share a read-aloud that has caught the interest of a class. We might also reflect on a brief article I've placed in teachers' mailboxes before the meeting. Most of all, we develop a sense of community as we keep track of what is going on in the various reading workshop classes.

Ongoing Assessment and Evaluation

Class Forms

Because we have chosen to try and meet the needs of a larger group of lifers rather than focus on a much smaller group of struggling readers, we need to use ongoing assessment and evaluation tools that are easy to administer and interpret and that give us an accurate picture of a lifer's progress as both a reader and a learner. These forms include:

1. Reading Workshop Weekly Progress Sheet and Agenda Check (appendix C). This form is filled out by students as they enter class each day and is checked by teachers at the end of the block.

2. Reading Journal Scoring Guide (appendix E). This form, filled out by the teacher, evaluates a reader's weekly journal entries.
3. Reading Log (appendix F). This form is a record of a student's silent reading.

These forms, kept in individual student folders arranged by class and stored in a file cabinet in the reading workshop room, are available to both teacher and consultant.

Beginning-of-Year Assessments: Getting to Know the Learner

Because we realize that reading failure is far more complex than a simple skills deficiency, we take time each fall to administer a variety of assessments, each of which fleshes out the portraits of the lifers enrolled in Reading Workshop I. By looking at a pupil's attitude toward reading, her familiarity with and use of cognitive reading strategies, and her understanding of where she stands as a reader, we come to know an adolescent as more than a standardized test score. There are many such tools available. The ones we find particularly helpful, in addition to being user friendly, include:

1. Reading Attitude Assessment (adapted from the Rhody Secondary Reading Attitude Assessment), a twenty-five-question survey that provides a quick indication of a student's attitude toward reading. It is easily administered in about ten minutes.
2. Reading Strategies Survey (from *The Stanford Diagnostic Reading Test*, fourth edition, Harcourt Brace 1995), a fourteen-question survey in which students indicate the thinking strategies they use during the reading process. It can be administered in five to ten minutes.
3. Reading Survey (Atwell 1987, 271–72), a twelve-item questionnaire that asks students to write sentences telling what they know, think, and do as readers. This is one of the first in-class writing activities.

Quarterly Evaluation and Goal Setting

One of the September minilessons introduces students to the Reading Workshop I Rubric (see appendix D). This one-page evaluation lays out clearly and concisely the method by which quarterly report card grades will be earned. The rubric itself accounts for forty percent of a student's mark; weekly journal grades, use of class time, and assigned projects make up the other sixty percent. During the final week of the quarter, each class member completes the rubric to evaluate his progress in the course. The reading workshop instructor also fills out a rubric for each class member. During their book chat that week, teacher and student compare the two rubrics. Any mismatches are discussed and realigned. Although this may well be the first stab at self-evaluation for these struggling readers, it is remarkable how accurately these adolescents can evaluate their progress when given the opportunity to do so.

Once the rubric has been discussed, the student is asked to rethink his view of reading and measure his progress as a reader. What makes a good reader? What is the best book he has read this quarter? Why does he like it? What has he learned about himself? How has he changed as a reader? Looking ahead to the next nine weeks, the pupil is asked to set individual reading and learning goals and then explain how he plans to reach these goals. Students who up till now have failed to see themselves as readers are beginning to revalue the reading process while revising their view of the readers they can become.

Midterm and Final Assessments and Evaluations

Just as with any other course, reading workshop students are expected to take a January midterm and a yearend final exam (see appendix G). In keeping with the emphasis on improving students' reading achievement while transforming the way they look at reading and themselves, this assessment has a dual focus. These reforming readers are asked not only to read but to evaluate their progress as well.

"Testing Out"

If you were to ask a reading workshop student the most telling assessment of all, most would be sure to point to the Nelson Reading Skills Test taken by all class members in late May. This is what these lifers have been working toward for nine months, the crucial forty-five-minute exam on which each student gets to prove to others and, perhaps more important, to herself or himself what many of us have been seeing all along, the remarkable and rewarding evolution from lifer to reader. It's a necessary assessment, a standardized acknowledgment of the success of our revised corrective reading curriculum. Yet when results are announced in each reading workshop class, when close to seventy-five percent of these once struggling readers exchange high fives over their success on the test, the teachers and I look at one another and smile. We don't need this test. We knew it all along.

Keeping Parents Informed

From the time that students are placed in Reading Workshop I, parents or guardians are kept informed of their child's progress. When quarterly report cards are issued, letters home explaining what is currently going on in reading workshop (see appendix H) are stapled to the reading workshop rubric. In addition, teachers meet and talk with parents one-on-one during regularly scheduled open houses and conferences. If more contact is needed, instructors make phone calls and encourage parents to do the same. When results of the Nelson Reading Skills Test are tabulated, a letter is sent home outlining the progress this student has made as a participant in the program (see appendix I). Gains are listed; if the student continues to need reading support, areas of weakness still to be tackled are also included. We want to make sure that parents know where their reading workshop student stands as a reader.

Chapter 6

Reading Rebound: Preliminary Footings for Those Who Need It Most

Can Reading Recovery, a program designed for first graders, be adapted to any age? I found that not only can it be adapted, but when it is paired with authentic, high-interest reading, older students begin to thrive. It is certainly more effective than continuing the worksheets and drills these older students have failed to internalize.

—KAREN BALLASH
"Remedial High School Readers Can Recover Too!"

The first time I met Brian, he was sound asleep on his desk in the middle of a reading test. While the other students in the class bit their lips and gripped their pencils tightly, trying to squeeze out enough correct answers to test out of reading workshop, Brian lay with his head on his front-row desk, legs outstretched in the aisle ready to trip anyone who ventured too close. Because the classroom teacher, Mrs. Patrick, needed to run a quick errand, I had volunteered to stand in for her for a few minutes. As I took my place at the front of the class, I threw my most teacherly glare toward the recalcitrant testee in front of me. But to no avail. He remained prone on his desk, eyes seemingly closed.

When Mrs. Patrick returned, I touched Brian on the shoulder and asked him to join me in the hall. Stifling a long yawn, he pulled in his legs, pushed back his chair, and ambled slowly through the doorway after me. "I don't think I know you," I started out as he stood facing me, arms folded across his chest. I tried unsuccessfully to hide the growing annoyance I was feeling toward this seemingly self-assured young man who had flaunted authority by sleeping through the year-end reading assessment. "I'm Mrs. Mueller, the reading consultant, and I'm wondering who you are and why you aren't taking the test with the rest of your classmates."

He looked me up and down, then replied with a cocky half grin, "My name is Brian." Barely missing a beat, he added in a confident voice, "I'm in tenth grade and I don't know how to read." Seeing surprise cross my face undoubtedly encouraged him to continue: "I don't have to do this reading test, Mrs. Mueller. You can't make me.

Mrs. P. is nice. She never makes me do this kind of stuff. She tells me that I can't learn to read so she will just have to read it for me. And she does." He paused, waiting for a response from the ticked-off reading lady standing next to him.

"What do you mean you can't learn how to read?" I challenged. After a moment Brian dropped his eyes; all the bravado disappeared as he answered in a subdued voice, "I just can't that's all. Ever since first grade. I've always stunk at it. Lots of people have tried, but nobody's ever taken the time to really teach me." I paused for just a moment, made fleeting eye contact with this suddenly vulnerable adolescent, then said in a firm yet kind voice, "I don't care what Mrs. Patrick says. I'm sure you can learn how to read. And you know what? Next fall I promise I am going to teach you."

"I'm a Reader Now"

My chance meeting with Brian was the inspiration for Reading Rebound, a program of intensive one-on-one remedial reading instruction for adolescents patterned after Marie Clay's Reading Recovery model of reading intervention for beginning readers. (The instructional components are outlined in figure 6–1) It's a program tailor made for students like Brian, who at the age of sixteen continue to be deeply mired in the reading acquisition phase of reading, stuck at the fourth-grade level despite year after year of remediation. It's a program for lifers at the very bottom of the barrel, students so needy that even the supportive environment of a reading workshop is not the answer.

As I was developing the program, well-meaning friends warned me that this inno-vative idea of mine might not work. "They say you can only use Reading Recovery methods in the first grade," one of them not very helpfully reminded me. But my response was simple: "What have we got to lose?" For years kind people like Mrs. Patrick had been telling Brian—by words and deeds—that he couldn't read, and by the time I met him he had long ago internalized their somber pronouncements of fail-ure. He now seemed to be taking this belief a step further: if everybody thought he couldn't read, he wasn't going to. Not on a test, not for a class assignment, not for any-thing. And yet if I believed that all children could learn to read, why not Brian?

In ten short months of Reading Rebound, Brian soundly disproved his critics. He became a reader, breaking the lifer bonds that had held him back for so long. Starting in September, when he confessed to me in the privacy of my office that if given the chance he "would like to read a little better," this proud eleventh grader spent three blocks a week working on his reading. Day after day, supported by Mrs. Daley, a kind teacher who believed in Brian and his abilities, he read familiar material, studied words, worked on metacognitive strategies, tackled new material, and read short selections over and over until he became fluent. In addition, he listened to Mrs. Daley as she read aloud, then spent time discussing what he had heard and exchanging jour-nal entries with her about the reading. Since he was notorious for his ability to wan-gle his way out of any class or assignment, both his teacher and I were delighted at his uncharacteristic dedication.

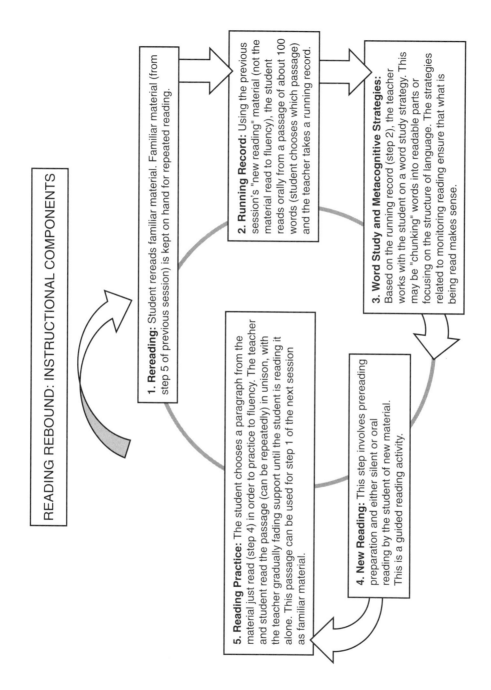

READING REBOUND: INSTRUCTIONAL COMPONENTS

1. Rereading: Student rereads familiar material. Familiar material (from step 5 of previous session) is kept on hand for repeated reading.

2. Running Record: Using the previous session's "new reading" material (not the material read to fluency), the student reads orally from a passage of about 100 words (student chooses which passage) and the teacher takes a running record.

3. Word Study and Metacognitive Strategies: Based on the running record (step 2), the teacher works with the student on a word study strategy. This may be "chunking" words into readable parts or focusing on the structure of language. The strategies related to monitoring reading ensure that what is being read makes sense.

4. New Reading: This step involves prereading preparation and either silent or oral reading by the student of new material. This is a guided reading activity.

5. Reading Practice: The student chooses a paragraph from the material just read (step 4) in order to practice to fluency. The teacher and student read the passage (can be repeatedly) in unison, with the teacher gradually fading support until the student is reading it alone. This passage can be used for step 1 of the next session as familiar material.

Figure 6–1. *Reading Rebound: Instructional Components*

In November I was a presenter at a regional reading conference, sharing my Reading Rebound experiences and ideas with middle and high school educators. When I first told Brian of my planned presentation, in a moment of daring he said he wanted to go with me: teachers needed to know what learning to read as a junior in high school was like, how Reading Rebound was affecting him as a reader and a student. At the last minute though, he got cold feet. I could use his words, he said, but he'd rather not appear himself. The message that he asked me to deliver was concise yet poignant:

> This program is helping me. It makes me understand the book. I could never do that before. Mrs. Daley and I talk about the book and it makes sense to me. She reads to me, we read together, I read by myself. She writes in a journal the things I've been thinking about. The word board helps a lot too. I get what words say now. I think this year is going to help me. I'm actually going to learn how to read. I may never like it, but I'll be able to do it.

Brian's words about reading were well received at the conference, but Brian the reader was not yet quite ready for prime time. That would come later.

When I had given Brian an Analytical Reading Inventory (Woods and Moe 1995) in September, I had been hard pressed to note any reading strengths. He was cooperative and seemed willing to put some effort into his reading; that was about it. On the weakness side of the ledger, though, I had a long list of areas he needed to work on: little or no self-correction of miscues; ineffective use of syntax and context; a lack of automaticity and fluency as he got bogged down in multiple mispronunciations, substitutions, and omissions; a weak vocabulary; and limited experiential background from which to build a context for understanding. Not surprisingly, when retelling a story he was unable to retain and put facts together to see the big picture, a problem compounded not only by multiple miscues but also by his inability to visualize what he was reading. During the first semester his desire to learn remained constant as he continued to work hard through lesson after lesson, and in time he started to pay more attention to his reading, to notice a miscue and attempt to correct it, to stop and think when something he read didn't make sense. His word identification skills became stronger as he developed a strategy for unlocking multisyllable words. And he began to enjoy what reading could hold for him, selecting a novel, *Wrestling Sturbridge*, that managed to capture his interest from day to day. *I wonder what we'll find out*, he would often say to himself and his teacher as he opened the book to the next chapter.

In January, as part of Brian's semester evaluation, Mrs. Daley and I asked him to reflect on his Reading Rebound experiences. His words tell of his growing knowledge of and faith in himself as a reader:

> I can read better now. I don't struggle as much. I have a place where I can read to somebody else and not be embarrassed. I am learning strategies and I know that I can get better with practice. My advice to anybody who wants to become a better reader is to read more, to read lower books and practice so you can move up to higher levels. If you want to know how to read better, just keep on reading.

Brian kept on reading. As part of his reading goal for the second semester he said, "I would like to prove to people that I have really learned how to read better. I want them to come and listen to me. They'll see what I know. I'm a reader now."

This nascent reader read and practiced, read and practiced, for the next three months. He finished the first novel he had ever read from start to finish. He picked out a book of short stories to read. He brought in magazines with articles about cars and trucks. He laughed at some Shel Silverstein poems. He even attempted *Ethan Frome*, required reading in English 11, with help from Mrs. Daley. At the end of April, Brian compiled a guest list of ten people he wanted to invite to a "private reading" scheduled for the morning of May 29. On the list were his parents, his grandmother, his favorite teachers and guidance counselors, special ed staff members, even the principal. He created an illustrated invitation on the computer (see figure 6–2), then sent a copy to everyone on his list.

After reserving a conference room and planning the refreshments he would serve his guests (the school cafeteria ladies were more than happy to help him out with cookies and lemonade), Brian tackled the most important task, deciding which selections to read aloud. He ran some questions by Mrs. Daley and me ("Do you think it's dumb to pick a picture book I read to the second graders during book buddies last year?"), but in the end the eclectic choices were Brian's own. To prepare for the private reading, he spent the two weeks before the presentation reading his selections over and over. "I gotta be sure to do this right," he told Mrs. Daley more than once. When May 29 arrived and his invited audience assembled in the conference room, a nervous but well-dressed Brian, his worn jeans and tee-shirt for once replaced by khakis, shirt, and tie, handed out typed programs to each of his guests (see figure 6–3).

When everyone had been seated, Brian moved to the front of the room. "I'm here to show you I can read," he began in a tone barely above a whisper. And show them he did, in a proud voice that grew louder and more confident as he demonstrated for himself and his audience what he had worked so hard to become—a reader.

A year later, as Brian gave an oral presentation on his senior project, which each graduate is required to plan and carry out independently, his subject was still reading. Fittingly, his words to his committee validated once and for all the innovative road to reading proficiency that Brian had traveled with Mrs. Daley as his guide:

> I chose literacy tutoring as my senior project because when I was young I had difficulty reading. No one had the time when I was younger to teach me how to read. I wanted to be a reading tutor for a first grader who couldn't read. I wanted to help Charlie to learn to read better. I wanted to help him know what letters and words are. I wanted to show him how to make fun out of reading. . . . During my sophomore year I had a 4.8 reading level and now I read at the eighth-grade level. I couldn't read then. I can now. I still don't like to read on my own. It's not easy for me to sit still and concentrate, so it's better if someone reads the hard stuff to me. But when I go out in the real world, I'll have to do it on my own. And the good thing is, I know I can do it. I'm not worried. I am a reader.

INVITATION TO A PRIVATE READING
BY BRIAN L.

THE DATE: MAY 29, 1998
THE LOCATION WHERE IT WILL BE HELD
WILL BE AT DANIEL WEBSTER REGIONAL HIGH SCHOOL
IN THE GUIDANCE CONFERENCE ROOM
THE TIME WILL BE FROM 11:30 A.M. - 12:15 P.M.

WE WILL PROVIDE SNACKS

AND BEVERAGES FOLLOWING THE READING

R.S.V.P. TO MRS. DALEY AT 537-6765 OR IN PERSON

Figure 6–2. *Brian's Invitation*

The Reading List For Brian L.

#1) *If You Promise Not to Tell*—Joe Wayman
- "I Hate to Wait" pg. 4
- "Bored" pg. 49
- "Questions without Answers" pg. 8

#2) *Where the Sidewalk Ends*—Shel Silverstein
- "Us" pg. 36

#3) *Children's Books*
- *Chimps Don't Wear Glasses* by Laura Numeroff
- *Tacky the Penguin* by Helen Lester

#4) *Wrestling Sturbridge*—Rich Wallace, chapter 11

Hope you enjoy the show!

Figure 6–3. *Brian's Reading List*

Background

After spending a year hidden away in the high school special education office and another marking time in reading workshop, Brian was not a reader. Mrs. Patrick didn't see him as one, and neither did Brian. And for good reason. First, Brian's well-honed learned helplessness served him as well in high school as it had throughout his earlier dismal school career. If he insisted that he couldn't read, kind teachers like Mrs. Patrick wouldn't expect him to. Then, too, even if Brian had wanted to read independently in reading workshop he would have had difficulty doing so; the library in Mrs. Patrick's room contained very few choices written at or below Brian's reading level. Indeed, as I discovered when searching for appropriate texts for him, most adolescent trade books that appeal to high school students are grade 5 level and above. Although there were shelves of novels and texts chosen to match the independent reading levels of his higher-performing reading workshop peers, selections that gave these lifers the opportunity to become readers by reading, there were very few books that a student still learning to read could simply pick up and get through on his own.

As a pupil still acquiring the reading basics, Brian needed an individualized instructional program that began where *he* was, not where a set curriculum was. He needed a curriculum that would, as the Reading Recovery model suggests, build on his strengths as it taught him how to solve problems in text, how to monitor his reading, how to check options, how to be an independent processor of print. He needed an adolescent version of Clay's Reading Recovery.

Goal

The goal of Reading Rebound is quite straightforward: to transform our neediest lifers into independent self-extending readers. According to Clay, a self-extending reader is one who becomes better as a result of his own efforts. As a child learns to read, this interactive system of processes becomes more empowering each time she picks up a new and more difficult text. Good readers learn to read by reading; poor readers, on the other hand, fall further and further behind with each new reading task assigned and never completed. Students like Brian, who arrive at high school reading below the sixth-grade level, have been unable to move beyond the acquisition phase of reading instruction. None of the worksheets, none of the drill sessions, have freed them from their prison of failure. Lacking the skills and strategies to read independently, they have come to rely on the support of others in order to make sense of text. They do not read; at best they are read to.

Instructional Model

I did not develop Reading Rebound in a vacuum. Initially I learned as much as I could about Marie Clay's early-intervention program, reading her books, identifying the assumptions and research that informed her practices, and examining studies that measured the effects of Reading Recovery on struggling beginning readers (Shanahan and Barr 1995; Center et al. 1995; Pinnell et al. 1990; Speigel 1995). Because I was eager to move from theory to practice, I also observed two friends who were Reading Recovery teachers in local schools. I noted the components included by these trained and competent teachers in every thirty-minute lesson: rereading familiar material, taking a running record, developing letter and word identification knowledge, writing and manipulating a short text, and reading new material. I also read Pikulski's (1994) review of Reading Recovery and four other successful reading programs for at-risk first-grade readers, noting the common components he identified.

Critical features that I felt could apply to the high school setting included:

- One-on-one or very-small-group instruction (maximum teacher-student ratio 1:3).
- High-quality additional reading instruction (not a substitute for regular reading instruction).
- Interesting, motivating, quality literature in place of workbooks meant for practicing isolated skills.
- A balance between the reading of meaningful, connected text and systematic word identification instruction (with a focus on word patterns).
- Repeated readings of text to build fluency, with the emphasis on reading as an act of constructing meaning.
- Writing activities that reinforce word recognition.
- Ongoing assessment.
- Additional reading outside the instructional setting.
- Consistent teacher training, to include ongoing consultation.

Finally, I took note of articles written by Lee and Neal (1993) and Ballash (1994), concerned educators like me who had successfully adapted Clay's Reading Recovery model and used it with at-risk adolescent readers.

Each segment of Reading Rebound's current instructional model has been fine-tuned by what our students have taught us about shaping Reading Recovery to meet the needs of adolescent readers. This framework evolved not only from our experience with Brian but also from our work with lifers who participated in the program the following year. It can be used either one-on-one during a traditional fifty-minute period or with two students working with one teacher in a ninety-minute block. In the latter case, the teacher works with each reader for forty minutes while the other listens and responds in writing to a book on tape of his or her own choosing. The last ten minutes of class are spent discussing the books the students are "reading" independently.

Rereading Familiar Material

Because we want the student to see—and hear—himself as a reader, each session starts with the student reading aloud a familiar piece of text he has read successfully in the past. This may be a short selection from a chapter or a short story, a paragraph taken from a news article, a poem, or an excerpt from his journal. Kept in an ever-expanding folder, these brief mastered texts are the tools by which the reader develops fluency and self-confidence. If he sounds like a reader, he is one.

Running Record

Using the previous session's "new reading" material (see below), the student chooses a passage of about one hundred words to read aloud. Following along on her own copy, the teacher takes a running record, a written analysis of oral reading that notes discrepancies between the spoken word and print. Each word pronounced correctly is marked with a check; any mispronunciation is noted by writing the incorrect pronunciation above the printed word. Self-corrections are also indicated. This running record (an example is shown in figure 6–4) is a window into the student's reading, establishing a focus for the explicit instruction in the next part of the lesson.

Word Study and Metacognitive Strategies

Based on what has been learned from the running record, the teacher works with the student on a word study strategy. The lesson may focus on using the analogy approach to decoding unknown words, "chunking" a troublesome multisyllable word into readable parts by comparing the unknown parts to familiar word patterns (R. Gaskins et al. 1992), or using semantic and syntactic cues to understand a difficult word or phrase. This is also the time to stress the metacognitive strategies used by proficient readers to comprehend text (Keene and Zimmerman 1997). Because we know that struggling readers like Brian have come to see reading as decoding, we use this time to encourage the student to monitor his understanding of what he has read. Does the text make sense? If not what can he do about it? Has he brought meaning to the text by using his prior knowledge? Has he asked questions or made mental pictures? Can he infer and draw conclusions? This sort of individualized instruction fosters the lifer's ability to become a self-extending reader.

New Reading

This step, modeled on Fountas and Pinnell's (1996) guided reading, enables the student to practice reading strategies on new text with the teacher's support. First, the student chooses a piece from a carefully compiled collection of texts written at his instructional level. When we began working with Brian we used a novel he had chosen as the instructional text. However, we soon realized that most novels don't move quickly enough to hold a student's interest; the story drags on from week to week, with never an end in sight. So, in order to foster a sense of completion and accomplishment, we are now apt to offer short stories, poems, and a variety of magazine or news articles. Once the piece has been selected, the teacher introduces the text in order to activate the student's prior knowledge and set a purpose for reading.

By the stick I am going into the same
year as all the fingers on both hands, fold them
down, then hold up the thumbs. Delie says it be
twelve but I don't know numbers to count so
that doesn't mean so much to me. I don't yet
have the trouble so I am still left to be as a child.
We work around the quarters and clean the yard
and gather eggs and help mammy with the
young ones. It's work, but it ain't dawn to dark
hard work like the field work and it leaves me a
bit of time to listen and see things. Mammy she
tells me some things to learn and I hear some
others from the field hands who come back at
dark and now and again I have to work in the
flower beds below the big window on the white
house.

The house women are fond of leaving
the window open and talking all their business
right there. So when I'm in the flower bed
below the window I hear…

RR - 11/3/99
Brian

Night John
G. Paulsen

Figure 6–4. *Brian's Running Record*

When necessary, key vocabulary, hard-to-pronounce names, and important concepts are also reviewed. Finally, the student reads the text softly to himself, asking for help when necessary. The teacher "listens in," giving appropriate support. Since the reader is now contextualizing the skills dealt with in the previous segment of the lesson, the teacher carefully observes whether the student is using these strategies, noting successes as well as areas where more instruction is needed. When the reading is completed, teacher and student briefly discuss the text. Personal responses are solicited and valued.

Reading Practice

The student chooses a paragraph from the new material to use to develop fluency. The teacher and student start out reading the passage in unison, and the teacher gradually drops out until the student is reading alone. Sometimes mastery will occur after one reading; sometimes it may take one or more rereadings before the student feels comfortable and satisfied. This text is then placed in the familiar-reading folder, to be used during another session.

With practice, the five components of a Reading Rebound lesson can be completed in forty or fifty minutes. A ninety-minute block also leaves time for independent reading (often a high-interest book on tape that struggling readers would be incapable of reading independently but the text of which they can follow as they listen); writing in a journal to support and extend the reading; and informal conversations that highlight the social aspect of literacy. Those who need to adapt this model to high school's traditional seven or eight periods have to build these components creatively into two periods. (As with Reading Workshop, Reading Rebound should not take the place of a regular English class. These struggling lifers need *more* not *less* time to revalue themselves as readers.)

Choosing the Student

When I started working with struggling readers, I had naively expected all lifers to benefit from reading workshop. Brian proved me wrong. His reading level on standardized tests had scarcely budged after two years of reading intervention. His predicament made it clear to me that we need to offer Reading Rebound to these neediest lifers as soon as they enter high school. The logic for this is quite straightforward. If we can move a student beyond the reading acquisition phase of instruction during his freshman year, then as a sophomore he can become a member of the Reading Workshop I class. There he will have the time to hone his newly developing reading abilities through extensive practice while feeling part of a caring and supportive community of learners.

It is not difficult to predict who will benefit from Reading Rebound; all I need to do is look at the eighth-grade NRST results collected in the spring. Anyone scoring below grade six is a prime candidate, and come September the administration of an informal reading inventory such as the Analytical Reading Inventory (Woods and Moe 1995) usually bears out this prognosis. During this assessment the student reads aloud a series of passages of increasing difficulty. By listening into his reading I can ascertain his strengths and weaknesses in both word identification and comprehension. At the start of this hour-long session I also conduct the Burke Reading Inventory (Burke 1988), for I want to understand not only how the student views reading but also how he sees himself as a reader. And I want to begin a personalized dialogue about reading, one that will last throughout the Reading Rebound experience.

If the ARI's results show a student still in the reading acquisition phase (below grade level 5.5), he is reassigned from Reading Workshop I to Reading Rebound. When I make this change, I share the test results with the student; it is important for him to be aware of the strengths and weaknesses he has exhibited during the testing session. Then, too, I want him to know his role in making a difference in his reading; without his commitment and desire for change there is little I, or anyone else, can do.

Training and Supporting the Teacher

All Reading Recovery teachers participate in a rigorous yearlong training class run by a certified Reading Recovery expert. During this time, each trainee tutors up to four children daily while attending two-to-three-hour weekly seminars. Part of the training includes "behind the glass" sessions, when trainers and peers observe and discuss each class member as she puts her book learning into action with a struggling first-grade reader. For a newly conceived program like Reading Rebound this sort of intensive and comprehensive training isn't an option. We are venturing into uncharted instructional territory; there are no manuals, no observation lessons, no experts to call on.

Instead, after deciding that I wanted to develop a high school model of Reading Recovery, I approached Mrs. Daley, the young special education teacher who was Brian's case manager. I knew she had established good rapport with this often-exasperating adolescent, a prerequisite for success in this sort of intimate intervention in which teacher and student must collaborate to effect substantive learning. She had taught some reading workshops and was therefore familiar with me as well as with the school's approach to corrective reading instruction. Like most of us she was frustrated with Brian's lack of academic progress during his first two years at Daniel Webster, and she reacted positively to my idea of creating a course to meet his literacy needs. She agreed on the spot to take on the role of Reading Rebound teacher-to-be.

During the spring Mrs. Daley and I discussed short articles describing Reading Recovery's philosophical assumptions and educational practices. She learned about running records and the individualized instruction that springs from these daily assessments. She was introduced to the phrases used by Reading Recovery teachers to support a reader as she monitors her understanding. She learned about teacher actions that seem either to interfere with or to accelerate a Reading Recovery student's progress. In order to help Brian develop a self-extending system, she reviewed the three cueing systems—graphophonic, semantic, and syntactic—used by readers to decode words, and she revisited the basic metacognitive strategies that proficient readers employ to construct meaning from text. After spending two days observing Reading Recovery sessions and seeing the program in action, she began to practice taking running records with some of her students; she began to think and act like a Reading Recovery/Rebound teacher. Throughout these months Mrs. Daley and I met weekly, discussing all she had read and seen and wrestling with any questions she had.

When school ended, she and I continued to get together during the summer to work on this instructional model, trying to visualize it in action. Once September came, Mrs. Daley and I continued our collaborative planning and troubleshooting, taking our cues from her sessions with Brian. With his permission I dropped in for informal class visits whenever I could. My observational notes, in concert with Mrs. Daley's experiences, gave us plenty to think and talk about. Indeed, Brian became our best teacher and agenda setter; what he said and did during his Reading Rebound sessions determined where the curriculum would lead.

Heeding Pikulski's (1994) conclusion about the place of training in effective intervention programs, I made sure that there was an opportunity for on-going consultation built into Mrs. Daley's schedule. Every week throughout the year, she and I met to debrief completed sessions and plan for coming ones. My goal was to keep one step ahead of this committed teacher as she piloted the evolving Reading Rebound model and give her whatever support she needed.

Once the year was over, she and I (with Brian's help) reviewed what we had accomplished, revised the model based on what we had learned, and planned for year two. Flush with success, I recruited another Reading Rebound teacher from our special education staff so we could expand the program during the coming school year. There were more Brians to be taught.

Assessing Progress

Ongoing Assessment

Because of the preliminary literacy assessment we conduct before a student is assigned to Reading Rebound, we already know a great deal about her. Results of the Analytical Reading Inventory and reading interview afford us a view of a pupil's strengths and weaknesses and reveal her perceptions of reading and herself as a reader. With these data as a baseline, the instructor then uses information gained through running records to drive the daily instruction.

This on-going assessment keeps the teacher abreast of the student's progress and allows her to individualize the lesson to meet that student's particular needs. If Sally substitutes *hovering* for *horrifying* and *revised* for *received* as she reads a paragraph aloud, the lesson focuses on noticing the middle chunks of multisyllable words. If Sally reads *was* for *saw*, her teacher encourages her to be on the lookout for syntactic cues: "Does that sound right to you?" In order to encourage Sally to think like a proficient reader the teacher asks, "What picture do you have in your head as you read those sentences?" In subsequent weeks the teacher notes the skills and strategies Sally is beginning to use independently as well as areas in which more work is needed. Instruction is guided by what the teacher observes every day.

Periodic Assessment

Quarterly rubrics and semester-end self-evaluations and goal setting are an integral part of Reading Rebound's assessments. For example, Brian's midyear self-evaluation shows us a glimpse of this lifer's transformation-in-progress:

How have you grown as a reader? *I have grown as a reader by learning how to understand the reading and to ask questions if I need to have a word or paragraph explained. I have learned to read different types of information. I've read different types of books. I can visualize more about the book. I have become a stronger reader since the beginning of the year. I am more patient with my reading. I'm not giving up so quickly. I have learned how to communicate with the book I guess. I understand the book better. As a student I can do a lot more things on my own. I can do my homework, which is usually reading a textbook.*

What are your weaknesses? *If I cannot read a certain book I will just put it down and not even try to read it. Another is putting words into places where I am not supposed to put them. I need to work on that.*

Which activities have helped you most as a reader? Why? *One activity was the reading of magazine and newspaper articles. They are not the same as books. There is always something new to read. I can learn about new stuff. It gave me the chance to read things that I like to read about. Running records helped me too. They helped me by showing me my mistakes and helping me to self-correct. The reading together with the teacher made me think of how I should read to other people, like using expression. Now I am able to read to other people. If I could change one thing it would be reading novels. I really don't enjoy reading the same book every day. It gets boring.*

How is reading important to you now? Later on in life outside of school? *Reading is important to me now because I need to finish school. I need to read my textbooks and do my assignments. Later on I will use it to read recipes and magazines. It will help me to educate my children. I will be able to read something to my children so that they can understand it. I want to do that.*

Evaluating Results

There is no body of data on which to judge the success of Reading Rebound. I have only the clear evidence of Brian's transformation and my knowledge of what transpired with the handful of students who participated in Reading Rebound during the program's second year on which to base my conclusions. But when combined with the case studies of Lee and Neal (1993) and Ballash (1994) and anecdotal evidence from other teachers across the state who have implemented the Reading Rebound model with their lowest-achieving adolescent readers, it seems safe to say that Reading Rebound is a practice with promise. In all cases, as a direct result of participation in Reading Recovery–type individualized intervention, hard-core lifers have taken the first step toward escaping the shackles of failure. They have begun to develop the strategies that will empower them to become independent self-regulated readers.

If an ARI can be seen as a measure of growth, then Brian's success is both obvious and remarkable. Before Reading Rebound Brian struggled while reading a fifth-grade ARI selection orally; he had an accuracy rate of 87 percent and made an error every seventh word. Not surprisingly his comprehension was below 50 percent. Just a year later, he was able to read a seventh-grade selection with a 96 percent accuracy rate, making miscues only once every twenty-one words. His comprehension had risen to 90 percent. Brian himself points with pride to his growth on standardized tests; in his senior project report he reminds us that in two years his reading scores had moved from below grade 5 to grade 8.

After several years of stagnant test results, this progress is truly exceptional. But what is more exceptional to me is the change I witnessed in Brian. An adolescent who had hated reading, who had written off reading as something he would never be able to or want to do, had begun to see it—and himself—in a new light. "I may never like reading," he confided to me. "But I can do it. And it's nice to know how to read because some day I'm going to have to."

Chapter 7

Reading Workshop II: Constructing the Framework for Success

In order to develop readers, we must encourage and foster the creative attitudes and activities of engaged readers. . . . By . . . focusing our instruction and support on the construction of meaning, the classroom can become a place where students not only produce and share meanings, but a place where they share ways of reading and being with text, becoming aware in the process of their own strategies and those of others.

—JEFF WILHELM
You Gotta BE the Book

Marie transferred to Daniel Webster toward the end of her freshman year. She was referred to me by her newly assigned guidance counselor, an educator who often uses my office and my services as a last resort for students who have nowhere else to turn as they struggle with the ever growing demands of high school. "She and her family just moved here from Riverside," Jim told me. "She's a discouraged student who seems to be afraid of her own shadow. She has no special education coding, but for whatever reason she's spent most of her life in self-contained classrooms. Her reading scores are low, and she's having a hard time in all of her classes here. It's too late to put her in reading workshop this year, so I think she could use your help."

When Marie arrived at my office that first afternoon I was quick to notice her slumped shoulders and downcast eyes. Yet even her body language couldn't prepare me for the first words out of her mouth: "My name is Marie, and you need to know that I'm stupid. I'm stupid, and I can never do anything right."

As I worked with Marie that spring, helping her as she struggled to make sense of her English and geo-political studies assignments, I soon realized that this needy and discouraged adolescent had misjudged herself. She wasn't stupid. When given the opportunity to complete an assignment with my support, she drew from a well of intelligence and abilities she didn't even think existed. It became painfully clear that I was rubbing shoulders with a poster child for learned helplessness, a pupil who through the words and actions of others had come to see herself as incapable and incompetent.

In time Marie started to see herself in a different light. She began to develop the ability to think and work on her own. She displayed the beginnings of self-assurance. Her sophomore year she participated in Reading Workshop I, and at the end of a year of becoming a better reader by reading she had shown remarkable growth. The student who had spent a lifetime saying "I can't" was now willing to give her courses and herself a try. One June day she delightedly informed me that the spring reading workshop test results had placed her just below the grade 8 reading level, the level at which students were said to "test out" of Reading Workshop I. "I guess I didn't really test out—but almost! My scores went up almost two years. My comprehension still isn't all that great, but look at how well I did on vocabulary!"

Marie was right. After a year of corrective instruction she had certainly made progress, and because the school curriculum had nothing more in place to support this developing reader, she was going to have to move ahead on her own. I wondered to myself that afternoon, *Is she ready?* Marie thought she was, and I hoped so.

"We Can Read and Talk, Read and Talk"

In October of her junior year, a "new and improved" Marie swooped unannounced into my office. I had seen her in the cafeteria earlier that fall, sporting a provocative miniskirt and an updated hairdo to match. "Don't forget that I'm here if you need me!" I had called to her across a throng of laughing adolescents jockeying for position in the lunch line. "Oh, Mrs. Mueller," Marie had giggled through a brightly lipsticked mouth that bespoke her march toward young adulthood and independence, "you don't have to worry about that!" I marveled at Marie's transformation from self-effacing ninth grader to poised upperclassman.

"So young lady," I said. "What brings you here today?"

"Not much really. I just need a little help in English," responded Marie with a smile. "Miss Sizer says that for the new quarter each of us has to pick out a novel and read it on our own. Then in six weeks, at the end of the book, we have to do a project. Geez, I don't know what to do. I really don't have a clue. We never had to do anything like this in any other class, not all by ourselves. If we had a book assigned in English class last year, Mrs. T. was always there to help us in reading workshop. Can you believe Miss Sizer really expects us to do this? We all tried to talk her out of it, but she won't change her mind. Mrs. Mueller, can you help me, *please?* If you want, I can come here three times a week during my study hall. We can do it then. We can read and talk, read and talk, just like they had us do in reading workshop."

Marie's request, so simple and yet so challenging, sent both of us on a journey of discovery, as she learned for the first time what it means to *engage* in reading, and I learned firsthand how difficult such a task can be for a newly re-visioning lifer like Marie. My teaching journal captured our belabored voyage, page by page and week by week.

October 28

Today I met Marie in the library. Miss Sizer had given me a list of novels Marie could choose from and I'd gone over the list carefully, discarding those over Marie's head. I want her to be successful. I gave the revised list to Marie and suggested she choose a book she really wanted to read. *Flowers for Algernon* was included; so was *Roll of Thunder, Hear My Cry*, my "secret" choice for her. As we were going over the list Miss Sizer walked by and said, "How about reading *Animal Dreams*, Marie? The kids always seem to like it and I'll bet you can really connect with it." I assumed she was alluding to the rumor that this woman-child sitting next to me had suffered a miscarriage that fall; Codi, the main character in the book, has had one too. Since none of the other books seemed to please Marie, she jumped at Miss Sizer's suggestion. I am excited because I love Kingsolver's writing. I don't know the readability level of the book, but if Marie really gets into it what does it matter? Word attack has always been a strength for her; she doesn't get thrown by multisyllable words like lots of her peers. We got two copies and we looked at the cover, a stylized painting of a Native American pueblo, I think. It didn't look at all familiar to Marie. I'll bet she has never been anywhere near a town like Grace, Arizona. Next class I plan to bring in pictures I took when our family was out there two summers ago. That'll give her some background for the setting of the book. I told Marie to go home and look over the book. I'll do the same.

October 31

After looking at my pictures and talking about the West (the farthest from New Hampshire Marie has been is Rhode Island, to visit her father after her parents got divorced), we scanned the book together, talking about how the book is written from different points of view, with flashbacks, dreams, and Native American legends all mixed in. She seems to be comfortable with all of that. She told me they had talked about flashbacks in Miss Sizer's class at the beginning of the semester. We reviewed the names of all the main characters so that Marie will know who's narrating each chapter. She liked the fact that this was about a girl who is looking for her own identity. "So am I," she told me. Maybe this book will do what good stories are supposed to do, letting Marie learn more about herself as she gets to know the people and the plot. We have six weeks to read this book, but I'm going to start off slowly. I asked her to read just the first chapter. I had wanted to read it in class but we ran out of time. We talked too much. Oh well, it's only two pages long.

November 2

Good grief. Here I thought this was a book Marie would enjoy reading on her own, and the first thing she told me was that she didn't get it. Two pages and she didn't get it. Not at all. She got the words, but she didn't know what they were saying. So I suggested thinking about it out loud. I'd read it and tell her what was going on in my mind when I was reading. She would follow along in her own book. I assured her this was the same as the shared readings she did in reading workshop, the book was just a little harder. When reading, I modeled the seven metacognitive reading strategies they'd gone over and over in reading workshop, and she seemed to understand. Then on to the next chapter, with another character narrating and including a flashback in his musings to boot. Marie wanted me to keep reading and thinking so I did. I questioned, I visualized, I predicted and read between the lines. I drew her into the conversation so she would know that she was a part of this reading and sense making. We covered sixteen pages in ninety minutes. I decided not to ask her to read on her own yet. I think she has to get comfortable in the book before she can go solo. But there are 325 pages to go and only five and a half weeks until the book has to be finished. Yikes!

November 4

Today I suggested that we take turns reading a paragraph aloud and then stopping to talk about any questions either of us had. Read and talk. Read and talk. I reminded her of how well that strategy had worked when Mrs. T. helped her make sense of *April Morning* last year. It only took me one two-and-a-half-page chapter to realize we are in way over Marie's head. With Kingsolver you have to think and reason all the time, pulling in what you already know to make sense of the multiple (and now it seems to me nonstop) nuances of her style and story. For struggling readers her style is truly inconsiderate. And for struggling readers with a limited experiential background it's even worse. We got through another two chapters today; we're on page thirty-six. Three hundred pages and five weeks to go. Still no independent reading. What's the point? Without the talk that goes along with the reading, there is nothing there for her.

November 9

What a disaster! When we started the book I told Marie that we were going to take turns reading (she likes to read aloud, and she's very "fluent"), discussing what we had read at appropriate points. Well, we're doing that, but let me tell you, we've been doing a lot of discussing. Hardly a sentence goes by without that panicky I-don't-get-it look crossing her face. We then stop while I try to pull out Marie's ideas and model what I want by sharing mine. After sixty-odd pages of hard hard work, it has become very clear to me that understanding this book goes far beyond the Barnell Loft strategies of picking out the main idea and supporting details. In order to grasp the essential, in order to construct meaning, I have reverted to one long "think-aloud." I am looking at comprehension in a totally new light. And I wonder how she's looking at herself. Marie has come so far in two years; I only hope this ordeal doesn't make her fall back into that helpless "I can't" pattern. Whose bright idea was this anyway?

November 14

Getting close to Thanksgiving, but there's not much to be thankful about when I think of what's going on between Marie and this book. She hates the book. She hates

Codi and her father and all the people in Grace. Not knowing what else to do in our quest to "conquer" this book, Marie and I spent today doing just what we've been doing for the past two weeks. Or almost—Marie has given up on reading aloud herself. She has realized that when she does, she puts all of her energy into words and none into meaning. So I read aloud. Marie doesn't get it. We talk in order to figure things out. And so on and so on. At the end of the session Marie told me once more how much she is disliking the book. So I made her a promise. We will keep plodding on until we get to page one hundred (twenty long pages from where we are now). If by then it is still a struggle, we will throw in the towel. I am almost looking forward to doing that. Don't know what I am going to say to Miss Sizer. . . .

November 16

Today we had worked our way through a *long* chapter, fourteen pages. I went to close the book and Marie surprised me by saying, "Let's keep reading. The next chapter's a short one." We did; and at the end of the chapter, without any prompting, Marie said, "You know why I think he did that, Mrs. Mueller?" Clearly understanding the essence of the text, she went on to make a thoughtful inference, then a prediction. I was taken aback; on her own she was beginning to reason, to make sense of the story as she read it. On her own she was beginning to see the point as she became an engaged and thoughtful reader. I think we are going to finish this book.

November 18

Suddenly we are moving faster. Marie is beginning to connect with Codi's pregnancy; without really telling me the details, she is using the novel as a way to come to terms with her all-too-similar history. I can see it in the way her thoughts are beginning to develop and grow, no longer the staccato of making meaning sentence by sentence, but rather the flow of page-by-page understanding. We have decided Marie will do some reading on her own. To try it out, we each read the same short section to ourselves. I told her that the thinking aloud I have been doing would now go on in her own head. When we finished, we talked. It wasn't smooth and easy; we still had a lot to go over. But some of the responsibility for making meaning is shifting to Marie. Atwell would be proud of this handover! And for the first time I gave Marie a reading assignment. Over the weekend she'll try to finish the rest of chapter 12 on her own. I suggested that she attach a sticky note every time she comes to something she doesn't understand or wants to talk about. I will do the same. We'll see what happens.

November 21

It's a start. Marie got through three pages on her own—and the sticky notes worked! One asked the meaning of "mortar" (it's so easy to forget how limited Marie's vocabulary is) and how a baby could be "mortared" into a wall (even when knowing what mortar is, that picture stretches a reader's use of the word, so typical of Kingsolver). The other gave Marie's surprised reaction to Codi and Loyd's lovemaking: "Do you think he planned all of this?" followed by "I don't get it. Does he know about her pregnancy or not?" We read a five-page chapter silently, then discussed it as a whole. It's hard, though, to get away from the little things that come up over and over to puzzle Marie. I've got to realize that what counts for her is the big picture the author wants her to come away with, not the nuances that go right over her head. She needs to make sense of her reading on a level that works for her. On her own she will read the next five-page chapter, again using sticky notes.

November 23

Marie is really beginning to get into the book now. Today as we read together silently, there was a part about Codi's attempt to teach birth control to her high school students. Marie laughed to herself, then suddenly looked up and said, "I'm surprised that I know so much!" Then she paraphrased what Codi had been telling her class: "If they're gonna do it, they'd better know what they're getting in for!" Of course, it's easy when Marie can connect with the text; it's much more challenging when there's a divide between what she knows and what the book is telling her.

November 25

For the first time I feel we're making progress. If Marie works hard over the weekend, we will be halfway through the book. I'm getting worried about her finishing on time; there are only two weeks left. I'm not sure what a stickler Miss Sizer is for deadlines, and I doubt she realizes what a stretch this assignment has been for Marie. Too often teachers are simply unaware of their students' abilities (but I'd better not forget that I was there when Marie picked this book). It's not as though Marie hasn't been working. She's surprised herself with what she has been able to accomplish. When I mentioned my concern, Marie told me that Miss Sizer is going to give them class time for independent reading. I think Marie will be able to take advantage of that. I asked if she thought keeping a journal would help her understand the book. She's used to doing journal entries; that was a part of reading workshop that she really liked. She's going to give it a try.

December 3

Things are going much better. Between reading with me, reading in English class, and reading on her own, Marie is really making progress. The journal entries seem to be helping her as well. They are taking over from the sticky notes, giving Marie a place to record what she is thinking—and getting her to think more. Here's part of one entry:

> I disliked how Codi's father wouldn't talk to her about their relatives. Why does he have to keep it hidden from her? She's old enough to know. I think that Codi is getting stronger. At first all she wanted to do was leave Grace after a year. Now I think she may hang around. I can just picture Codi standing up and talking to all the ladies

in town. She must have been afraid. But she must have been proud too. I thought the cockfight was disgusting. I wonder how anybody could do that to an innocent bird.

December 6

Because I want Marie to think about how she is growing as a reader this semester, I have asked her to use her journal as a place to reflect not only on the book but also on the strategies she has used to make sense of it. My goal is to help her realize that she is capable of doing independently what we have done together. I want her to become Clay's self-extending reader. I'm beginning to think she's well on her way. Here is an entry in which she honestly and successfully evaluates herself:

> As a reader I have learned that I can read anything as long as I ask questions or stop to think about what I read. I feel that I am pretty good at visualizing what I read. I ask a lot of questions too. I sometimes can predict what's going to happen next. I need to work realizing that books take time and patience and understanding in order to read them.

December 8

I must admit that I have not stressed synthesizing with Marie. The act of synthesizing is one of the most sophisticated cognitive strategies used by good readers, so with Marie I have stressed other things. We have put a lot of effort into visualizing (she's good at that now), asking questions/predicting (another emerging strength) and inferring (ditto). She has been using fix-up strategies and working at picking out what's important in the reading. And then today, as we finished reviewing some reading that Marie had done on her own (that's how we spend most of our time now, going over text she has read independently), she turned back to a page that had really been puzzling her. "I still don't get this whole thing," she said. After we talked it out together, she wrapped up our discussion with, "I know. Codi feels so alone." A slight pause. Then "Oh, so that's what the whole book is about, isn't it?" She seemed slightly disgusted when she said this, as if she should have known this all along, as if perhaps I should have told her this before we even opened the book. "I know how she feels. I often feel alone, even in the middle of a room full of people."

December 10

For the past week I've been worried about what's going to happen if Marie doesn't finish the book on time. But I decided to let Marie take care of that; after all, it's her responsibility. It turns out I shouldn't have been so concerned. As break ended today, Marie flew into my office, her face flushed with excitement. "Mrs. Mueller, guess what? I'm not gonna get marked down for being late finishing the book. Miss Sizer has decided to give all of us an extra week. When she asked me how much I have to read, I told her that I had only four chapters left, that I can't wait to find out if Codi is going to leave Grace or not. I can't understand why she would; doesn't she understand how much Loyd and Emmelina and everybody else really need her? I wouldn't go if I was her. See you this afternoon." As quickly as she had entered my office, she turned to leave, intent on catching the bus to the vocational center. "I really love this book, don't you Mrs. Mueller?" *Yes, Marie,* I thought to myself as I watched her rejoin her laughing group of friends. *I really love it too. More than you'll ever know.*

Background

As strange as it seems now, it took more than two years before I dealt with the fact that for some Daniel Webster lifers there is no light at the end of the academic tunnel after a year of reading workshop. Since I corrected the Nelson Reading Skills Test given to all reading workshop classes each spring, I knew that some students fail to "test out," not only those like Marie who are on the cusp of success but also those who still have a long way to go before reaching grade 8 on the standardized test. But my mind was on those who were successful, those who proved ready to use their practiced strategies independently and without support. And my energies as a consultant were focused on making sure that the new reading workshop classes ran smoothly and successfully. The lifers who were unable to make the grade as self-extending readers retreated to special ed, welcomed back and fostered by the nurturing staff members. Or like Marie, they laid claim to the seats in the back of their English and history classrooms, hoping against hope that they could somehow manage to conquer the texts assigned to them.

Working with Brian and Marie forced me to see that one year of reading workshop is not a panacea for all literacy ills. Despite our best efforts, there will always be students who need more than Reading Workshop I, adolescents who after a year of reading, keeping a journal, attending to minilessons, and sharing remain passive readers lacking the knowledge and ability to monitor their own reading process. Some are pupils like Marie, who have more trouble with comprehension than vocabulary, who can decode words fluently but who are unable—or perhaps unaware of how important it is—to make sense of what they are reading. Others continue to trip over multisyllable words, expending all their energy on word identification rather than making meaning. These students, usually eleven or twelve out of a group of forty-five, require more intensive and explicit instruction in what proficient readers do to engage themselves in and comprehend text. They need a curriculum geared to their individual needs. And whatever their differences, they all need more time and support to come to understand who they are as readers in order to take control of their own literacy development.

Goal

The goal of Reading Workshop II is twofold:

1. To continue to provide a supportive classroom community in which these lifers can persevere in their growth as readers and learners.

2. To replicate in a small group the kind of one-on-one instruction, practice, and interaction Marie and I shared as we worked our way through *Animal Dreams*.

What Marie referred to as "read and talk, read and talk" is a shared reading experience, a time when struggling readers receive the support they need to make sense of meaningful text while building the self-confidence to voice their ideas without fear of failure. It's a time for these students to understand that the facility they show for making sense of oral language can be transferred to the written word.

I chuckle when a teacher says of a lifer, "He never has anything to say!" Just listen to them as they cluster in the hall sharing stories with their friends during break. Eavesdrop on their animated chatter as they congregate during lunchtime. It's not that these lifers have nothing to say; it's that for too long they have been relegated to classrooms where meaningful talk has been all but eliminated for at-risk readers like themselves. Whether working in "special" classes where most learning is done in isolation or attempting to fit into mixed-ability classes where they feel inferior by virtue of their reading struggles, they are "not accustomed to expressing their opinions, solving problems, or gaining group consensus in collaborative decision making" (Allen 1995, p. 112). For all intents and purposes these silenced students have been disenfranchised from traditional classroom discourse.

In the Reading Workshop II community, on the other hand, lifers can discover the power of language, both oral and written. Through lots of shared and independent reading, lots of teacher modeling, lots of focused discussion about interesting books, lots of opportunities to become immersed in a wide range of language activities, these adolescents can take the next step toward reading engagement and independence. Once they learn to tell and value their own stories in a safe and supportive setting, they can move on to reading and valuing the stories of others. They can become readers.

Learning More About Our Students

When the results of the Nelson Reading Skills Test are announced in the spring, pupils who fail to "test out" of reading workshop meet with me individually. My goal is to assure these disappointed—and often frustrated—students that their time in Reading Workshop I has been time well spent, that although they may have failed to reach the elusive grade 8 reading plateau, they have nonetheless made a move toward reinventing themselves as a reader. My sales pitch is based on fact, for in almost every case test results document meaningful growth over the past ten months. So do the numbers from the spring Reading Attitude Assessment and the students' year-end self-evaluation. Generally speaking, it's not that these adolescents haven't found success in reading workshop; like Marie, they simply need more time and focused support in order to attain reading independence. My concentrated PR blitz usually succeeds; with my gentle nudge, the Reading Workshop II students-to-be accept the importance of an additional dose of reading support, albeit grudgingly.

In the fall I invite each class member to meet with me individually once more, this time in an effort to gather the assessment data needed to plan our classroom instruction. Whereas the large group of Reading Workshop I participants necessitates a fairly generic approach to reading improvement, the reduced number of Reading Workshop II students allows the teacher to focus the curriculum on the specific needs of the participants. To evaluate these needs, I administer the one-on-one assessments I use when learning about a Reading Rebound student. In addition, I choose one oral selection on which to do a detailed oral reading miscue analysis, an exercise that affords me a "window into the reader's mind" (Goodman 1991), letting me share with the student his reading process in action while at the same time examining how he predicts and monitors his reading for meaning. As I explain what I have learned from these assessments, the student comes to know the individual strengths he brings to reading as well as the areas in which additional growth is needed. This is a crucial part of my assessment. If this adolescent is to continue to grow as a reader, he must be made aware of where he needs to go and what he can build on in order to get there.

The information gathered from these sessions, along with results of the Metacomprehension Strategies Index (Schmitt 1990) administered to the entire class and the data carried over from Reading Workshop I, fleshes out the portrait of each Reading Workshop II class member. It replaces the sterile NRST numbers by which these students have been identified (7.7 vocabulary, 6.8 comprehension, 7.2 composite) with flesh-and-blood descriptors of skills, attitudes, and strategies that can be comprehended, acknowledged, and worked on by a committed re-visioning reader.

Logistics

Like Reading Workshop I, Reading Workshop II meets three blocks a week for either fifty or ninety minutes depending on the day and is limited to a maximum of eight or nine students per class. The course continues to incorporate the traditional workshop elements of time, choice, and response, and students read, keep journals, and have conferences. However, the schedule is not as regimented. Depending on the needs of the students in the class, lesson plans differ from day to day and week to week. Nevertheless, there are some common elements. For instance, each block includes opportunities for all areas of language development—reading, writing, listening, and speaking. Also, whole-class activities are interspersed with individual and small-group work. The teacher begins every block by reading aloud, and direct instruction takes place along with independent reading and journal writing. Sometimes minilessons are presented to all students. At other times explicit instruction is presented only to those two or three students who need support in a particular area. An instructional theme lasting between six and eight weeks gives continuity to much of the daily work: units include choosing what to read (culminating in a class shopping trip to a bookstore), author studies (Gary Paulsen is a favorite), and favorite picture books (everything from *Green Eggs and Ham* to *Knots on a Counting Rope*). A sample weekly schedule is shown in figure 7–1.

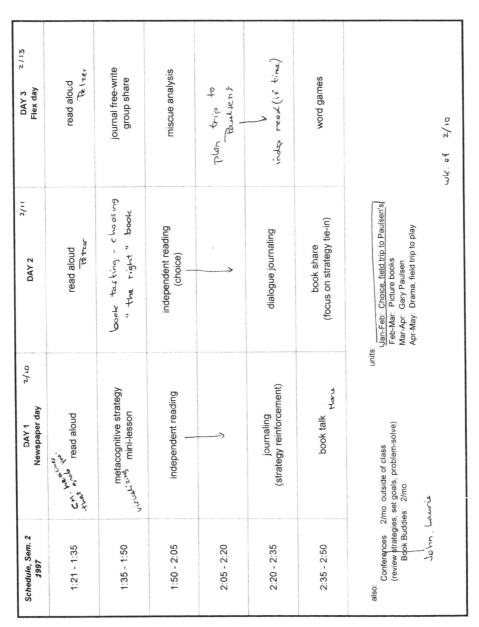

Figure 7–1. *Reading Workshop Schedule*

Reading Beyond the Classroom

Once the class settles into the Reading Workshop II routine, once students and teacher develop a cohesive sense of community, it's time to move literacy learning beyond the classroom so that these students can experience the value and joy of reading in the outside world. It may be a one-time event (going to dinner and the theater at the end of a creative drama unit, for example) or an ongoing activity. In the highly rewarding book-buddies program, for example, these re-visioning adolescent readers become twice-a-month reading mentors to local primary-grade children.

Another popular outreach project, at least after the first timid foray, is "supper club." Each Reading Workshop II student chooses an adult from the community as a reading companion. The paired readers then pick a book acceptable to both of them and read it within a reasonable amount of time, exchanging journal entries while they do. Finally, all the twosomes meet at the high school for an evening of pizza and book sharing. At the start of the evening the air is pregnant with silence, but with a little urging these reticent readers/thinkers/speakers begin to talk. "Did you like the way it ended?" "What did you think of the main character?" "I couldn't believe how he reacted when his brother ran away." Spontaneous questions and comments fill the hour and a half as adolescents once disenfranchised from literacy discourse find their voices in a social setting. This is often the first time these students have been a part of such a discussion outside of the safety of their reading workshop classroom; judging from the sense of camaraderie and the laughter interspersed with the talk, it may not be the last.

Introducing Effective Reading Practices

Our work with Reading Workshop II students has identified a number of reading practices that encourage students to become more aware of their active role in making sense of text as they revalue both the reading process and themselves.

Cognitive Strategies

Good readers are *metacognitive*—that is, they think about their thinking as they read. In their ground-breaking *Mosaic of Thought* (1997), Keene and Zimmerman demystify reading comprehension by pointing out the seven cognitive processes that all proficient readers use as they seek to bring meaning to the written word: activating prior knowledge, determining importance, asking questions, creating images, drawing inferences, synthesizing, and using fix-up strategies to repair comprehension when it breaks down. Starting the first week of class, the Reading Workshop II teacher models these strategies, introducing them one by one in a series of explicit think-alouds. (A lesson on activating prior knowledge is shown in figure 7–2) Once the strategy has been modeled, students are encouraged to practice it, first as part of a group setting, then as they read independently. If I had to pick the element of Reading Workshop II instruction that is most

METACOGNITIVE LESSON STRATEGY #1
Activating Prior Knowledge (Schema)—Connecting the Known to the New

1. Explain that when proficient readers read, they think about things they already know; they relate the experiences they have had to what they are reading. There are three kinds of connections that can be made:

- Text-to-self connections.
- Text-to-text connections.
- Text-to-world connections.

2. Using a book that you have previewed in order to find places where you as a reader make these three types of connections, do a "think aloud" in which you share with your students your use of the strategy.

3. Be explicit about what you are doing. For example:

   Okay, this is how it's going to work. When I'm reading you'll see me looking at the text and sharing it as I always do during our read-aloud sessions. But instead of reading straight through, I'll stop and think aloud about things I know or have experienced that are like the book in some way. You may notice that I stop to think before I speak; after this pause I'll let you know what I was thinking.

4. Model the strategy for your students, showing examples of all three types of connections. Don't be shy—they need to know exactly what your brain is doing!

5. Remind students that proficient readers activate prior knowledge (usually without even thinking about it) in order to comprehend, to make sense of what they are reading. The meaning, then, comes from our interaction with the text as we read; without the reader there are words but no meaning. It's a two-way street—our prior knowledge gives meaning to the book, and the meaning we gain from the book expands our knowledge.

Figure 7–2. *Metacognitive Strategy Lesson*

beneficial to these struggling adolescent readers, this is it. These strategies are the means by which readers embark on mind journeys rather than become lost on dead ends.

Retrospective Miscue Analysis

This powerful instructional practice, adapted from Goodman and Marek (1996), is another tool by which students come to know and understand themselves as readers. In the session, the teacher plays a tape of a short oral reading. The students follow along in the written text, on the lookout for reader miscues ("an instance in reading when someone reads a text in a way that another person listening would not expect," p. ix). By analyzing these miscues (see figure 7–3), the students begin to see how effectively the reader is using the three basic cueing systems—semantic, syntactic, and graphophonic—that proficient language users employ instinctively as they speak and as they read. They learn that all readers make some miscues, but that proficient readers carefully monitor their comprehension, correcting the miscue when it detracts from the meaning of the text.

Struggling readers not only make a great many miscues but also fail to monitor and correct them when necessary. Without this all-important monitoring and correcting step, they lose control of the reading process and forfeit their ability to construct meaning from the text. Once Reading Workshop II students understand that the same cueing systems they use naturally in their speech can make a difference in their reading, they begin to predict, infer, sample, confirm, and self-correct as they read. Where they once rushed through a selection with barely a thought for what the words meant, they now begin to pay attention to the meaning they are constructing as they read.

Reciprocal Teaching

This comprehension-fostering and -monitoring activity trains the instructional spotlight on the reading of high school textbooks. Since efficient word callers like Marie "read" the words of a textbook but fail to monitor meaning on their own, they need to be taught to do so through direct instruction and modeling. Then, in order to incorporate this strategy into their daily reading, they need many opportunities to practice and internalize it.

In a reciprocal teaching session (Palincsar and Brown 1984), the teacher works with three or four students. Using a text at their independent (or instructional) decoding level, she reads a short passage aloud as the students follow along. Then she points out and models four activities that help her derive meaning: she summarizes the selection, asks a thoughtful question about what she has read, clarifies the meaning of a particular word or phrase, and predicts what may come next. When the students seem comfortable with these activities, one of them becomes the "teacher." The next paragraph is read (either silently or aloud, as the group chooses), and the new "teacher" performs the four thinking tasks for his peers. The real teacher provides whatever

Recorder: ___David, Leon, Pat (group work)___ **Reader:** ___Leon___

Date: ___April 30, 1997___ **Read from (text):** ___Face on Milk Carton___ **(pages:** ___82-83___ **)**

Text / Miscue	**Semantic:** Does the miscue mean the same thing as what is in the text?	**Syntactic:** Does the miscue sound like language? (correct grammar)	**grapho-phonic** Does the miscue look or sound like what was in the text?	**Did the reader self-correct?**	Did the reader **need t** self-correct?
1. Rehearsed/reassured	no	yes	no	Yes	Yes
2. has/was	Yes	Yes (but the change was syntactic, tense)	No	No	No
3. come/came	Yes	Yes (but the change was syntactic, tense)	no	No	No
4. Miranda/Martha	Yes	Yes	No	No	No
5. shuddered/shrugged	No	Yes	No	No	No
6. mother/father	No	Yes	No	Yes/yes	
7. Some/so	No	Yes	No	Yes/yes	

Figure 7–3. *Retrospective Miscue Analysis*

guidance is necessary, giving praise and specific feedback. When a particular task needs improvement, she once again models it for the group. All readers get the chance to become the "teacher" and always receive whatever support they need.

Since almost all Reading Workshop II students bask in the feeling of being "in charge" of a lesson, reciprocal teaching is a popular small-group activity. With practice students are able to participate in the sessions with less and less support, and the teacher moves from responsive coach to confirming audience. As the students complete these activities successfully, they transfer their newly developed self-monitoring ability to other expository reading.

Analogy Approach to Word Identification

How often I've heard frustrated high school teachers say, "These reading workshop kids just don't know their basic phonics!" Based on my experience working with at-risk adolescent readers, I can say this statement is untrue; I can count on my fingers the students who have fallen into that category over the past twenty years. It's not the individual symbol-sound relationships, the short *a* and the digraph *ch*, that these readers struggle with; it's the application of these phonetic generalizations to multisyllable words, the terrifying "big words," that gives them trouble. When I give the ARI, I easily spot the readers who need direct instruction in word identification. They're not the students who unlock the words ever so slowly; those kids just need practice to become more automatic and fluent. Rather, they are the students who when trying to decode a multisyllable word, zero in on the beginning and the end but ignore what's in between. For years they have been told to "sound it out," but they have never figured out how. For these struggling readers, usually three or four pupils in a class of nine, the analogy approach to word identification has proved to be the most successful instructional approach to decoding.

Developed at Irene Gaskins' Benchmark School, a school for struggling readers grades 1–8, this systematic decoding program is based on explicit instruction, teacher modeling, guided practice, and feedback. It is grounded in research showing that when good readers come to an unfamiliar word, they use what they already know to figure out what they don't know (Cunningham 1975–76; Mason and Au 1986; Gaskins, Gaskins, and Gaskins 1991). In the analogy approach to word identification, students are taught to use common words (key words) to decode unknown words. After chunking a multisyllable word into spelling patterns they recognize, they compare these segments to the key words they already know in order to come up with the new word. For example, by dividing an unknown word into *in*, *cum*, and *bent* and comparing these parts to the key words *in*, *drum*, and *tent*, the reader decodes *incumbent*.

For many lifers, this new approach to word identification is the piece of the reading puzzle they have been searching for through years of frustration and failure. Gone are the syllabification rules that have never made any sense, the isolated sounds that rarely seem to connect with real reading. In their place is a systematic strategy that with practice leads to the automatic recognition these lifers need in order to succeed as readers and students.

Learning Together: A Team-Teaching Approach to Instruction

I first began to think about the need for a second year of reading workshop as I was sitting in my office one October afternoon talking to a young special ed case manager about some of her lifers who had not tested out of Reading Workshop I. Michelle was wondering what kind of reading support she could offer these struggling students. "It seems so unfair that we have given them a year of help and now they're right back in special ed," she confided. "I can help them with their homework like I always have. Read their English books with them. Be sure they hand in their assignments. Work on their research papers. But that's not going to do them any good as readers."

"I know they need something more," I replied, "but there's no way with my schedule that I can do anything else."

"And what about kids like Marie?" she continued. "Uncoded kids who can't keep up on their own? Most of them are getting no help at all, unless you decide to work with them—or unless we sneak them into the special ed office when nobody's looking. "

As a part-time reading consultant I was really feeling the pinch. Perhaps if I were at school every day I could have launched a class for these needy students on my own. But not when I was only there three days a week. Not when I already had a full-time job to do in little more than half the time. "I guess I need somebody to job-share with," I suggested. "That was always the plan, but somehow with the tight budget and all, it's never materialized. If only there were another reading person in the building. . . ." I trailed off into silence.

"You know what?" Michelle glanced at me with a half smile. "Did I ever tell you how awful I was at reading growing up? How much I hated reading aloud, being expected to read textbooks I couldn't begin to understand? I'm not a 'reading person' now, far from it. But with a lot of work I've learned to love books, and maybe I could help you do the same with these kids. I know what they're going through. I've been there myself. Maybe with your support I could become that other reading person."

Such was the impetus for the team-teaching approach Michelle and I developed together that year. I was the consultant who created an instructional framework to meet the needs of the students; she was the enthusiastic brainstormer who came up with curriculum ideas and activities to go along with it. When I pointed out the importance of teaching metacognitive strategies to these unengaged readers, Michelle had a collection of favorite picture books she wanted to use to introduce these strategies to the class. When I mentioned how crucial I felt it was to get these adolescents talking about and feeling a part of literacy events, she couldn't wait to get the class involved in creative drama.

During the rest of the semester I supplied her with books and articles about teaching at-risk adolescents, and every week we discussed how to put the best practices we had read about into action. Together we went to Bob and presented our idea of extending reading workshop for a second year. We needed his okay for a case manager like Michelle to teach a regularly scheduled class. "What do we have to lose?" Bob asked. "You'll all be learning together, right?"

By January we had a classroom, an assigned block, and an overflowing roster of nine students. We had access to the reading workshop library and a weekly schedule to follow. Michelle was the Reading Workshop II teacher; I was her mentor, ready to support her in her new teaching venture. Having tested each student individually, I knew what they needed as readers and I shared this information with Michelle. We chose a curriculum that would build on the students' strengths and attend to their needs. As the weeks passed I introduced Michelle to the reading practices she was unfamiliar with. I came into the Reading Workshop II classroom and worked with groups of students on reciprocal teaching; I tried out the analogy approach to word identification with deficient decoders; I modeled effective instructional practices. In time Michelle was able to do more of the teaching on her own.

Building on the Reading Workshop I support group already in place, all of the educators involved in the corrective reading curriculum—the Reading Workshop I and II teachers, the Reading Rebound teachers, and I—had monthly meetings to plan for the weeks ahead and share what was going on in the different classrooms. Mrs. Daley told us about Brian's success with the analogy approach to word identification, and I was able to take what she had learned and apply it to some of Michelle's struggling decoders. When Mrs. T. said she was worried about the students in her room who didn't seem to be "buying in" to reading, Michelle mentioned that she gave her recalcitrant students comic books. We brainstormed ways to improve the journals our students were keeping, and I suggested we learn more about Atwell's dialogue journals for our next meeting. We discussed the lifers who were making gains and those who might need another dose of reading intervention in the year to come.

Assessment and Evaluation

Ongoing Classroom Assessment

Since by its very nature the Reading Workshop II class fosters a more intimate teacher-student relationship, Michelle didn't need weekly progress sheets to keep track of her students' behavior and learning. Instead, her anecdotal notes about what she observed in the classroom became a large part of the ongoing evaluation. In addition, she adapted other Reading Workshop I progress and assessment forms to meet her needs. First, she incorporated reading logs into each student's journal. Then, as she grew more confident in her evaluative skills, she transformed the Reading Journal Scoring Guide into a rubric assessing the deeper understanding that was a cornerstone of the Reading Workshop II curriculum (see appendix J). "I hope this is okay," she said when she asked for feedback on her first stab at developing assessment tools.

It was more than okay; Michelle's work was clear evidence that she was learning how to learn more about her students. She continued to use quarterly rubrics as an impetus for self-evaluation and goal setting; and like the Reading Workshop I semester-end assessments, her midterm and final exams gave students the opportunity to reflect on their growth as readers while assessing their ability to use the reading strategies taught and practiced in class. At the end of each quarter letters home kept parents informed of class literacy goals as well as the progress of their son or daughter.

Periodic Assessment

We also administered an oral reading miscue analysis for each Reading Workshop II student at the end of every quarter. By collecting each oral reading on a student's personal tape, we created an ongoing record of his or her progress as a reader, one that could move from class to class and teacher to teacher as the reader's development dictated. In individual conferences, the students and I reviewed each reading and the miscues it contained; together we applauded the growth shown and set goals for future learning based on what we were able to see through this revealing "window."

Testing Out

"Testing out" of reading workshop was never far from these adolescents' minds. It was something they knew they had to do—but something they dreaded. And with good reason. As lifers they had never had any success picking out vocabulary definitions or answering comprehension questions. More often than not they had entered their answers to standardized tests in visual patterns, as if decorating a Christmas tree. But because we live in a world where standardized test results continue to hold clout, we needed to use one to document these readers' growth.

To prepare her students to take the Stanford Diagnostic Reading Test, Michelle coached them in class. She introduced them to tried-and-true test-taking strategies—narrowing down multiple choices, reviewing the questions before reading the comprehension selections, pacing one's progress through the different sections of the test. She talked of the importance of getting a good night's sleep the night before, of relaxation techniques that can help stressed-out test takers during the session itself. And she gave them plenty of chances to practice, letting them work with alternative forms of the test to bolster their self-confidence.

When testing week came, the class was ready. With the exception of two pupils who had tried our patience all semester, who had refused to commit themselves to making a difference as readers and learners, the Reading Workshop II students took the year-end test seriously. During the long and arduous sessions these invested students gave the test questions their fullest attention in their desire to prove themselves as re-visioning readers. These lifers had worked hard for two years, and they wanted their efforts to pay off. That first year, in a class of nine students, five reached the required grade 8 reading level needed to remove themselves from the lifer roll. Not only that, both in their year-end self-evaluations and in the readministered attitude surveys, nearly all could point to areas of substantial growth, not only in reading achievement but also in how they viewed reading and themselves as readers and learners. They—and we—were making progress.

Chapter 8

Literacy Workshop Electives for Those Who Still Need Support

Jerome Bruner (1986) refers to this phenomenon—when an adult intervenes and gradually provides less assistance to a learner—as the "handover phase." In handover, understanding and strategies that emerge during an interaction between a more competent person and a less competent person gradually become internalized in the learner's mind.

—Nancie Atwell
In the Middle

At about the same time that I was setting up my interviews for this research project, Laura Rogers (1998) was completing her analysis of the Reading Workshop I class. Pleased to see that my work with at-risk readers had been validated, I was inspired by her findings to search out one of the original reading workshop students still at Daniel Webster, ideally a student who had benefited from two years of corrective reading instruction by participating in Reading Workshop II as well. If the freshmen and sophomores in Laura's study felt that Reading Workshop I was making a difference for them, imagine what a senior would have to say of its lasting effect on his academic career.

Thinking about whom I could approach, I immediately recalled Joe, a personable young man who as a sophomore had impressed me with his ability to interact with teenagers and adults alike. When I first met him two years before, he had been a student in the original Reading Workshop II class, an adolescent who had worked hard that second year to improve his reading skills so that he could make the grade on the spring test. I remembered the concentration he had showed during the testing sessions. Unlike some of his classmates, he had used every minute in his determination to succeed. And he did succeed—that May he had scored well above the grade 8 cutoff, high enough to leave corrective reading instruction behind once and for all.

I knew Joe wouldn't be intimidated by my position, wouldn't just tell me what he thought I wanted to hear. I could count on him to tell it like it was. And tell me he did, opening my eyes once again to the fragility of change, to the lot of re-visioning lifers who after two years of personalized corrective instruction have their reading support pulled out from under them just as they are savoring the intoxicating air of achievement. These newly successful readers confidently insist that they want to "do school" on their own but too often find out that they are not yet fully prepared for the academic independence this demands. The hard-won confidence of these vulnerable students is too easily shattered by classes and teachers demanding too much, too soon. An eloquent representative of this group, Joe offers a lesson educators of at-risk readers need to learn.

I've Got the Knack of It All Right, But Only to a Point

I'll let Joe tell it in his own words.

"When I was in reading workshop the second year all I wanted to do was get out. Because I felt there was something better on the other side. Not that I didn't like it. It gave me time to read the book and get credit for doing it. I mean, I knew I was getting something out of it, learning to read better and a credit on my transcript too. And it was fun most of the time. It's kind of not cool that my classes aren't fun any more. The people, too—I liked the people in that class. Just the other day I was thinking about the teacher, Mrs. Morrison. Oh, she was a good teacher. I liked her. She was so nice. She always, like when I didn't do something, she didn't just go, 'Well, if you don't do your work you're not graduating.' Not that that's not logical. But when we didn't do something, and all of us didn't get it, she'd take a step backwards and do it in class. And even if only one person out of everybody didn't get it, she'd reteach it. That's good for the kid who doesn't get it and it's also good for the people who do get it to learn more about it. Most of the times you don't get everything, you pretty much get a concept of it but you don't get everything. It's not going to happen. So then people get an even better understanding of what happened.

"I felt smart in that class. I felt like I was one of the smartest kids in that class. Maybe it's because of who I was up against. Plus it was like I was competing with everybody and I knew I had a chance to win. That's the way I've always been. Even where I work part time, at Market Basket, I have a friend and I'll go to stocking and if he tries to get faster than me, then I'll turn it up a notch so that I'm faster than him. In Reading Workshop II when I'd go to read something I knew I'd have more time to read it, and I'd be the first one flipping the pages. Not like in my English class now. We read a lot more. We do a lot harder stuff, and sometimes I just can't do it. Like, we have really smart people in my class, where if they have to read something, they'll complain about it and everything else but they'll read it and they'll get it done; and when time comes for conversation or whatever they know all the questions and the answers. I can't compete against them. I don't know, maybe I got lazy or something. Or I'm just lazy when it comes to reading.

"I'm a slow reader. In English 12 Mrs. King tells us to read page one to sixty in *Catcher in the Rye* and then the next day we'd come in and have kind of a circle group and discuss what we read. I really get into discussions, I really get into talking and what not, like I'm the voice of the automotive class at the vocational center, and I'm really good at that you know? But sixty pages? I tried to read it but I only got through twenty. It probably took me, well, I got up and got a drink, but it still took me about an hour and a half to read those twenty pages. That's a lot of time to spend reading. I mean, come on. So we go into class and start to talk. I'm talking about the first twenty, everybody else is up to sixty. I definitely get behind, because if I'm reading the next twenty pages, everybody else is reading the next eighty. Okay, I can talk a little bit. But then they're reading the next eighty and I'm still back here on page forty. I'm going, 'I want to talk about what we were talking about yesterday.' I get left way behind. Because I don't . . . it's not really that I don't have the time, well, I really don't have the time to use up reading eighty pages at a time, because there's no way that I can do that.

"For me now a good reader is somebody that can read up to a certain speed and remember what they're reading. Maybe I could do that in reading workshop but not now. I try to fool people, like I have another class where the teacher passes out a paper and it's four pages long and he says, 'Take five minutes and read this and we'll discuss it.' So he gives us our five minutes; we read it. It seems like when I look around the room everybody's turning pages and reading. I don't know if they're actually doing it, because that's what I'm doing. I'm turning pages but I'm only pretending like I'm reading. I read as much as I can, until I hear a few people turn pages, and then I'll turn the page. And read as much as I can on that page, until I hear some more people turn pages and then I'll turn the page. It's not just the kids getting farther than me that bugs me, because when I'm at my house I'm the only one reading so I don't know what everybody else is doing there. All I know is that it's taking me way too long. I thought I was a good reader when I got out of reading workshop. Now good readers are everybody but me.

"But the speed thing doesn't bother me when I'm reading something that's important, when I'm reading the procedure on how to do a tune-up on my '94 Z24 Cavalier. I mean you have to pull the bottom engine out, you have to rock the motor forward to get to the back spark plugs. I'll read that; if it's a paragraph I'll read it four or five times just to make sure I can understand it. And the time thing won't bother me; if it takes me an hour to read it, it won't bother me. It won't bother me because first off I want to make sure I do it right, and second off no one else is standing around and turning pages faster than I am.

"Reading is part of my life now. You teachers have always told me that. Now I know you're right. Every time I work on a car I have to read something. That's the way it is. You can't go in, you can't even pop the hood of a car and actually go for what you're looking for most of the time without picking up a book. A lot of the cars I work on are in no-start conditions. They won't idle. They won't run. You can't just go under the hood and go, 'Okay, I know the problem's over there.' It's not possible. You need a book. And even when you know what the problem is, like it's a speed sensor let's say, you don't know where it is. You gotta read, you gotta remember, you gotta understand. That kind of reading I can do.

"It's the school reading I have trouble with. When I have to go home and read and understand sixty or eighty pages or something it's just not going to happen. The problem with reading is that if I have to read something that doesn't apply to me or my life, like a fictional book, it's not important so I won't remember it. My memory has like this filter in it. Whether I want to or not, the story itself just won't get let in. It's weird. Give me a used-car buyer's guide or something along those lines, I'll read specs, dimensions, I'll read wheel bases, I'll read sizes of motors and what not. I'll remember every word of it, you know? I could tell you the torque specs of any part of a 350 right off the top of my head because it's important to me. But *Catcher in the Rye*? I can barely remember who the main character was. Even though he did a lot of things like I do, so it does kind of connect with me, it's like who cares about this type of thing? It's a fictional book. Oh, once I read about a concept car, they call it a jeepster, with four-wheel drive, eighteen-inch aluminum rims, nice tires, big motor. I can remember it and that's fiction, that's not fact. So I guess it's not the fiction that doesn't interest me, it's what's in the fiction that doesn't interest me.

"I'm not sure how I even tested out of reading workshop, because the reading on the test couldn't have been something that I was interested in. It was hard work. But I wanted so bad to test out. I had to read things over and over again, to make sure I got the answer right. I'd read it the first time, I'd go to the question and if I didn't remember it I'd have to read it again. I think that nobody finished before me. Because when somebody finishes a test before me, especially comprehension questions, that's when I just start marking boxes. If I'm first to finish, if I'm not pages and pages behind, it makes me feel more confident about my reading. It's not that being first makes me a better reader; it just makes me feel that way. I've already been reading for a while, let's say ten years or so, and I've got the knack of it all right. But only to a point. Being behind when I read in school, like with *Catcher in the Rye*, makes me truly believe in my mind that I can't do it. And most of the time I don't. I give up.

"At the end of tenth grade I felt good about me and my reading. Not now. I hate to say it, I wouldn't want to ruin it for everybody else, but probably you should have kept me in reading workshop. I know I have been forced to learn more from Mrs. King, because that's just the way it is. I mean we just keep going on to other things, and we keep having to learn other things no matter if you've learned the first thing or not, and eventually you get the knack of it because the first thing always leads to the second. But there's got to be another place in there somewhere. I'm like in between as a reader. It's not that those kids in English class are smarter than me, because that's just not possible. But maybe they are better readers. And reading is I think the only thing in my whole life I won't try to get better at, to beat other people at, except when I'm in a place like reading workshop. I worked real hard to pass the test; I thought the grass was greener on the other side. But now I'm not so sure."

Background

For most lifers the Reading Workshop I and II classes supply the foundation and framework on which to build both reading and academic success. After two years of hard work, lifers long imprisoned by their reading failure are finally "free," viewing both themselves and reading in a new light. They have learned the key strategies for reading proficiently; they have had many opportunities to apply these strategies successfully in a variety of situations. They feel smart; they feel good about themselves; they see themselves as successful and capable readers. As Joe says, they've finally "got the knack of it." And we hope that these newly confident adolescents will apply what they've learned in their other classes, becoming eager and ready contributing members of learning communities that value their literacy achievements. And some of them do.

But as Joe so eloquently points out, this isn't always the case. In a regular classroom setting, Joe's hard-won confidence in his revalued status as reader and learner begins to diminish. He discovers that reading sixty pages of *Catcher in the Rye* for a senior English class is not the same as completing a similar assignment within the supportive comfort of reading workshop. Nor does it compare with reading, at his own pace, a novel he's chosen himself. And it's certainly not like reading, remembering, and understanding the used-car guides he devours in his free time. Although the loquacious Joe has found his voice by participating in lively reading workshop discussions, he is unable to keep up with classroom conversations based on the nightly English assignments.

So like the lifer he used to be he quits taking part in literate talk. He falls back on other abandoned habits as well, pretending to read in class while simply turning the pages when everybody else does, reading just a part of the assignment before giving up in frustration. In time, lifer thoughts begin to resurface: the other students in his class are smarter than he is; they can read quicker; they know all the questions and the answers. Good readers used to be people who could read fast and remember everything they read. They seem that way again. In fact, good readers are once more everybody but him. No longer confident about himself or his reading, he thinks, *Maybe I'm not a good reader after all. Or maybe I'm just lazy.*

Goal

For "in between" readers like Joe, as well as for the lifers who have yet to attain basic competency on their standardized tests, literacy workshop electives offer the consistent scaffolding they need to meet success in their academic lives. We purposely call the courses electives, because by this time in their education the students' motivation and effort will mean the difference between continued reading growth and stagnation. If a junior or senior in our school elects to work at becoming a better reader, with our help she will; if not, there is little any of us can do to make a difference for her. Our students all know this.

The semester-long literacy workshop electives are highly individualized courses developed to meet the specific needs of a particular student or a small group of students. Some focus on reading; others emphasize the reading-writing connection. In each one, however, there remains a common element: the independent reading and journal keeping that are the hallmarks of all our corrective reading instruction. Independent reading and writing are the means by which readers develop the fluency Joe lacked, the fluency necessary to be successful in their other classrooms.

Even before I interviewed Joe, we had begun to create and offer these electives. For example, after Brian completed Reading Rebound, he needed to review and practice the metacognitive strategies proficient readers use to make sense of print. He also needed more work decoding unknown words and using the three cueing systems effectively. So we developed literacy tutoring. By coaching a struggling beginning reader, Brian reviewed the very lessons he continued to need for himself. Joe's words, however, inspired us to offer such support to a wider range of ex-lifers.

Courses

The following courses have either been offered at Daniel Webster or are on the drawing board as brainstorms, awaiting both students who are interested and a teacher with the time and energy to help develop and teach the course.

Literacy Tutoring

A cross-age tutorial that pairs a high school student with a struggling primary reader, with the goal of reinforcing basic reading strategies for both participants. It includes weekly instructional sessions with a teacher/mentor and is intended for students who need to review basic reading strategies. It may be used as a senior project.

Independent Learning Seminar (ILS)

Students use basic reading strategies while completing their content area reading assignments. Students taking the same content area class receive teacher and peer support. Both the individual and the group set goals. It is intended for students whose comprehension and vocabulary are adequate but who need support transferring those abilities to their content area reading.

Oral History

In this course, which is based on Wigginton's (1985) Foxfire program, students go into the community to interview senior citizens as a way of preserving oral history. It incorporates reading, writing, speaking, and listening, and allows students who feel confident as speakers to use their strengths to improve as readers and writers. It may be used as a senior project.

The Play's the Thing

In this course, students develop automaticity and fluency by working with TV and movie scripts, plays, etc. The student's ability to understand text is enhanced by dramatic interpretation. It often includes an outreach component in that the plays are presented at senior-citizen centers, day care centers, or elementary schools. It is intended for students for whom lack of fluency and comprehension is the biggest deterrent to reading success.

Real-Life Writing

In this seminar, adapted from Huntley-Johnston et al. 1997, each student researches, writes, and publishes a how-to book on a subject of his or her choice. It links students' literacy development and achievement to their interests and provides an authentic motivation for reading and writing. It may be used as a senior project.

The Reading-Writing Experience

Field trips are the focus of this experiential learning curriculum. Reading and writing become integral components of a particular experience (for example, a visit to New York City, a sailing trip, mountain climbing/camping). These authentic motivations for reading and writing are particularly suited to students who learn best outside the classroom.

Breakfast Club/Lunch Bunch

Students read and discuss books chosen by the group. With teacher modeling and guidance, they learn to lead their own book conversations. The experience helps students strengthen their reading skills and develop self-confidence as competent readers and thinkers.

Afterword: What's the Point to All This?

In his 1994 article on corrective reading programs Pikulski shares a frightening discovery made in the course of his research: there was little evidence that remedial programs undertaken after second grade were effective. I read this sobering fact just as I was developing the first reading workshop at Daniel Webster. For someone less stubborn than I am, this might have been a deterrent. If the experts agreed that it couldn't be done, who was I to think otherwise? I found myself in a lonely position, acting on little more than the courage of my convictions.

And yet my beliefs were too strong to ignore. As a secondary school reading educator I have always seen my role as one of empowerment, supporting all students in their quest to become independent learners capable of succeeding when they leave high school. With each group of lifers that arrives at Daniel Webster, my challenge has been to do what I can to help these at-risk readers escape the label. Where in the past many educators have stressed keeping up as they interact with this group of adolescents, I prefer to emphasize catching up. My reasoning is simple: if Alexis, Kayla, and Mick manage to keep up with *Of Mice and Men* but fail to catch up on their ability to read novels independently, what will the future bring for them except more of the same? Once a lifer always a lifer.

Therefore, over the past six years I have sought to change the way we teach these students, creating a corrective reading curriculum that helps them improve their abilities to decode and make sense of text while transforming the way they look at reading and themselves. As lifers change their view of themselves, it often happens that teachers who work with them do the same, eradicating once and for all this insidious label and all the baggage that comes with it.

Developing, implementing, and sustaining a corrective reading program in high school is hard work. It's a curricular change that asks educators and students alike to re-envision their respective roles, priorities, and actions. Administrators need to lead as visionaries and risk takers, abandoning the safety of the status quo while allowing innovative faculty members to embrace an unproven idea. Teachers have to let go of content in favor of process, learn to empower rather than enable, and treat struggling students as able learners rather than incapable lifers. Students must admit the failure they have always felt in order to escape it, reassess the power and purpose of reading, and work hard at something they have long shied away from. All need the patience to allow change to take place.

But when it does—and it can at your school, just as it has at mine—each and every one of us can revel in the results. And that, my old friend Paul, is the point to all of this. Wherever you are now, I want you to know that.

Appendices A–K

Appendix A: My Way of Knowing

Finding the Students

It's not that I found the students for this study; they found me. They found me each March as I administered the Nelson Reading Skills Test to the eighth graders who would become the incoming freshman class. They found me each April as I corrected those reading tests and compiled a long list of students who had been unable to perform at grade level, students who experience had taught me would need help in order to succeed in high school. They found me each June as I scheduled each of these struggling students into our required Reading Workshop I classes, the first level of corrective literacy instruction and academic support for our school's at-risk readers. And they found me each September, as I put names and test results to the faces of students who arrived for their first year of high school—angry or accepting, uncommunicative or disruptive, arrogant or self-effacing, but most of all afraid of what lay ahead.

During the first week of the 1998–99 academic year, I sought out the forty-eight Reading Workshop I students, our newest batch of at-risk readers, the usual mixed bag of adolescents: coded and regular ed, buttoned-down and tee-shirted, soccer players and skate boarders. I wanted to interview freshmen so that I could hear about their reading histories before they adapted to the learner-centered culture of Daniel Webster, an award-winning school where teachers strive to recognize and meet the needs of all students, a school that stands out in its work with at-risk high school readers. Also, I knew that at the beginning of a new school year most students, even those who are most apt to be turned off to reading and academics, tend to be open and willing to volunteer. Once the newness of the setting had worn off, my pool of accessible and amenable adolescents would likely diminish.

I was delighted when twenty-five of these students agreed to participate in my study; of those twenty-five students, twenty-two (thirteen boys and nine girls) stuck with it till the end. All but Sergio came from an English-speaking family; he grew up speaking Portuguese at home. At the time of my research seven of the pupils were getting special ed support, although most of the others had been tested for learning disabilities at some point. Half of the students had grown up in this school system; the others had moved from place to place during their academic careers. Since New Hampshire has no required public kindergarten, the students' preschool experiences were varied, ranging from those who started school in a day-care center at the age of three to those whose introduction to formal education was the first-grade classroom. A fair number were readiness graduates and grade repeaters. Among these twenty-two students, pupils who are considered to be at the very bottom rung of the academic achievement ladder, only Kayla qualified for a free or reduced-price lunch. Their parents' occupations ran the gamut from heavy equipment operator and secretary to English teacher and building contractor.

I did not have the luxury of picking and choosing from a large and diverse student body; indeed, I included in my research whoever offered to share his or her thoughts with me. Yet these twenty-two adolescents offered a broad range of views about literacy and reading instruction. In interview after interview they worked hard, sharing their perceptions of what had happened to them over the years in the name of reading education. They recounted their learning experiences from the at-risk reader's perspective, conceptualizing a world of frustration and failure into which few teachers have gained entry. It's a world that goes far beyond the boundaries of Daniel Webster and the surrounding communities, that supersedes any classroom, school, or town in our country. Can we as educators learn anything from the world these adolescents have fabricated for us? Can we generalize from the voices and memories of these twenty-two individuals? Peacock (1986) talks of "revealing the general through the particular, the abstract through the concrete." He leaves it up to the reader to "decode the description in order to grasp the underlying values, then juxtapose these implicitly abstracted patterns to illuminate their own experience (p. 83)." My fervent hope is that educators who read the stories of these twenty-two reading workshop students will do just that.

Wolcott (1992) points to three useful qualitative ways to come to know your subjects: interviewing/inquiring, observing/experiencing, and researching/examining (p. 19). In trying to cast the widest net possible, I chose to employ all three.

The Interviews

I used Seidman's (1991) in-depth phenomenological interview technique as my primary research tool. According to him, looking at phenomena in the context of a person's life leads to the construction of meaning. In my study, I set out to make sense of the phenomenon of the at-risk adolescent's own experience of failure, understanding that the meaning these students would make of their past reading experiences would affect the way they were dealing with reading now. I looked at each adolescent not as another struggling reader sitting in the office of an all-knowing reading consultant but rather as a unique and knowledgeable human being with a story to tell.

In order to do this I had to learn to keep enough distance to allow the student to respond as independently as possible (p. 73). During the first series of interviews this proved difficult; at the start most students, undoubtedly conscious of the power differential, had little to say to the teacher sitting across from them. "Tell me about your earliest memories of learning how to read," I asked at the start of our initial interview. More often than not this request was met with silence, at which point I nervously jumped in: "Let me show you my first-grade report card from Miss Peek. My mother has kept it for almost fifty years!" In time though, as the students began to feel more at ease with the setting, the dialogue began to flow; and once it did, I had to remind myself that this was meant to be an interview rather than a conversation. For me, that meant listening more and talking less, a challenge for any teacher who finds the normal thirty-second wait between a classroom question and an answer to be interminable.

But listen I did, using open-ended questions posed in a series of three separate hour-long interviews with each participant spaced over a two-to-three-month period. The three interviews provided a meaningful and understandable context. Interviewers who set out to explore their topic in a single meeting with someone they have never met "tread on thin contractual ice" (Mishler, quoted in Seidman 1991, p. 10); I wanted to avoid this pitfall. (My interview questions are provided in appendix K.)

During the first interview I set out to establish the context of each student's experiences by asking them, in groups of two or three (to ease their initial discomfort), to explore and share their reading histories. I also invited each one to bring along a reading artifact, something that held particular significance. I hoped that talking about these articles would set the scene for comfortable sharing. However, I had forgotten about the inherent dislike most reading workshop students have for reading. Given the negative impact reading has had on their lives, how many of them would voluntarily spend the time to find and show such an artifact? The answer, quite simply, was none. Only Sierra admitted that her mother had saved a poem Sierra had written in first grade, and it wasn't until our second interview that she dared to share the poem with me. Instead, we used my yellowed report card, a serendipitous last-minute addition to my school bag the morning of the first interviews, as an impetus for talk. And once the floodgates were opened, the hurtful reading memories began to flow. One after another the students regaled me with long-forgotten stories of words they could not unlock and books they were unable to read, of teachers who didn't seem to care and peers who were always ten pages ahead of them in class. The context began to emerge.

In the second interview, in which I spoke with only one student at a time, I asked what reading and writing was like now. I spent the first part of this hour filling in the gaps of the student's early reading history. Carol, for instance, had had little opportunity to share her reticent thoughts during her first interview; each time she had begun to speak, either Mick or Bob was sure to interrupt. Shy students like Sierra had hung back during our first meeting, patiently waiting for an interviewing rapport to emerge. Revisiting some of their sparse comments during our second interview helped enrich the context. Then I moved on to the concrete details of the student's current literacy experiences, encouraging him to tell his story while at the same time staying on track. It would have been easy to sit back and listen as garrulous Cody recounted yet another long and convoluted tale of his preschool library trips with his mother. Having a focus in mind was easy; with experience, I became better at remaining true to it.

During the third interview I wanted the students to reflect on the meaning their literacy experience held. In order for these fifteen- and-sixteen-year-olds to tackle this somewhat weighty question, I realized that I would first have to "prime the pump." Selecting phrases I had heard them use over and over again as they spoke of their reading experiences, I asked them to react to dichotomous words like *hate* and *love*, *boring* and *interesting*, as they pertained to reading. I also asked them to delve more deeply into their own reading processes: What is there about *The Outsiders* that grabbed you? What is going on for you when you read? Only then, with their minds attuned, did I ask them to make sense of their reading histories and its impact on their lives now and in the future.

That the reading experiences of at-risk students like these are dismal may be a foregone conclusion; it's what many researchers have been saying all along. But hearing the students themselves create and make sense of the context of failure in which they find themselves inextricably caught, a context with severe implications for their future, has been a powerful learning experience.

Recording and Taking Notes

I used a small unobtrusive tape recorder equipped with an external microphone to record what was said during the sessions. Rather than inhibit the conversation as I had feared it might, this tool became an ice breaker—almost every student expressed interest in hearing the sound of his or her voice. I then had the tapes transcribed verbatim into a double-entry journal, so that the thoughts I was going to interpret were the adolescent's rather than my own. The double-entry journal gave me a place to add any personal comments, impressions, and insights that emerged as I reread the transcription. I looked for words that validated my assumptions as well as for those that went against what I thought I might find. The words and phrases I encountered over and over, the categories that arose, the questions I wanted to bring up with the students, all found a place in this journal. Not only did I keep an accurate account of what I heard during the interviews, but also I was able to identify what I did *not* hear.

I also brought my "interviewer's journal" to each interview. In it, in blue or black ink, I jotted notes as the student and I talked. Immediately afterward I reviewed these notes and, in red ink, added anything that seemed pertinent—an impression, a reaction, a thought about where to go next. Following my notes on each interview I also listed the topics that had been discussed. Looking through this journal, I could quickly review what had taken place during an interview weeks ago before moving on to another session; this helped me maintain my three-interview format. I also used it to record informal conversations with participants outside the interviews and to jot down random thoughts that struck me in the course of my research. (On more than one occasion, this journal saved the day when the occasionally temperamental tape recorder failed or when I pushed the wrong button: the essence of the interview was not lost.)

The Observations

Although the bulk of my research was via the in-depth interviews, I planned to augment my data by observing a ninth-grade reading workshop in action, once a week, for three and a half months. I naively expected the curriculum I had thoughtfully outlined and patiently explained to Mrs. Thomas, the aide-turned-teacher we had hired to teach the classes, to be incorporated into her classroom. I expected to share in this environment firsthand, observing students within a natural school setting, participating in minilessons, and taking part in formal and informal discussions. The sharing took place all right, and the setting may well have been natural, but the environment into which I stepped was a literacy nightmare in which Mrs. Thomas struggled to keep control of a restless group of turned-off readers. Chairs tipped, paper clips flew, books dropped, and little or no reading was done. After two weeks of mayhem I stopped going. With help from me and the administration, Mrs. Thomas regrouped. Once she had the class under control, she invited me to return. In mid-October, I came back, not as the insider I had hoped to be but as a nonparticipant observer, acknowledged by the students but not involved in their class activities. It was a far more comfortable role.

Knowing that the tape recorder, so useful during my interviews, would be a burden in my classroom observations, I kept longhand field notes in a spiral notebook. After the first week, the students got used to me and my scribbles. Occasionally they would ask whether I had written about what seemed to them to be a particularly irregular event ("Hey, Mrs. Mueller, did you see that Kim and Carol were talking during silent reading time?"). I always invited them to look over my shoulder, but one look at my illegible handwriting usually dampened their enthusiasm for such firsthand knowledge. More often than not I sat at the center table observing and writing my notes undisturbed. When the bell rang, I was usually granted a departing "see ya"; but in time I came to be just another "furnishing" in the reading workshop classroom

To expand my growing understanding of the lifer's world, I spent the month of January observing (with their consent) Alexis, Mick, Kayla, Cody, Sergio, Paul, Kim, and Carol as they moved through their school day. After checking in with the teacher, I usually sat toward the back of the room at an empty desk. At Daniel Webster, visitors are always popping into classrooms unannounced, so to most students I was just another person checking out their award-winning school. Shadowing these students from subject to subject, I noted similarities and differences in the roles they played in a range of classes. These observations gave me a broader perspective into their school lives, particularly in the area of literacy, and helped me develop richer pupil profiles.

Research: Examining Academic Files

In order to develop a clear picture of the twenty-two at-risk readers' academic and literacy histories, I spent several afternoons reviewing each student's school records, part of the permanent files in the high school guidance office. In addition, all special ed students had a separate file, a much thicker one, kept separately under lock and key in the special education office. I collected the following data: schools attended; report card grades from kindergarten through grade 8; general comments by teachers at each grade level; behavioral patterns noted by educators or parents (usually as part of a report card or a conference summary); standardized test results; special ed referrals and testing; psychological testing; and family information (family size and configuration, parents' occupation, whether or not they qualified for the free or reduced-price lunch program). When a student had a special ed history, I researched that file as well. It was in these files particularly—files that can hold inches of repetitious documentation of yearly IEPs, teacher-parent meetings, and school-home communications—that I became acquainted with the behavior and feelings of parents toward their child's ongoing struggle with reading.

Analyzing and Sharing What I Found

Once all the interviews had been transcribed and my field notes had been gathered, I set about trying to make sense of my imposing pile of data. I highlighted whatever struck me as interesting and important, not necessarily what I had expected the students to say, trying to keep my preconceived notions of what I had thought I would hear apart from the words they had spoken.

Words and phrases began to stand out and categories started to emerge. I was struck for instance with how many times the word *boring* was used as these at-risk readers talked about reading. Everything about reading, it seemed, was "boring" for these students. Once I started noticing the word, it began to take on subtle nuances. Mick's use of "boring" was not the same as Frank's. "What's the point?" was another phrase that kept bubbling to the top. Just what do these students mean when they label reading as pointless?

I also began to look for what was not being said. Why was it that students never talked about understanding what they read? Was the "remembering" that teachers asked them to do, something they all seemed to struggle with, synonymous with what the reading consultant in me called *comprehension*? Was that the only kind of understanding these readers knew?

Next, if I felt my findings were worth sharing, I had to present them in a way that would invite other teachers to read and reflect on them. Because my goal had always been to highlight the voices of at-risk readers, I decided to profile the students whose words best captured the major themes that emerged. Here's how I went about it.

During the preliminary reading of each transcript, I marked and labeled passages that "jumped out at me." Keeping the original transcript as a reference for placing excerpted words in context, I then made two additional copies, one to be used in the thematic development of materials and one to use to create the profile. In developing the profile, I cut out all the marked passages and taped them together into a single transcript. Rereading this copy, which was about one third the length of the original three-interview transcripts, I culled it for words that best exemplified the theme this student's words established. In Alexis's case for example, I looked for comments that best depicted a lifer. (I forced myself to omit compelling material that would not have added to the power of the particular narrative I had in mind.)

Once I'd selected the material, I set down the student's story, determined to use his or her actual words. Since part of the strength of these narratives lies in the chronological depiction of their academic lives, with one literacy experience inexorably building on another, I assumed it would be simple to build the narrative just as the words had been spoken, with little or no rearrangement. After all, the sequence of the three interviews had led the students from past to present to future as they recounted their stories.

But I was wrong. For one thing, in the second interview I'd asked students to clarify comments they'd made in the first group interview. Kayla, for example, had briefly mentioned her struggle with reading "harder words" during her first interview; I needed her to expand on that thought when I met with her again. Then, too, a particularly potent memory would often recur in our conversations, whatever the focus of the session. Again and again Mick revisited his what's-the-point stance as he wrestled with his feelings about reading; this phrase became an integral part of all three of my interviews with him.

The biggest challenge, then, was fitting the speaker's words together without changing the context in which they had been said and thus distorting their meaning. Therefore, I referred again and again to the broader context in which the words had been spoken, making sure that the decisions I was making as I crafted the profile were fair to the interview as a whole (Seidman 1991, p. 93). I was also careful to note those few times when the words included in the narrative belonged to me. Occasionally, for instance, I needed to change a verb tense or add a word in order to ease a transition or clarify a passage; I include these in brackets. However, I decided to delete an overabundance of repetitive teenage terms (*like* and *you know*), leaving just enough to authenticate the adolescent voice without driving the reader to distraction. Nowhere in the profiles will you read more than a word or two of mine; instead, you will find the students' words, far more compelling than mine could ever have been, woven into powerful first-person narratives.

To augment the representative profile, I assembled comments spoken by peers that connected with and enriched the theme the profile embodied, words that in their haunting repetitiveness had enabled me to construct this truth in the first place. For instance, if Alexis's angry yet poignant words best captured the plight of the at-risk lifers for whom reading has always been a struggle, what did her classmates have to say that echoed a common understanding? I needed their words to flesh out hers.

Once I had crafted my profiles, I wanted to make sure I had "gotten it right." So I returned to Daniel Webster and invited the three profiled students to sit with me in the guidance office and go over what I had written. *Have I misinterpreted your words? Is this what you meant when you said these phrases?* I asked them as they crowded around a table with me. All three were excited to see my finished product. "I thought you had just disappeared," admitted Kayla. Both Kayla and Mick got right down to work, turning pages and chuckling. Mick's comments as he finished reading were brief and to the point.

"That's it, all right," he said as he pulled back from the table. "You got me exactly." "Hey, are we gonna make any money off of this?" were his last words to me as he hurried off to break and his friends. A quieter and more serious Kayla was equally affirming. "That's exactly what I said," this gentle reader murmured. Then as if to underscore her acceptance of my work, "I'm glad you put the part in about my mother."

Alexis was not nearly as enthusiastic. "You expect me to read all this?" this ever disaffected adolescent muttered as she picked up the five-page-long interview. "Would you like me to read it to you?" I asked. "Just read it with me," she suggested. And so we began reading together, silently but in tandem. All went well until Alexis came to the word *stupid*. "Did I say that about myself? I really didn't mean it. I don't want it in there," she barked in no uncertain terms. "My mother won't like to read that. She'll kill me when she sees it." Remembering my adviser's wise comments about negotiating rather than arguing with an interviewee who decides to renege on her words, I took a deep breath and suggested that she pick another way to describe herself. "How about saying that I just didn't feel so good about myself?" And so it went, as Alexis, in revisiting herself, met a student she would just as soon not have known. Her reaction, every bit as much as Mick's and Kayla's, told me that my analysis was indeed on track. In presenting insights that disturb those who read them, I hope to move people to think about what has brought us to this place.

Although qualitative research does not necessarily lend itself to interpretation, I believe that my work addresses Wolcott's question: "What is to be made of it all?" Indeed, as I have come to know these twenty-two lifers, I believe that I have begun to understand them and their world of frustration and failure as no researcher has before. By sharing what I have learned from them, I hope to initiate a discussion of how we might better meet the needs of the at-risk adolescent reader, a population of students that deserves far more from the educational establishment than we have thus far been able to offer them.

Appendix B: Letter to parents of incoming ninth graders

READING DEPARTMENT
DANIEL WEBSTER REGIONAL HIGH SCHOOL

June, 1997

Dear Parent(s)/Guardian(s):

Daniel Webster Regional High School is moving toward a performance diploma. One of the criteria for graduation will be basic competency in reading. Based on a reading test administered to _____, s/he has been identified as needing extra help in order to meet this reading requirement. We are fortunate at Daniel Webster to be able to offer Reading Workshop, a program of supportive instruction for students who are experiencing reading problems.

Reading Workshop, which meets three times a week, has as its goal the building of skills necessary for success at the high school level. To do so the class integrates the teaching and reinforcement of essential reading, writing, and study strategies. As a Reading Workshop participant, each student receives intensive reading instruction and academic support from teachers and tutors. Reading Workshop students earn one credit for meeting the requirements of this year-long course.

Your student has been scheduled into a Reading Workshop taught by _____ during block _____. We look forward to _____'s participation in the class. Please feel free to contact me with any questions that you may have about the program.

Sincerely,

Pamela N. Mueller
Reading Consultant
Daniel Webster Regional High School

Appendix C: Weekly progress sheet and agenda check

Name _____   Week of _____

READING WORKSHOP WEEKLY PROGRESS SHEET/AGENDA CHECK

Day 1: Today I need to: Agenda Check: _____
    1) read for thirty minutes.
    2) write a journal entry.
    3) _____
    4) _____

I still need to complete the following work:

            teacher initials: _____

Day 2: Today I need to: Agenda Check: _____
    1) read for thirty minutes.
    2) write a journal entry.
    3) _____
    4) _____

I still need to complete the following work:

            teacher initials: _____

Day 3: Today I need to: Agenda Check: _____
    1) read for thirty minutes.
    2) write a journal entry.
    3) _____
    4) _____

I still need to complete the following work:

            teacher initials: _____

Appendix D: Reading Workshop I rubric

READING WORKSHOP I RUBRIC

NAME _____ GRADE _____

TEACHER _____ QUARTER ____ DATE _____

CATEGORY	consistent	inconsistent	comments
exhibits positive attitude			
thoughtfully completes journal			
keeps reading log up to date			
participates appropriately during class time			
selects books carefully			
participates thoughtfully in book chats with teacher			
works towards individual reading goals			
completes daily progress sheets			
participates in group book share			
uses Student Agenda			

RUBRIC GRADING SYSTEM

A–consistent in all areas (9/10 out of 10)
B–consistent in most areas (8 out of 10)
C–consistent in many areas (7 out of 10)
D–inconsistent in many areas (6 or fewer out of 10)

QUARTER GRADE FOR READING WORKSHOP I

READING WORKSHOP RUBRIC	40%
READING AND RESPONSE JOURNAL/READING LOG	30%
EFFECTIVE USE OF READING WORKSHOP TIME	20%
SKILLS DEVELOPMENT	10%

COMMENTS:

Appendix E: Reading journal scoring guide

READING JOURNAL SCORING GUIDE

Name _____   Week of _____

Block _____   Teacher _____

Journal Entry #1

0	1	2	3	Heading (book title, date, pages read)
0	1			Use of reading log
0	1	2	3	Length of entry
0	1	2	3	Personal connection with book
0	1	2		Neatness
0	1	2		Extra credit—originality, creativity

POINTS _____

Journal Entry #2

0	1	2	3	Heading (book title, date, pages read)
0	1			Use of reading log
0	1	2	3	Length of entry
0	1	2	3	Personal connection with book
0	1	2		Neatness
0	1	2		Extra credit—originality, creativity

POINTS _____

Journal Entry #3

0	1	2	3	Heading (book title, date, pages read)
0	1			Use of reading log
0	1	2	3	Length of entry
0	1	2	3	Personal connection with book
0	1	2		Neatness
0	1	2		Extra credit—originality, creativity

POINTS _____

2 Entries	3 Entries	TOTAL POINTS _____
A range = 26 to 28	A range = 39 to 42	
B range = 22 to 25	B range = 34 to 38	GRADE _____
C range = 17 to 21	C range = 30 to 33	
F = Below 17	F = Below 29	

Appendix F: Reading log

READING LOG OF _____

DATE	TITLE		GENRE	PAGES	COMMENT

Appendix G: Reading Workshop I final exam

READING WORKSHOP I
END-OF-YEAR SELF-EVALUATION

DUE: _____

Write a well-developed paragraph of at least 5 sentences to answer each of the following questions. Your answers must be typed on a separate piece of paper. Be prepared to discuss your answers with your Reading Workshop teacher. This will take the place of a final exam in Reading Workshop, so answer these questions thoughtfully and honestly. The grade earned on this *end-of-year self-evaluation* will appear on your report card as your **final exam grade**.

1. What does someone have to do to in order to be a good reader?

2. What do you feel are your strengths as a reader?

3. In what area(s) do you feel you still need to improve as a reader?

4. In what ways has Reading Workshop helped you to grow as a reader? (Remember that reading involves all reading, not just novels. You read textbooks, newspapers, manuals, recipes, even test questions.)

5. Using your journal and reading log as a guide:
   a. How many books have you completed this year? Have you read more this year than in past years? If yes, why? If no, why not?
   b. Name the title of your favorite book this year. Explain what you liked about the book (eg. characters, plot, subject matter, writing style, etc.).
   c. Who was the favorite character you met in a book this year? Why?

6. Think about the reading goals you set for yourself this year. Which ones did you reach? What did you do to reach them? Which ones were you unable to reach? Why?

7. How could you and your teachers work to further improve your reading?

8. Which parts of Reading Workshop were most helpful to you as a reader (silent reading, journals, book talks, minilessons, conferences, field trips, etc.)? Why were they useful?

9. How could we improve the current Reading Workshop program?

Appendix H: Quarterly Reading Workshop letter

Reading Department
Daniel Webster Regional High School

November, 1997

Dear Parent(s)/Guardian(s):

It is hard to believe that one fourth of the 1997–98 school year is over. During the past quarter I have enjoyed getting to know my Reading Workshop I students. In our nine weeks together we have accomplished a great deal.

We have learned how to choose books that interest individual readers and have discussed different strategies that good readers use when reading a variety of materials from textbooks to novels. Minilessons are presented weekly to teach students effective reading strategies. Students now know how to activate background/prior knowledge with both fiction and textbooks. They have learned how to preview chapters in textbooks to assist them in developing a framework of understanding before reading.

Class members are also reading books of their choice twice a week for thirty minutes. Then each student writes in a personal response journal, an activity that helps the reader make personal connections to the text. In addition, students are provided time to work on homework at the end of each block. During the second quarter we will continue to reinforce useful reading strategies through the use of novels, textbooks, plays, newspapers, and poetry.

Since Reading Workshop is a credit class, your student is receiving a report card grade showing his/her progress over the first quarter. This grade is based in part on a rubric, an assessment tool in which students are taught to evaluate themselves as readers and learners. Because we see parents as an integral part of our students' success in Reading Workshop, I have enclosed a copy of your student's rubric for you to read. Please note areas in which s/he shows consistency as well as areas in which improvement is needed. After looking at the rubric, please sign the back of this letter and have your student return it to me. If you have any suggestions, questions, or concerns about your student's progress, please write them in the space provided on the back of this letter. If you prefer, you can call me at Daniel Webster at your convenience.

I have enjoyed working with the Reading Workshop I students this quarter. The classes are wonderful, and each class member's active participation ensures a positive and engaging learning environment. I look forward to working with your student during the coming months.

Sincerely,

Lori Thomas,
Reading Workshop I teacher

Appendix I: Year-end letter to parents

<u>READING DEPARTMENT</u>
<u>DANIEL WEBSTER REGIONAL HIGH SCHOOL</u>

June, 1998

Dear _____:

As the school year draws to a close we want to share with you _____'s
progress in Reading Workshop I. Our class literacy goals have been many, and your student has shown much growth this year. S/he currently exhibits strengths in the following
highlighted areas:

      understanding the reading process
      comprehension strategies
      vocabulary enrichment
      positive attitude toward reading
      literate self-awareness
      respectful and responsible class participation
      organizational and study skills

Areas in which s/he needs continued work include:

      understanding the reading process
      comprehension strategies
      vocabulary enrichment
      positive attitude toward reading
      literate self-awareness
      respectful and responsible class participation
      organizational and study skills

Although _____ has exhibited improvement this year, his/her class
achievement and test scores indicate that an additional year of Reading Workshop support will aid him/her in moving towards the goal of independence in reading. For this
reason, s/he has been enrolled in Reading Workshop II for the 1998–99 school year.

We look forward to working with _____ in the fall. Please call if
you have any questions or concerns about the Reading Workshop program.

Sincerely,

, Reading Workshop teacher

Pamela N. Mueller, reading consultant

Appendix J: Reading Workshop II Journal Rubric

Reading Workshop II Reflective Journal Rubric

NAME: _____   BLOCK: ____

WEEK OF: _____   GRADE EARNED: A   B   C   F

PERSONAL RESPONSE	consistent	inconsistent	comments

makes discoveries:
    expresses amusement, sadness,
        excitement, fright, inspiration			

interprets/makes judgments:
    agrees/disagrees
    compares/contrasts
    makes connections
    reads between the lines			

determines importance:
    points out main lesson(s)
    synthesizes ideas			

asks questions:
    expresses confusion
    asks questions of self,
        of author, of teacher			

predicts: thinks ahead to what may happen			

uses sensory images:
    makes a movie in mind
    employs other senses			

ORGANIZATION, LANGUAGE	consistent	inconsistent	comments
pulls ideas together, using good organization, smooth transitions			
formulates ideas in own words			
uses correct spelling			
uses appropriate grammar and punctuation			

RUBRIC GRADING SYSTEM:

A–consistent for all areas (9/10 out of 10)
B–consistent for most areas (8 out of 10)
C–consistent for many areas (7 out of 10)
F–inconsistent in many areas (6 or fewer out of 10)

Appendix K: Interview Questions

Interview One: Focused Life History

What has reading and writing been like for you from the first time you remember until the present?

- How did you learn to read and write?
- What are your earliest literacy memories, before you began going to school?
- What literacy memories do you have from elementary and middle school?
- What is the place of literacy in your family?
- What/who has helped your literacy?
- What/who has hindered your literacy?
- What good and bad literacy events stand out for you?

Interview Two: The Details of Experience

What is reading and writing like for you right now?

- What kinds of things do you read and write during a typical day?
- What literacy experiences do you have in school?
- What literacy experiences do you have outside school?
- What's easy to read? What's not?
- What/who helps your literacy?
- What/who hinders your literacy?
- How do you use reading and writing in your life?

Interview Three: Reflection on the Meaning

1. On a reading continuum from *hate* to *love*, where did you stand before you went to school? Where do you stand now? What has precipitated the movement (if any)?
2. People use the word *boring* a lot when they talk about reading. When is reading boring? When is it interesting?
3. Think about a book you have really liked. What was there about that book that grabbed you? What was going on as you read that fostered that reader/text connection?
4. People look at reading as either an active or passive experience. How do you see it? What goes on in your head when you read? Do you ever:
   - Think of your prior experience, what you already know, before you begin to read a new book?
   - Figure out the most important ideas as you read?
   - Ask questions as you read?
   - Make a picture in your mind as you read?

- Read between the lines or infer? Use what you already know and what you are reading to come up with a prediction, a conclusion, or a new idea about what you are reading?
- Go over in your mind what you have read in order to make sense of it?
- Fix up your comprehension when you know you're not understanding what you are reading?

5. *(If appropriate)* How does doing this help you?
6. Thinking back on your reading history, are you realizing anything through these interviews about reading and its effect on you? How has your experience with reading been? How do you understand that?
7. OR Taking your reading history into account, how has it impacted you?
8. What things are important to you in your life? How do you see reading fitting into your future?

References

ADAMS, M. 1995. *Beginning to Read: Thinking and Learning About Print*. Cambridge, MA: MIT Press.

AGAR, M. 1980. *The Professional Stranger*. New York: Academic Press.

ALLEN, J. 1995. *It's Never Too Late: Leading Adolescents to Lifelong Literacy*. Portsmouth, NH: Heinemann.

ALLEN, J., AND K. GONZALEZ. 1998. *There's Room for Me Here: Literacy Workshop in the Middle School*. York, ME: Stenhouse.

ALLINGTON, R. 1994. "What's Special About Special Programs for Children Who Find Learning to Read Difficult?" *Journal of Reading Behavior* 26(1): 95–115.

ALLINGTON, R., AND P. CUNNINGHAM. 1996. *Schools That Work: Where All Children Read and Write*. New York: HarperCollins College.

ALLINGTON, R., AND S. WALMSLEY. 1995. *No Quick Fix: Rethinking Literacy Programs in America's Elementary Schools*. New York: Teachers College Press.

ALM, R. 1981. "Educational Causes of Reading Difficulties." *Journal of Research and Development in Education* 14: 41–49.

ANDERSON, H. C. 1997. *The Little Mermaid: The Original Story*. New York: Random House.

ANDERSON, R., ET AL. 1985. "Becoming a Nation of Readers: The Report of the Commission of Reading." Washington, DC: National Institute of Education.

ATWELL, N. 1998. *In the Middle: New Understandings About Writing, Reading, and Learning*. 2d ed. Portsmouth, NH: Boynton/Cook.

——— . 1987. *In the Middle: Writing, Reading and Learning with Adolescents*. Portsmouth, NH: Heinemann.

ATWELL-VASEY, W. 1998. *Nourishing Words: Bridging Private Reading and Public Teaching*. Albany: University of New York Press.

AU, K., AND J. MASON. 1981. "Social Organizational Factors in Learning to Read: The Balance of Rights Hypothesis." *Reading Research Quarterly* 17(1): 115–52.

BALLASH, K. 1994. "Remedial High School Readers Can Recover Too!" *Journal of Reading* 37(8): 686–87.

BARRINGTON, B., AND B. HENDRICKS. 1989. "Differentiating Characteristics of High School Graduates, Dropouts, and Nongraduates." *Journal of Educational Research* 82(6): 309–19.

157

BINTZ, W. 1993. "Resistant Readers in Secondary Education: Some Insights and Implications." *Journal of Reading* 36(8): 604–14.

BOND, G., AND R. DYKSTRA. 1967. "The Cooperative Research Program in First-Grade Reading Instruction." *Reading Research Quarterly* 2: 5–142.

BRISTOW, P. 1985. "Are Poor Readers Passive Readers?" *The Reading Teacher* 39: 318–25.

BRUNER, J. 1986. *Actual Minds, Possible Worlds*. Cambridge, MA: Harvard University Press.

BURKE, C. 1988. "Burke Reading Inventory." In *Whole Language Strategies for Secondary Students*, edited by X. Gilles et al. Katonah, NY: Richard C. Owen.

BUTKOWSKY, I., AND D. WILLOWS. 1980. "Cognitive-Motivational Characteristics of Children Varying in Reading Ability: Evidence for Learned Helplessness in Poor Readers." *Journal of Educational Psychology* 72(3): 408–22.

CALKINS, L. 1994. *The Art of Teaching Writing*. Portsmouth, NH: Heinemann.

CENTER, Y., ET AL. 1995. "An Evaluation of Reading Recovery." *Reading Research Quarterly* 30(2): 240–47.

CHISERI-STRATER, E., AND B. SUNSTEIN. 1997. *Field Working: Reading and Writing Research*. Upper Saddle River, NJ: Prentice Hall.

CLAY, M. 1991. *Becoming Literate: The Construction of Inner Control*. Portsmouth, NH: Heinemann.

CLEARY, L. 1991. *From the Other Side of the Desk: Students Speak Out About Writing*. Portsmouth, NH: Boynton/Cook.

CUNNINGHAM, P. 1975–76. "Investigating a Synthesized Theory of Mediated Word Identification." *Reading Research Quarterly* 11: 127–43.

CUNNINGHAM, P., AND R. ALLINGTON. 1994. *Classrooms That Work: They Can All Read and Write*. New York: Harper Collins College.

DAHL, R. 1996. *James and the Giant Peach*. New York: Penguin.

———. *Matilda*. 1998. New York: Puffin.

DIONISIO, M. 1991. "A Journey to Meaning." In *With Promise: Redefining Reading and Writing for "Special" Students*, edited by S. Stires, 9–17. Portsmouth, NH: Heinemann.

FAST, H. 1983. *April Morning*. New York: Bantam Books.

FOUNTAS, I., AND G. PINNELL. 1996. *Guided Reading: Good First Teaching for All Children*. Portsmouth, NH: Heinemann.

FRAZIER, C. 1997. *Cold Mountain*. New York: Atlantic Monthly Press.

FRIEDEL, M., AND D. BOERS. 1989. "Remedial Reading Instruction of the AROBAR Student." *Reading Improvement* 26: 37–42.

GASKINS, R., J. GASKINS, AND I. GASKINS. 1991. "A Decoding Program for Poor Readers—and the Rest of the Class Too!" *Language Arts* 68 (March): 213–25.

GASKINS, R., ET AL. 1992. "Using What You Know to Figure Out What You Don't Know: An Analogy Approach to Decoding." *Reading and Writing Quarterly: Overcoming Learning Difficulties* 8: 197–221.

GEISEL, T. 1957. *The Cat in the Hat*. New York: Random House.

GEORGE, J. 1991. *My Side of the Mountain*. New York: Viking.

GOETZ, J., AND M. LECOMPTE. 1984. *Ethnography and Qualitative Design in Educational Research.* New York: Academic Press.

GOFFMAN, E. 1973. *The Presentation of Self in Everyday Life.* Woodstock, NY: The Overlook Press.

GOODMAN, K., 1991. "Revaluing Readers and Reading." In *With Promise: Redefining Reading and Writing for "Special" Students,* edited by S. Stires, 127–33. Portsmouth, NH: Heinemann.

GOODMAN, Y. 1995. "Miscue Analysis for Classroom Teachers: Some History and Some Procedures." *Primary Voices K–6* 3(4): 2–9.

GOODMAN, Y., AND A. MAREK. 1996. *Retrospective Miscue Analysis: Revaluing Readers and Reading.* Katonah, NY: Richard C. Owen.

GRANT, R., AND J. METSALA. 1996. "Engaging At-Risk High School Students: Perspectives from an Innovative Program." *Reading Today,* April/May, 41–42.

GRAVES, D. 1994. *A Fresh Look at Writing.* Portsmouth, NH: Heinemann.

GULLO, D., ET AL. 1984. "Prediction of Academic Achievement with the MST and the MRT." *Psychology in the Schools* 26: 37–42.

HAHN, A. 1987. "Reaching Out to America's Dropout: What to Do?" *Phi Delta Kappan* 69(4): 256–63.

HANSEN, J. 1987. *When Writers Read.* Portsmouth, NH: Heinemann.

HARRIS, T., AND R. HODGES. 1995.*The Literacy Dictionary: The Vocabulary of Reading and Writing.* Newark, DE: International Reading Association.

HARVEY, S. 1998. *Nonfiction Matters.* York, ME: Stenhouse.

HINTON, S. E. 1997. *The Outsiders.* New York: Puffin.

HONIG, B. 1987. "Reading the Right Way." *The School Administrator,* September, 6–15.

HUNTLEY-JOHNSTON, S. MERRITT, AND L. HUFFMAN. 1997. "How to Do How-To Books: Real-Life Writing in the Classroom." *Journal of Adolescent and Adult Literacy* 41(3): 172–79.

INTERNATIONAL READING ASSOCIATION AND NATIONAL ASSOCIATION FOR THE EDUCATION OF YOUNG CHILDREN. *Learning to Read and Write: Developmentally Appropriate Practices for Young Children.* 1998. Newark, DE: International Reading Association and National Association for the Education of Young Children.

JOHNSTON, P. 1985. "Understanding Reading Disabilities." *Harvard Educational Review* 55: 153–77.

JOHNSTON, P., AND R. ALLINGTON. 1991. "Remediation." In *Handbook of Reading Research,* vol. 2, edited by R. Barr, M. L. Kamel, P. Mosenthal, and P. D. Pearson, 984–1002. New York: Longman.

JOHNSTON, P., AND P. WINOGRAD. 1985. "Passive Failure in Reading." *Journal of Reading Behavior* 17: 279–301.

KEENE, E., AND S. ZIMMERMAN. 1997. *Mosaic of Thought.* Portsmouth, NH: Heinemann.

KEYES, D. 1984. *Flowers for Algernon.* New York: Bantam.

KING, S. 1978. *The Shining.* New York: Penguin.

KINGSOLVER, B. 1990. *Animal Dreams.* New York: Harper Perennial.

KLETZIEN, S., AND B. HUSHION. 1992. "Reading Workshop: Reading, Writing, Thinking." *Journal of Reading* 35(6): 444–51.

KOHL, H. 1973. *Reading, How To.* New York: E. P. Dutton.

KOS, R. 1991. "Persistence of Reading Disabilities: The Voices of Four Middle School Students." *American Educational Research Journal* 28(4): 875–95.

KOZOL, J. 1991. *Savage Inequalities: Children in America's Schools.* New York: Crown.

KROGNESS, M. 1995. *Just Teach Me, Mrs. K.* Portsmouth, NH: Heinemann.

LEE, N., AND J. NEAL. 1993. "Reading Rescue: Intervention for a Student 'at Promise.'" *Journal of Reading* 36(4): 276–82.

LEINHART, G., ET AL. 1991. "Reading Instruction and Its Effects." *American Educational Research Journal* 18: 343–61.

LESTER, H. 1988. *Tacky the Penguin.* Boston: Houghton Mifflin.

LITTLE GOLDEN STAFF. 1995. *Snow White and the Seven Dwarfs.* New York: Golden Books Publishing Co.

MASON, J., AND K. AU. 1986. *Reading Instruction for Today.* Glenview, IL: Scott Foresman.

MCDERMOTT, R., AND H. VARENNE. 1995. "Culture as Disability." *Anthropology and Education Quarterly* 26(3): 324–48.

MUEHL, J., AND E. FORELL. 1973–74. "A Follow-up Study of Disabled Readers: Variables Related to High School Reading Performance." *Reading Research Quarterly* 9(1): 110–23.

MUELLER, P., AND L. STRAUCH. 1996. "At-Risk Ninth-Grade Readers: Tracing Their Academic Histories in Search of Predictors of Reading Failure." Unpublished paper. University of New Hampshire, Durham.

NUMEROFF, L. 1995. *Chimps Don't Wear Glasses.* New York: Simon and Schuster.

OPITZ, M., AND T. RASINSKI. 1998. *Goodbye, Round Robin.* Portsmouth, NH: Heinemann.

ORWELL, G. 1990. *Animal Farm.* Orlando, FL: Harcourt Brace.

PALINCSAR, A., AND A. BROWN. 1984. "Reciprocal Teaching of Comprehension-Fostering and Comprehension-Monitoring Activities." *Cognition and Instruction* 1(2): 117–75.

PALMER, P. 1998. *The Courage to Teach: Exploring the Inner Landscape of a Teacher's Life.* San Francisco: Jossey-Bass.

PATERSON, K. 1994. *Lyddie.* New York: Penguin Putnam Books for Young Readers.

PAULSEN, G. 1996. *Hatchet.* New York: Aladdin.

PEACOCK, J. 1986. *The Anthropological Lens: Harsh Light, Soft Focus.* Cambridge: Cambridge University Press.

PEARSON, P., ET AL. 1992. "Developing Expertise in Reading Comprehension." In *What Research Has to Say About Reading Instruction*, 2d ed., edited by S. Samuels and A. Farstrup. Newark, DE: International Reading Association.

PEARSON, P., AND M. GALLAGHER. 1983. "The Instruction of Reading Comprehension." *Contemporary Educational Psychology* 8: 317–44.

PEARSON, P., AND D. JOHNSON. 1978. *Teaching Reading Comprehension.* Orlando, FL: Holt, Rinehart & Winston.

PELZER, D. 1995. *A Child Called It.* Deerfield Beach, FL: Health Communications.

PIKULSKI, J. 1994. "Preventing Reading Failure: A Review of Five Effective Programs." *Reading Teacher* 48(1): 30–38.

PINNELL, G., ET AL. 1990. "Reading Recovery: Learning How to Make a Difference." *Reading Teacher*, January, 43(4): 282–95.

PRESSLEY, M., ET AL. 1998. "The Nature of Effective First-Grade Literacy Instruction." Albany, NY: Center of English Learning and Achievement.

PURVES, A., AND E. JENNINGS. 1991. *Literate Systems and Individual Lives: Perspectives on Literacy and Schooling.* Albany: State University of New York Press.

RIEF, L. 1992. *Seeking Diversity.* Portsmouth, NH: Heinemann.

RIST, R. 1970. "Student Social Class and Teacher Expectation: The Self-Fulfilling Prophecy in Ghetto Education." *Harvard Educational Review* 30: 411–51.

ROGERS, L. 1998. "Reading Workshop at John Stark Regional High School: An Analysis." Unpublished paper. University of New Hampshire, Durham.

ROLLER, C. 1996. *Variability Not Disability: Struggling Readers in a Workshop Classroom.* Newark, DE: International Reading Association.

ROMANO, T. 1995. *Writing with Passion: Life Stories, Multiple Genres.* Portsmouth, NH: Boynton/Cook.

ROSENBLATT, L. 1978. *The Reader, The Text, The Poem: The Transactional Theory of the Literary Work.* Carbondale, IL: Southern Illinois University Press.

ROSENTHAL, N. 1995. *Speaking of Reading.* Portsmouth, NH: Heinemann.

RUBEN, A. 1989. "Preventing School Dropouts Through Classroom Guidance." *Elementary School Guidance and Counseling* 24: 21–29.

RUMELHART, D. 1977. "Toward an Interactive Model of Reading." In *Attention and Performance*, edited by S. Darnic. Hillsdale, NJ: Erlbaum.

SALINGER, J. D. 1951. *The Catcher in the Rye.* Boston: Little, Brown.

SAMUELS, S., AND A. FARSTRUP. 1992. *What Research Has to Say About Reading Instruction.* 2d ed. Newark, DE: International Reading Association.

SCHMITT, M. 1990. "A Questionnaire to Measure Children's Awareness of Strategic Reading Processes." *Reading Teacher*, March, 43(7): 454–61.

SEIDMAN, I. 1991. *Interviewing as Qualitative Research: A Guide for Researchers in Education and the Social Sciences.* New York: Teachers College Press.

SHANAHAN, T. 1990. *Reading and Writing Together: New Perspectives for the Classroom.* Norwood, MA: Christopher-Gordon.

SHANAHAN, T., AND R. BARR. 1995. "Reading Recovery: An Independent Evaluation of the Effects of an Early Instructional Intervention for At-Risk Learners." *Reading Research Quarterly* 30(4): 958–98.

SILVERSTEIN, SHEL. 1974. *Where the Sidewalk Ends.* New York: HarperCollins.

SMITH, F. 1997. *Reading Without Nonsense.* New York: Teachers College Press.

SPARKS, B. 1994. *It Happened to Nancy.* New York: Avon.

SPEAR-SWIRLING, L., AND R. STERNBERG. 1996. *Off Track: When Poor Readers Become "Learning Disabled."* Boulder, CO: Westview Press.

SPEIGEL, D. 1995. "A Comparison of Traditional Remedial Programs and Reading Recovery: Guidelines for Success for All Programs." *Reading Teacher* 49(2): 86–92.

STANOVICH, K. 1986. "Matthew Effect in Reading: Some Consequences of Individual Differences in the Acquisition of Literacy." *Reading Research Quarterly* 21: 360–402.

STAUFFER, R., J. ABRAMS, AND J. PIKULSKI. 1978. *Diagnosis, Correction, and Prevention of Reading Disabilities*. New York: Harper and Row.

STEINBECK, J. 1993. *Of Mice and Men*. New York: Penguin.

STIRES, S. 1991. *With Promise: Redefining Reading and Writing for "Special" Students*. Portsmouth, NH: Heinemann.

TAYLOR, M. 1997. *Roll of Thunder, Hear My Cry*. New York: Puffin.

TAYLOR, S., AND R. BOGDAN. 1984. "In-Depth Interviewing." In *Introduction to Qualitative Research Methods: The Search for Meanings*, 2d ed, 76–105. New York: John Wiley.

THARP, R., AND R. GALLIMORE. 1988. *Rousing Minds to Life: Teaching, Learning and Schooling in Social Context*. Cambridge: Cambridge University Press.

TIDWELL, R. 1988. "Dropouts Speak Out: Qualitative Data on Early School Departures." *Adolescence* 23: 939–54.

TWAIN, MARK. 1987. *The Adventures of Tom Sawyer*. New York: Viking.

ULLMAN, J. 1995. *Banner in the Sky*. New York: Harper Trophy.

VACCA, R. 1997. "The Benign Neglect of Adolescent Literacy." *Reading Today*, February/March, 3.

VACCA, R., AND N. PADAK. 1990. "Who's at Risk in Reading?" *Journal of Reading* 33 (7): 486–90.

VYGOTSKY, L. 1978. *Minds in Society: The Development of Higher Psychological Processes*. Cambridge, MA: Harvard University Press.

WALLACE, R. 1997. *Wrestling Sturbridge*. New York: Random House.

WAYMAN, J. 1991. *If You Promise Not to Tell*. Houston: Heartstone Press.

WEHLAGE, G., ET AL. 1987. "A Program Model for At-Risk High School Students." *Educational Leadership* 44: 70–73.

WELLER, L., C. SCHNITTJER, AND B. TUTEN. 1992. "Predicting Achievement in Grades Three Through Ten Using the Metropolitan Readiness Test." *Journal of Research in Childhood Education* 6(2): 121–130.

WELLS, G. 1986. *The Meaning Makers: Children Learning Language and Using Language to Learn*. Portsmouth, NH: Heinemann.

WELLS, M. 1996. *Literacies Lost*. New York: Teachers College Press.

WHARTON, E. 1997. *Ethan Frome*. New York: Scribner.

WHITE, E. B. 1999. *Charlotte's Web*. New York: Harper Trophy.

WIGGINTON, E. 1985. *Sometimes a Shining Moment: The Foxfire Experience*. New York: Doubleday.

WILHELM, J. 1997. *"You Gotta BE the Book": Teaching Engaged and Reflective Reading with Adolescents*. New York: Teachers College Press.

WOLCOTT, H. 1992. "Posturing in Qualitative Inquiry." In *The Handbook of Qualitative Research in Education*, 3–52. New York: Academic Press.

———. 1994. *Transforming Qualitative Data: Description, Analysis, and Interpretation*. Thousand Oaks, CA: SAGE.

WOODS, M., AND A. MOE. 1995. *Analytical Reading Inventory*. Upper Saddle River, NJ: Prentice Hall.

Index